MAN AND HIS
WORLD

People and Culture

Contributors and Consultants

People and Culture

NOBLE AND NOBLE, PUBLISHERS, INC.

Manufactured in the United States of America.
J430-1

Photo credits and acknowledgments for excerpts and
quotations appear on pages 469 through 471.

Library of Congress Cataloging in Publication Data
Main entry under title:

People and culture.

(The Noble and Noble basal social studies series.
Man and his world)
SUMMARY: Explores the reasons for the development
of different cultures and compares their social
structures.
1. Ethnology—Juvenile literature. 2. Culture—
Juvenile literature. [1. Ethnology. 2. Civilization]
GN330.P44   301.2   73-6712
ISBN 0-8107-2560-6

10 9 8 7 6 5 4 3 2 1

Contents

UNIT 1

CULTURE 1
People and Their Ways of Life 2
From Culture to Culture 16
The History of Culture 35

UNIT 2

NORTH AFRICA AND THE
MIDDLE EAST 49
Yesterday and Today 50
The Land and the People 79
Case Study: Immigrants
  Make a Nation 99

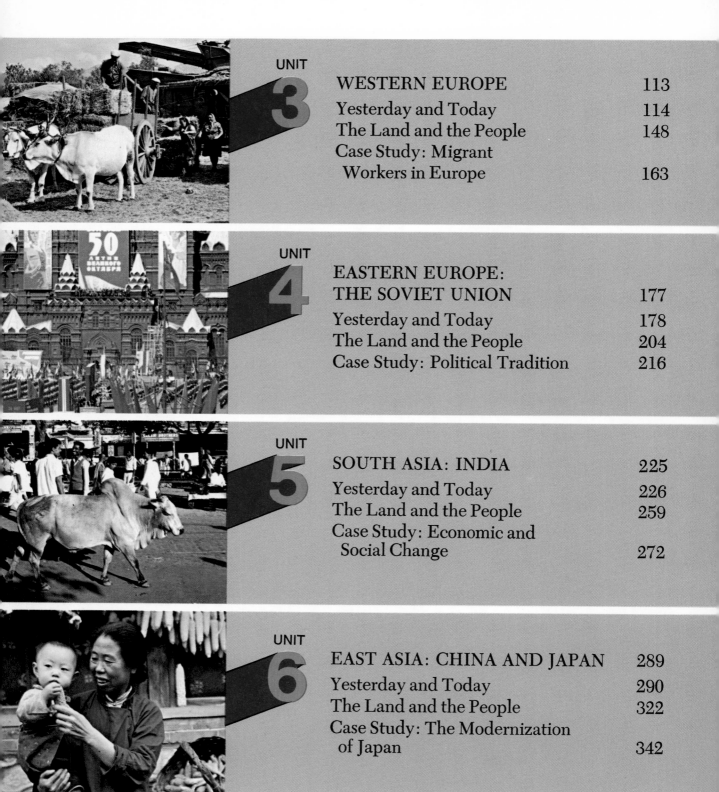

UNIT 3

WESTERN EUROPE   113

Yesterday and Today   114
The Land and the People   148
Case Study: Migrant
  Workers in Europe   163

UNIT 4

EASTERN EUROPE:
THE SOVIET UNION   177

Yesterday and Today   178
The Land and the People   204
Case Study: Political Tradition   216

UNIT 5

SOUTH ASIA: INDIA   225

Yesterday and Today   226
The Land and the People   259
Case Study: Economic and
  Social Change   272

UNIT 6

EAST ASIA: CHINA AND JAPAN   289

Yesterday and Today   290
The Land and the People   322
Case Study: The Modernization
  of Japan   342

UNIT **7**

AFRICA   353
Yesterday and Today   354
The Land and the People   383
Case Study: The Ibo of Nigeria   403

UNIT **8**

LATIN AMERICA   417
Yesterday and Today   418
The Land and the People   436
Case Study: Chile and Marxism   451

SOCIAL STUDIES DICTIONARY   465

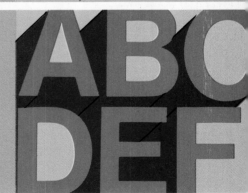

INDEX   472

artifact (är' tə fakt)—Any materi
caste (kast)—A Hindu social grou
chattel slavery (chat' l)—A form
collective farm—A type of farm i
cuneiform (kū nē' ə fôrm)—A sys
domestic slavery—A milder form
domestication (də mes' tə kā' sh
economic system—The way tha
ethnocentrism (eth nō sen' triz
extended family—A more comp
feudal system—The medieval v

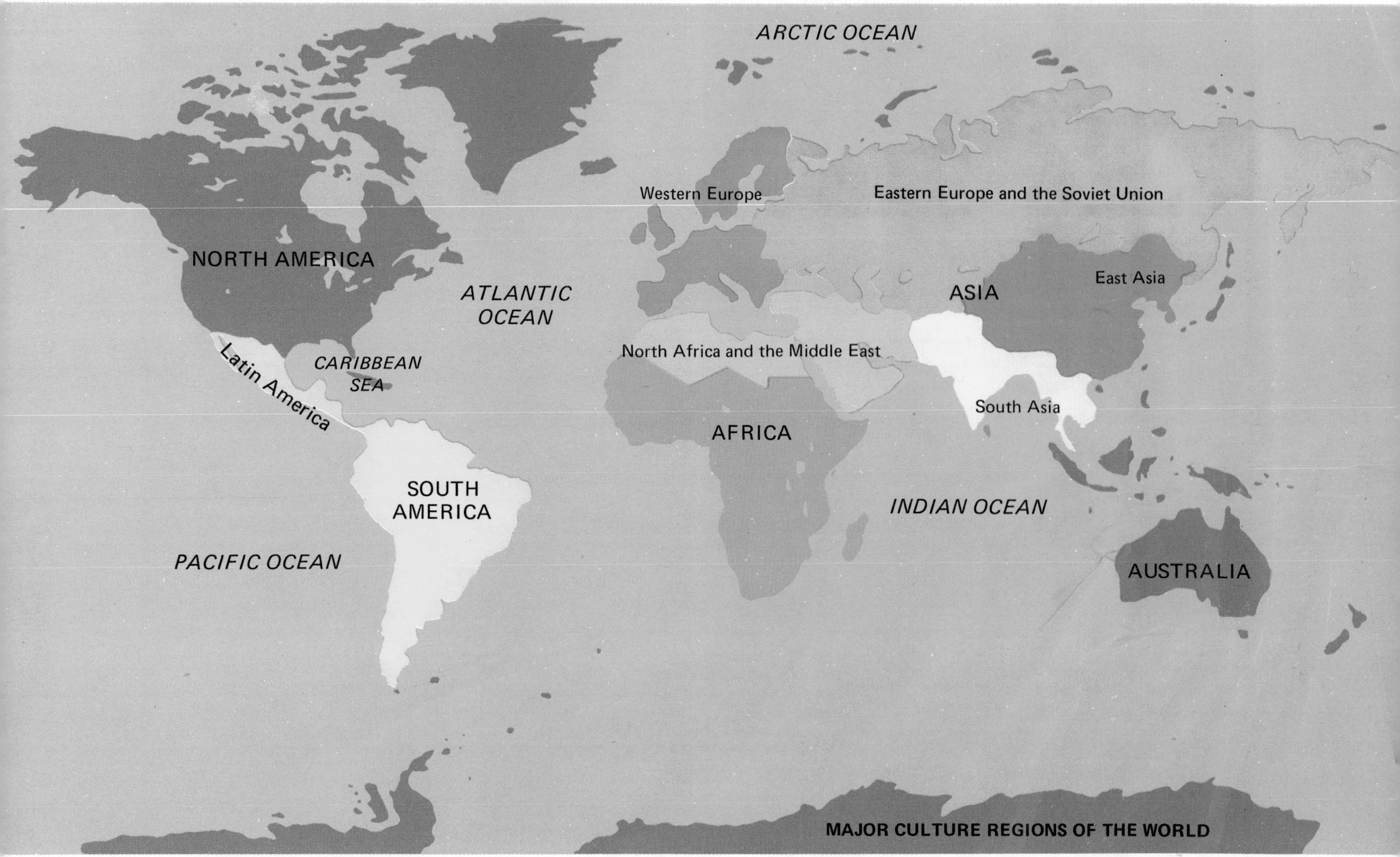

MAJOR CULTURE REGIONS OF THE WORLD

ARCTIC OCEAN

Eastern Europe and the Soviet Union

East Asia

ASIA

South Asia

INDIAN OCEAN

AUSTRALIA

Western Europe

North Africa and the Middle East

AFRICA

NORTH AMERICA

ATLANTIC OCEAN

CARIBBEAN SEA

Latin America

SOUTH AMERICA

PACIFIC OCEAN

CULTURE

Through the centuries mankind has learned to solve the basic problems of keeping alive. And although the solutions differ, there are some things that human beings everywhere know about—the things necessary for people to live together.

MARGARET MEAD

People and Their Ways of Life

THE FASHION OF MY COUNTRY

In 1863, a young Englishman named William Winwood Reade wrote a book about a journey he had made through West Africa. Traveling with only a few guides, Reade went deeper into Africa than any other white man before him. At that time, people in Europe and the United States knew very little about Africa. Reade's writings tell a great deal about Africa and about people.

In West Africa I stopped for a while to visit with the Rembo people. I stayed with their headman and his daughter, Ananga.

♪ rem′ bō
♪ ə nan′ gə

One day after dinner, Ananga asked me what made me wear so many clothes. I replied that it was the fashion of my country.

One day Ananga came into my house with a pipe in her mouth. Angrily, I took it from her. Ananga did not understand why I objected to her smoking. She saw her father smoke in front of me. She offered not to smoke if I objected, but she asked why I was so upset.

I explained that it was proper for men to smoke, but it was not proper for women to smoke. She quickly asked if that was another fashion of my country. When I said yes, she was eager to know why. Before I could explain, Ananga cried, "I know why. Tobacco is very expensive in your country. You will not give any to your wives!"

I assured her that she was wrong. Men and women had the same rights.

"Then why don't women smoke tobacco?" Ananga questioned.

"Because they do not like it," I said desperately.

"Then if they like tobacco, they can smoke it," she continued.

"No, men in our country know that tobacco is not good for the women. They would not like it."

Ananga shook her head a little.

3

"If women try it, they might like it," she said. "You do not let them try it because you are afraid they might like it. Tobacco is good to smoke. You do not let your women smoke. I would not like to go to your country. The women must work very hard there."

"Oh, no," I said, brightening up. "A fine lady in my country has no work to do at all. Even though you are the King's daughter, you must prepare and cook your father's dinner. In my country, the servants do all that. The fine lady has plenty of money, beautiful clothes, and someone to fix her hair all day long if she likes."

"Oh!" cried Ananga, "that country is a fine place. If I was a fine lady there, I would take my canoe and my slaves and go where I pleased. I would not have to ask my father's permission."

"No," I said, "our fine ladies cannot do that. They must not go out alone."

"Why not?"

I was puzzled again. What could I say? How could she understand our rules? I could only reply that it was a fashion of my country.

What did Reade mean by "the fashion of my country"? What things were different in each country?

Why do you think Reade and Ananga had trouble understanding each other's ways of life?

PEOPLE AND CULTURE

Nearly 4 billion people live on earth today. They speak thousands of different languages and dialects. They have many different **customs** and ways of life. Why do people from different parts of the world seem to be different from each other? Are there things about all people that are the same? We call all the ways of life of any people their **culture.**

◗ Dialects are different ways of speaking the same language.
◗ Customs are the particular ways a group of people do things.
◗ Culture is the complete way of life a group of people practice and pass on to their children.

4

Cultures can be very different from one another. Yet the people of all cultures are **ethnocentric.** This means that people judge the world from their own society's way of looking at things. Ethnocentrism does not have to be a serious problem. But at times it has been. What might result from the failure of nations to respect other peoples' ways?

Learning a culture Are you born with culture? Is it inherited along with freckles or brown eyes? Or is culture learned? And, if so, how? Some scientists think that the most important

◗ eth nō sen′ trik

◗ Ethnocentrism is the point of view that one's own way of life is better than all others.

◗ Do you think ethnocentrism affected William Reade and Ananga? Explain.

What custom does this picture represent? Thanksgiving is a custom, too. Name some other customs.

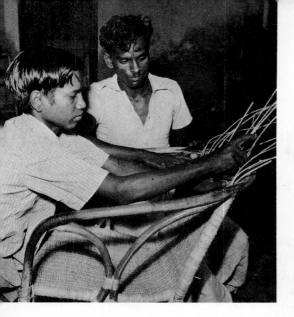

The boy in the picture above is making a chair from palm stems. What skills do you think he would learn in the class on the right?

◗ hot′n tot
◗ zü′lü
◗ ti bet′n

thing about people is that they *learn* to act human. Babies cannot grow up to be adult human beings unless other people teach them.

All people, everywhere in the world, raise their children to be very much like themselves. They do this by teaching them their way of life. Babies learn to be Eskimo or Russian, Chinese or Hottentot, Zulu or Tibetan when they learn the culture of the group to which they belong. Human life as we know it is not possible without culture.

The human infant learns to talk, dress, eat, work, and think in the special ways his people think are proper. People take most of these things for granted. We forget that they are learned. These things are part of culture. Each group likes to think that its own way is the proper way to do things. Most people learn to behave in ways similar to what their culture teaches.

6

People learn to dress like others in their culture. The woman in the picture lives in India. She must dress a certain way. Do you have to dress according to rules, too?

CULTURE AND EATING

All human beings have to eat. Food is necessary for life. We call it a natural need. Natural means something that comes from nature and does not have to be learned. However, different cultures even treat their natural needs differently.

What We Eat Is Learned

All human beings are able to digest all kinds of fruits, vegetables, and meats. But most people learn to eat only what their cultures teach them is good.

Hindus (hin'düz) are people who follow the religion of Hinduism. Most Hindus live in India. Hindus will not eat beef. They use their cows for milk. They use cows to help fertilize the soil. But they will not eat a cow's meat.

Religious Jews will not eat pork, or shellfish like lobsters and shrimp. But to many other people, lobster is a good food. Americans usually do not consider insects as food. But ants are accepted as food in parts of Africa and Asia. The food people of one culture eat is no more "natural" than that of another.

How We Eat Is Learned

In some places, like China, children learn to eat with chopsticks. In other places people pick up food with the thumb and the third finger. What do most children learn to eat with in our culture?

Most of us eat sitting on chairs at tables. But many Americans now eat standing up at hamburger counters. In some parts of the world, like Japan, most people sit on the floor to eat, or rest on cushions, or squat on their legs.

We are taught not to make noises when eating. But in some places, noises show appreciation for food, and quiet eating is considered rude. The things we call good manners are really the ways the people of our culture approve of doing things.

When We Eat Is Learned

We are taught to eat three meals a day—breakfast, lunch, and dinner. In some places in the world, lunch is the main meal of the day. In other places, people eat only breakfast and dinner. When do you think is the best time to give the stomach food?

In some places, children eat before adults do. In other places, adults eat before children do. Sometimes women eat with men. Elsewhere they eat separately.

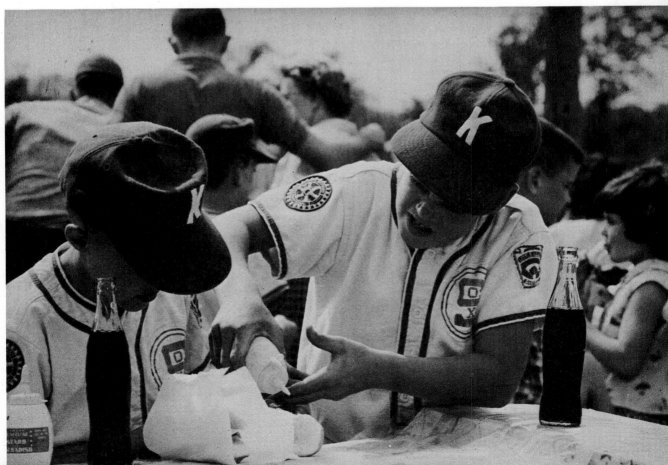

Raigili's father helped teach her rules of behavior. Have you ever taught anyone how to do something?

◗ Society is the group of people in a culture.

◗ sō′shə lə zā′shən

Raigili Here is a short story about an Eskimo child. As you read, ask yourself how Raigili learned. Who taught her? Did you learn in much the same ways?

There were only a few things Raigili was forbidden to do. She was not supposed to rummage in the household storage box or eat the food that had been saved for her sister. If she did these things or if she failed to run an errand, she earned a "moo" of disapproval.

Laughter and silence were used to encourage more adult-like behavior. Children were expected to learn reason and to control their anger.

If Raigili got angry and began to cry, her father would say, "There's a dog howling." If Raigili sobbed and shrieked, her father would respond to each shriek with an amused, "Thank you, thank you." Then he would quietly start to sing to himself. Soon the sobs were muffled. Then there was silence.

The lesson takes a remarkably short time to learn. By the time they are 10 years old, the children have great self-control.

Think about what you have studied and make a guess: Were you born with culture or did you learn it?

Making culture possible As human beings, we depend on what we have learned, while animals depend more on what they are born with. Learning to be part of a culture or **society** is called **socialization.** People's ability to learn from others makes culture possible. And culture makes human survival possible.

Each new generation of children has more to learn than its parents. But we cannot say the same about animals. Birds have built their nests the same way for thousands of years.

Americans sometimes say that their culture has spread throughout the world. Does the picture of the African village below support such statements? What signs of cultural contact can you see in the picture of Ecuador on the right?

HOW CULTURES CHANGE

Culture contact Cultures change in many ways. One important way is through contact with other societies. It is easy to see that the people of different cultures have always copied each other. When cultures meet, borrowing occurs. And cultural borrowing is a two-way street.

Soldiers and traders travel to other lands and find new ways of doing things. Spanish explorers brought the horse to America. American Indians soon learned to use and raise horses. The explorers, meanwhile, learned to grow corn from the Indians. They took it back to Europe. Later, Europeans introduced corn to Africa. Today, corn is an important food in Africa. Can you think of other examples of change through cultural contact?

In recent years, nomads have come into contact with people who have a more settled way of life, and who own more things. Today some nomads carry transistor radios with them and ride in trucks instead of on camels.

WHY ARE CULTURES DIFFERENT?

Geography and climate Sometimes the place where people live makes a difference in their culture. The Tiv are people who live in the Sahara Desert of Africa. In the desert they cannot hunt seals or build ice houses. And the Eskimos who live in the Arctic cannot ride camels or grow grapes and figs. Geography often determines the things that are possible or impossible for a culture.

Geography and climate do not determine how people live. There are often very different kinds of culture within the same climates.

◗ təv

The houses on the right are in Syria—a hot, dry land. They are made of earth and have no windows. This makes it cooler inside. Would you like to live in the kind of houses shown below? How would you visit a friend?

GETTING TO KNOW THE EARTH

People have always needed to know about geography. They have needed to know where there was a water supply and what the soil was like in a place. Why do you think this kind of knowledge was important?

Several centuries ago, geographers stayed home and drew maps of the world. They knew nothing about many places in the world. Sometimes they made up the places they put on the maps. Often the early map-makers drew pictures of great monsters to represent the unknown areas. Why do you think the map-makers picked monsters for symbols of the unknown?

Later, explorers began to map the world more carefully. They brought back better records of coastlines, rivers, deserts, and mountains. Geographers themselves traveled to far corners of the earth to make their observations. What do you think happened to the old maps after geographers brought back new information?

As people become familiar with their world, maps grow more and more accurate. Today satellites help to make maps. What area beyond the earth are scientists now making maps of?

Teams of strong huskies often pull Eskimo sleds. These dogs have thick, double coats. Do you think huskies are well-suited for their job?

The Eskimos hunted animals. Another people of this cold region, the Chukchi of Siberia, herded reindeer and used their milk for food.

Today Eskimos are moving into villages and towns. They often travel by snowmobiles instead of dog teams. They live in wooden houses, which often have electricity. Eskimo children go to schools very much like yours.

The geography and climate of these Arctic people have not changed. But their way of life has.

◗ chuk′ chē
◗ sī bir′ ē ə

1. Imagine you are living with a family of a different culture. Would there be customs of our culture that you could explain only by saying: "It is the fashion of my country"? Explain.

2. Have you ever helped socialize a younger brother or sister? If so, describe what happened.

3. Do you think that Raigili learned anything about the rules of her culture? Explain.

From Culture to Culture

All cultures are different from one another. But all have certain things in common. To study culture, scientists have divided people's ways of life into patterns. Some scientists say there are six patterns:

1. the ways we act together
2. the things we make and use
3. the ways we earn a living
4. the religions we believe in
5. the languages we speak
6. the ways we see beauty

In many ways, all of these things are related. They are parts of the picture of human culture —the ways in which all people live. As you read the following pages, ask yourself about your own culture. Compare your own culture with those you are reading about. How are the cultures alike? How are they different?

THE WAYS WE ACT TOGETHER

Every culture is made up of many different groups to which people belong. And culture affects the ways people act when they are with others. People belong to groups like families or athletic teams. Sometimes people become part of a group just by being in the same place at the same time. Shoppers in a store are grouped together, but they may never see each other again. Culture still affects their actions, however.

Our culture affects the ways we organize ourselves and the groups we belong to. For instance, very advanced countries usually have more complicated educational systems and governments than small, simple societies. We call such things as governments and educational systems **social institutions.**

▶ in stə tü′ shənz

Here are three different groups. Do you think each group has different rules for its members? Why or why not? Would different styles of dress be a sign of different rules?

Different cultures have different kinds of groups. Many Americans belong to bowling groups. Once a week or once a month, the members of such groups bowl together. Eskimos may belong to hunting groups. The men may go out together to hunt whenever the village needs food.

These are two examples of groups human beings belong to. What are some groups you belong to? Do you think every culture has groups like those?

The family, the educational system, and the government are three important groups in which people act together. All of these affect the ways we act. In turn, we affect what our families, schools, and governments do.

The family The family is perhaps the most important social institution. It helps to satisfy basic physical and social needs. The family provides food and shelter. It provides love and the training of the young.

Not all family groups are the same. In the United States, most families are **nuclear families.** This means that they are made up of only parents and their children.

▶ nü′ klē ər

A hundred years ago, however, most American families were **extended families.** This means that grandmothers and grandfathers, aunts and uncles, and, often, grown children lived in the same household.

▶ Who lives in your house? What kind of family are you a part of?

The way people are governed People set limits on their own behavior. For this reason, all cultures have rules. Members of the group are expected to obey the rules.

Where the population is large, the rules become laws that are written down by the

▶ Why do you think rules are often written down where there is a large population?

Extended families like the Mexican one above are still common in Africa, India, and other parts of the world. What kind of family is in the picture on the left?

▶ pig′mē

▶ Beaters are women and children who bang sticks and yell to scare animals into nets.

government. In smaller societies, such as that of a Pygmy band in the Congo, the rules and punishments may be simple. But they are just as effective as in larger societies.

Here is a social scientist's description of how a society can be governed by unwritten rules.

During the long day's hunt, Cephu had not trapped a single animal. Secretly, he had slipped away from the other hunters and set up his net in front of them. That was how he had captured the first of the animals fleeing from the beaters. But before he could escape with his catch, he was discovered.

Back at the camp, nobody spoke to Cephu. He went up to where a youth was sitting on a chair. Normally, the young man would have offered the seat. Today he did not.

The young man arose. "Who but an animal," he cried out, "would steal meat from others?"

Cephu tried weakly to excuse himself. He said that he had lost touch with the hunting party. He had only set up his net when he had heard the beating. But the others would not listen.

Cephu knew he was defeated. Alone, his band of four or five families was too small to make a good hunting unit. Survival depended upon cooperation with the others. At last, he apologized.

▶ What rule had Cephu broken? Why did his community think it was such an evil act?

PEOPLE WATCHERS

Some scientists do not wear long, white laboratory coats. And only rarely do they squint into microscopes. These scientists are called **social scientists.** They study people.

There are many different kinds of social scientists. But all of them search for similar clues. They want to find out how people act and why they do certain things.

Some scientists study the people of different cultures to learn their ways of doing things. These scientists are **anthropologists** (an thrə päl′ ə jists).

Anthropologists often live with the people of the culture they are studying. They try to watch, listen to, and feel the world of these people. But an anthropologist must be a good reporter when he describes other cultures. He must report facts, not opinions. Do you think it would be difficult for an anthropologist who believed in one God to write about a people who believed in many gods? Why or why not? Do you think his report might be mixed with opinion?

Looking at the Past

Another group of social scientists study how people lived long ago. These scientists are **archaeologists** (är kē äl′ ə jists). They dig in the ground to find pieces of pottery and old tools that have been buried for thousands of years. Sometimes archaeologists even uncover buried buildings!

Make a list of some things often found in junkyards. What do you think a time traveler from the future could learn about our culture from these things?

Social scientists often work together. An archaeologist might find a Greek vase somewhere in the Middle East. To find out how the vase got there, he might ask a **historian** for help. Historians work like detectives. They investigate clues—written ones—to solve the mystery of how people in the past lived. A historian might find the diary of a Greek officer with stories about his travels to the Middle East. How could the diary help the archaeologist?

Like detectives, historians often follow false clues. Not all written records give facts. Letters, government records, and a schoolboy's scribbles all tell different things. In some periods of history, many poor people could not write. How would this affect a historian's picture of how people really lived?

Looking at Today

Other social scientists study today's world. **Sociologists** (sō sē äl′ ə jists) are interested in how different people in societies live with each other.

Sociologists want to know what groups—families, schools, religious organizations, government departments—people belong to. Sociologists also study people who do not belong to the same groups as most other members of their society. They want to know why these people are different, and how these differences affect the rest of society.

There are social scientists who study governments, too. **Political scientists** are government watchers. Why? Because governments often determine how people live. Governments influence societies through laws and taxes and even leaders. Political scientists study and compare different kinds of governments. And they try to understand why people vote the way they do.

Does "money make the world go round"? **Economists** might think so. They are social scientists who study how goods and services are exchanged, owned, and managed. Economists want to know about the jobs people do, the things they buy, and the places they spend their money. Economists also study how money spreads throughout a society.

▶ What are some other roles you play?

▶ stā′təs

▶ Can you think of any other things on which status might depend?

▶ kasts

Role and status Culture affects how we act in other ways also. Sociologists and anthropologists talk about the importance of roles which people play. For instance, you play the role of a child in your family. To your brothers and sisters, you also play the role of a brother or sister. In school, you play the role of a student. In Scouts, you may play the role of a leader.

Culture also affects how we think about ourselves and how high or low the rest of society considers us. The degree of importance we have in society is called **status.**

Many years ago, a poor boy was born in Greece. He worked hard, and in time he became very rich. Today he has a very high status in Greece and in the United States, too. In many countries, like the United States, high status may depend on how much money a person has. It is possible to be born poor with low status and work your way up to a high status.

But in India, birth often determines status for life. Society there is divided by tradition into many levels called **castes.** The people who belong to the lowest level are called untouchables. Untouchables are expected to do the most unpleasant jobs. Often they are not allowed to get water from the same wells as people of higher status. Years ago they were not allowed to go to school. In India, birth affects both the roles people play and their status in a very special way.

Complete the chart on page 25. In your notebook, fill in the blanks with the social groups to which you belong. To the right, show the role you play in each, and give an example of the rules the social group makes.

SOCIAL GROUP	ROLE	RULE
family	*child*	*call if you will be late*
school	*student*	*be quiet during fire drills*
____	____	____
____	____	____
____	____	____
____	____	____

THE THINGS WE MAKE AND USE

Artifacts and archaeologists An ape may use a stone to crack a nut. He may sharpen a stick with his teeth or put two sticks together to push an object. But that is as far as he can go. People are the only living things with the ability to *make* tools and to *keep* them for future use.

This ability to use tools is necessary to provide people's **material culture.** Material culture is the tools, clothes, houses, art, and other objects people make and use.

Any item made by people is called an **artifact.** An artifact is any material object that people use as part of their culture. Tools are artifacts. Natural iron is not an artifact. It becomes an artifact when people use it in the objects they make.

Archaeologists often investigate ancient cultures by examining artifacts. The remains of the things people made and used long ago give the archaeologist clues to how people once lived.

Scientists know that cultures change. The deeper down an archaeologist digs, the farther

▶ ärt′ ə fakt

▶ Think of all the material things in your life. Name some of the objects of your material culture.

▶ Think about the items of material culture you named. Are they artifacts?

Dr. Louis Leakey, below, is using a small tool to clean a small piece of bone. The man on the right is an archaeologist, too. What special tools does he need?

▶ ōl′də vī gôrj

back in history he goes. Each layer of earth shows some change in a culture. Each layer has some artifacts like those above, but it also has some that are different.

Upper layers of earth may have pots like those below. But more recent pots will use new colors or better dyes. Sometimes cultures change for the worse. After wars or floods, workmen may forget how to weave cloth or glaze pots. Artifacts may show poorer workmanship.

Dr. Louis Leakey was an anthropologist and an archaeologist. He believed that people's tools tell much about them. For many years, Dr. Leakey and his wife, Mary, worked in East Africa. At Olduvai Gorge, they found many stone artifacts. Most were tools chipped out of stone that could be used as axes and cutting instruments. From these artifacts, Dr.

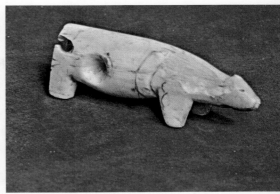

All of the artifacts on this page help archaeologists learn about ancient cultures. Hunting cultures often make beautiful models or drawings of the animals they hunt. More settled farming cultures often decorate the bowls and pots they use to store the things they grow. Can you tell which of the objects above belongs to an Inca farming culture and which to an Eskimo hunting culture? Tools, like the Eskimo hook on the right, show how different cultures get their food.

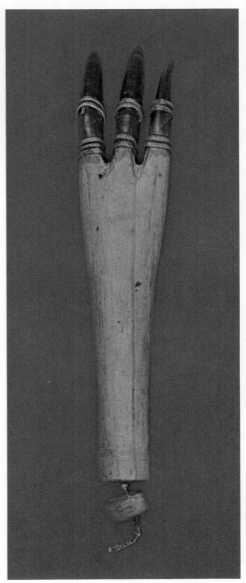

Leakey hypothesized—made an educated guess—that the earliest people lived in East Africa.

In 1959, after years of searching and digging in the area, he proved his **hypothesis.** The Leakeys found a skull of an early man over $1\frac{3}{4}$ million years old.

▶ How did bits of material culture help Dr. Leakey form his hypothesis? What other knowledge did Dr. Leakey need for an educated guess?

Technology Technology is the ways in which artifacts are produced. American culture creates many items. We use many different kinds of tools and machines. We have an advanced, or complex, technology. Name some things that are part of your culture's technology.

▶ Technology (tek nol′ ə jē) is all the skills and ways of doing things that a people develop. Tools + knowledge = technology.

▶ What is one important problem of our advanced technology?

▶ ab ə rij′ ə nēz

The people of some other cultures, such as Australian aborigines, have a simple technology. Their tools consist of bows and arrows, traps, and cooking tools.

THE WAYS WE EARN A LIVING

People in all cultures earn their living. We call the ways in which people do this an **economic system.**

All cultures have economic systems. This means that they have ways to produce goods and services. Goods are things like food and clothing that people buy. Services are things like the work of a doctor or a librarian.

▶ Economics (ē′ kə nom′ iks) is the way in which goods and services are produced and distributed.

Barter A very long time ago all people lived by **bartering.** If, perhaps, you were a potter and your neighbor was a farmer, he might bring wheat to you. In return, you would give him a pot to store oil or water.

▶ Barter (bär′ tər) means trading one thing for another without using money.

▶ Would it be possible to live by bartering in your community? Why or why not?

Some people still live by bartering. But in most of the world's cultures, economic systems are much more complicated.

The boats on the left are transporting coconut husks. What kind of technology do the boats represent? What kind of technology do the trucks below represent?

▶ Are complex means of trade and transportation important in a complex economy? Why do you think so?

Most people work for money. With the money they earn, they buy goods and services. In very complicated places, like our own country, we sometimes buy with credit. We say "charge it." This means that we promise to pay later. Sometimes we pay for this convenience by paying an extra fee called interest.

All of these ways of getting the things we want and need—barter, money, credit—are part of economic systems.

THE RELIGIONS WE BELIEVE IN

In spring, when some Mexican Indians take honey from beehives, they leave a little "for the gods." In the fall, they offer some ears of ripe corn to the gods before they eat the rest of the harvest. These offerings return what they call "the property of the gods." This is their way of dealing with those forces of nature they cannot control.

People have always tried to understand the natural things they cannot control. They have tried to explain illness and death, hurricanes, earthquakes, and eclipses. They have asked themselves such questions as "Why is my luck bad?" or "Why did the baby die?" These questions have led people to religion.

Beliefs and practices Societies differ in their religious beliefs. In some societies, people believe in one god. In others, they may believe in many gods.

Cultures differ in the way they practice religions, too. A religion is not only the gods people believe in but also the ways in which people worship their gods. What are some different ways of worship that you know about?

THE LANGUAGES WE SPEAK

Sounds People speak to each other with sounds. But so do other living creatures. Birds call one another, some with lovely songs. Dogs bark, cats purr. Frogs croak to each other. But there is a great difference between the sounds made by people and the sounds made by most other animals. The highly developed brains of human beings make it possible to use sounds in very complicated ways.

Symbols People can do more than just call out to signal danger or pleasure. They can also talk. They can tell stories about things that happened to them or to people who lived long ago. They can even talk about things that they have never seen. This is because the sounds people make are **symbols.**

A symbol is something that stands for another thing or idea. The sounds *rob ən* are a symbol for a robin. They are not the bird itself. All normal human beings have this ability to use language.

▶ Are words symbols? Do they stand for something else?

Uses of language Human beings pass on their cultures through language. But the cultures created by human beings change. New generations often find different ways of providing for their needs.

Like human beings, animals teach their young. Yet the dam that a beaver builds is almost identical to the ones beavers built 500 years ago. Why have new generations of beavers not developed different ways? One answer is language. Beavers do not have language. How do you think language enables people to improve on the past?

Why do you think it is important to keep written records?

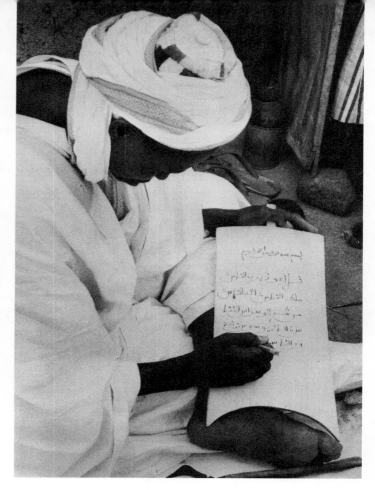

▶ There are thousands of different languages and dialects in the world. Why do you think there are so many? Are some languages better than others? Should all the people of the world speak one language? Which one do you think each group would choose?

▶ The Space Age brought new words into our language. What are some of them? Can you think of other things that have made new words necessary?

▶ Why do you think the Eskimos need 14 words for snow when we have only one?

Time-binding The ability to pass on knowledge from one generation to the next is called **time-binding.** By hearing how things *were* done, we are able to copy and improve on these ways. We learn from people's past experiences. Each generation is able to build upon the knowledge of those who came before.

Sometimes a language seems strange to people who do not know it. But anthropologists have found that every language is a **complete language.** This means that there is a way to express whatever people need to say in every language. New words are added for new things or ideas.

Needs and values Words themselves can show what a culture needs and values. The Eskimo language, for example, has 14 words for snow.

32

Here are some of them:

Mauyak is soft snow.

Ayak means snow on clothes and boots.

Opingaut is falling snow.

▶ mä yak'

▶ â yak'

▶ ô peng'ät

THE WAYS WE SEE BEAUTY

A means of expression People have other needs besides food, clothing, and shelter. They need to express their feelings and ideas to others.

Ideas and feelings are not expressed only through spoken language. Music may be used to express love or fear. A painting or a piece of sculpture may reveal hate, anger, or any other human emotion.

Poetry is one of the arts many cultures share. Poetry can reveal the concerns and interests of the people.

Voodoo dolls, like the one on the right, often represent enemies of the doll-maker. The nails are supposed to make the enemy feel pain. The needlework below shows an artist's view of a cat. Do these works of art show feelings and ideas?

One of the types of traditional Japanese poetry is *haiku*. Haiku has three lines. Usually, the first line has five syllables, the second line has seven, and the third line has five. Here are two examples of haiku:

Ha! The butterfly!
—it's following the person
who stole the flowers!

Anonymous

A giant firefly:
that way, this way, that way, this—
and it passes by.

Issa

The next poem was written by an African. It was to be sung by miners.

Stones are very hard to break
Far from home in a foreign land.
Far from home in a foreign land,
Stones are very hard to break.

What things interested the Japanese poets whose poems you read? Does the African poet write about the same subjects?

1. What do you think Cephu learned about the rules of his culture? How did he learn? Do we learn about the rules of our culture in the same way?
2. If you belonged to a family of higher or lower status, do you think that would change the way you learned your roles? Explain your answer.
3. Did Indians once live in your area? What are some of the ways that you could learn about Indian culture there 100 years ago?

The History of Culture

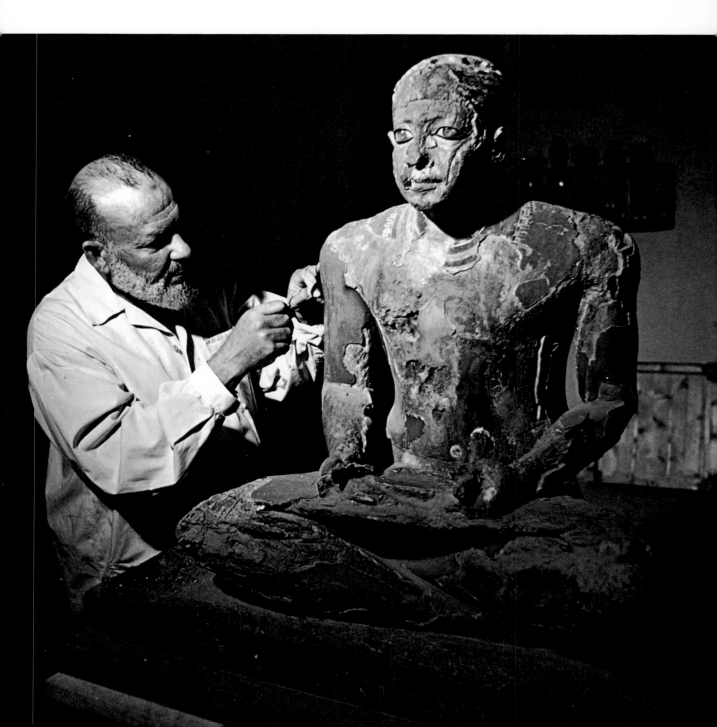

THE OLD STONE AGE

Culture is as old as people—and that is very old indeed. You are probably in your second decade of life. It is hard for any living person, young or old, to imagine people living as long ago as 2 million years.

We may never know exactly how early cultures began and developed. But we do have a good idea of how the earliest people lived.

▶ A decade (dek′ād) is ten years.

BONE DIGGERS: THE LEAKEYS

Richard Leakey's father, Louis Leakey, taught him how to dig for bones. But Richard Leakey is an anthropologist—not a gravedigger. And he does his digging on the banks of a lake in Africa.

Richard's father spent his whole life searching for old human bones. He wanted to find out what these ancient human beings were like and how they lived. Now Richard and his wife, Maeve (mēv), are looking for the oldest traces of human life on earth.

Other archaeologists have found bones and tools that seem very old. They have dated the oldest of these remains to about a million years ago. This seems very old to us, but geologists have learned that this is a very short time in the earth's history.

But the Leakeys are searching for evidence that human beings have been here much longer than a million years. Recently they discovered hundreds of bone fragments in the bank of an African lake. Mrs. Leakey spent months putting the fragments back together to form a skull much like a human skull. Meanwhile, geologists tested the soil where the fragments were found. The soil is nearly 2.6 million years old.

The other archaeologists are not sure if the skull is really that of a human being. But if it is, and if it is really that old, the Leakeys will have discovered the oldest remains of human life on earth. Does part of the credit belong to the geologists, too?

We know they used tools made of stone, and probably of wood, leather, and bone, too. Scientists still find and study stone tools. Because stone was so important to the way of life then, this ancient time is called the **Old Stone Age.**

Life in the Old Stone Age What sort of life did Stone Age people live? There were not many people. They lived in small bands. Men and women cared for each other and their children. They hunted animals. They gathered wild fruits and vegetables to eat. This is called **food-gathering.** People knew how to fish and to make and use fire.

Usually these small groups were independent of each other. Large tribes of people were not organized. Nothing like modern governments existed.

The cultural revolutions Most changes in a culture are very small. They take place over a long period of time. The discovery of fire was probably a very slow change. People long, long ago might have seen lightning strike a tree and burn it up. In time, perhaps, they learned to save embers from a burning tree. Perhaps they carried a pot of fire with them as they moved about. Finally, someone learned to make fire. Over thousands of years other people learned to make fire, too.

Sometimes, though, cultural changes are very great. Though these changes occur slowly, scientists call them revolutions. A revolution marks a great change in ways of living — whether it happens quickly or slowly.

Scientists often describe three major cultural revolutions: agricultural, urban (the growth of cities), and industrial. What do these mean?

▶ Food-gathering is finding things to eat, rather than growing them. Have you ever picked wild berries?

▶ The word *urbs* (erbz) means city. Urban means about cities.

38

THE OLD STONE AGE TODAY

A small group of 27 people called the Tasadays (tas a dīz′) live in caves in the southern Philippine Islands. The Tasadays are a friendly, peaceful group. These 27 people are the only Tasadays in the world.

Find the Philippine Islands on the map. In what ocean are they located?

Until recently, the Tasadays had never met anybody outside their own group. A thick jungle separated the Tasaday caves from a nearby village. Then, in 1972, the Tasadays and their neighbors from the outside world met.

When these peoples met, the Tasadays were still practicing an Old Stone Age way of life. They knew how to make only a few simple stone tools. They knew a great deal about how to use the plants that grew wild about them. They used some of these plants for food, and they also fished, but they did not farm. Now people visit the Tasadays in a helicopter.

Do the Tasadays have their own technology? How do you know? Do you think the Tasadays can preserve their Stone Age way of life? Why or why not?

THE NEW STONE AGE

Domestication A great, peaceful cultural revolution began about 10,000 years ago. It greatly changed people's ways of life. For the first time, people could control their own food supply.

This revolution was an agricultural one. Early people learned to work the soil with sticks and other tools. They were no longer forced to gather or hunt for food. They could grow their own grain and fruit. They could breed their own goats and sheep. This was known as **domestication** of plants and animals. This knowledge made a great difference in the cultures of mankind. Stone tools were still used, so this time is called the **New Stone Age.**

The domestication of plants and animals brought new riches — more food — to mankind. Now it was possible to feed more people. Now it was easier for people to settle in one place. Why do you think domestication made it possible for people to stay in one place longer?

▶ Domestication (də mes′ tə kā′-shən) of plants and animals means that people have some control over where the plants grow or the animals live.

▶ Which do you think would be a safer way of life — farming or food-gathering? Which would give more food?

In India, we can still see why the domestication of animals was important. In some other countries, however, farmers depend more on gasoline than on animals to produce crops. Why?

Ancient cultures were completely changed by the discovery of metals like copper, tin, and iron. An ancient Egyptian king wore the necklace in the top picture. People once wore suits of armor for protection. What are some other ways people have used metal since its discovery?

CULTURAL KNOWLEDGE GROWS

People invented and discovered new things. Sometimes these made life better, sometimes worse. People invented new ways to grow and store food, and to build. But people also invented new and better ways of warfare.

New materials were made. At first, copper was used. But copper is too soft for tools to keep their shapes. Then bronze, a stronger metal, was invented. Bronze, gold, and silver were used to make beautiful decorations and jewelry. Bronze was also used for weapons.

▶ Bronze is made by melting copper and tin together.

◗ Remember the Tasadays? The Tasadays had only a few stone tools before they met their neighbors. Then someone gave them an iron knife. The Tasadays quickly recognized the greater strength and sharpness of the knife compared with their stone tools. Now they use iron. Do you think the introduction of iron changed the material culture of the Tasadays? Explain.

◗ A surplus (ser′pləs) is extra food and goods.

Iron   Soon people learned to use another metal—iron. In China, Africa, and the Middle East, iron ore was mined. The iron was used to make plows for farming and pots in which to store food. It was also used to make even stronger weapons—like swords.

Metal tools and weapons, especially iron, were better than those made of stone. Iron did not break easily. It could be sharpened and shaped into useful objects. How do you think better weapons of metal affected people?

The use of metals changed people's lives. People with metal tools could produce more goods. People traded to get iron or the things made from it.

More great changes came. People began to produce more food than they needed. There was a **surplus.** This surplus could be traded, or used to support people who did other jobs.

Our technology depends on metal. Natural materials such as wood are not as strong or long-lasting. But the special qualities of metal objects can be a problem, too. Can you explain why?

Here is an early potter, drawn over 100 years ago. Do all cultures have artists and craftsmen?

Do you think the development of a surplus affected a culture's economic system? Why do you think so?

Specialization In time, some groups learned to make pottery and to weave cloth. The work of people became more specialized. We call people who do different jobs **specialists.** What does your father or mother do? Are they specialists?

◗ spesh' ə ləsts

In many societies, an **urban revolution** followed the food-producing revolution. As people gained greater control of their food supply, they began to settle in villages. Different ways of life developed. Settlements grew larger. Cities developed.

◗ Why do you think people learned to do new things, like weaving, after they began growing their own food and herding? How did they spend their time before?

Look at this painting as an archaeologist would. Was Egypt an agricultural society?

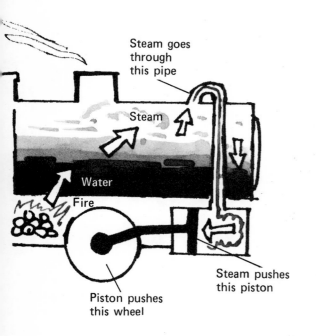

Steam goes through this pipe

Steam

Water

Fire

Steam pushes this piston

Piston pushes this wheel

PEOPLE CHANGE TECHNOLOGY

New sources of power Until a few hundred years ago, people and animals provided the energy for most machines. In coal mines, human beings pulled carts loaded with coal. On the roadways, horses hitched to wagons pulled people and products.

Around 200 years ago, people began to use steam as energy. New kinds of engines and machinery were created. Some steam engines could pull coaches. These developed into trains and railroads. Steam engines that could power ships replaced sails that had used the wind.

New machines While new sources of power were being developed, new machines were also being invented. There were machines for spinning cloth, machines for weaving cloth, and even new machines for sewing cloth.

These machines were big and expensive. So people with money to invest bought large buildings and machines and hired workers. We call the buildings factories. The new machines plus the new sources of power and new factories make up what is called the **Industrial Revolution.**

The Industrial Revolution was a major change in the ways people produced things. It caused a major change in other ways of life, too.

New methods of selling were needed. New methods of transportation were needed. More farm machines produced more crops, and fewer farmers were necessary. People moved from farms to the cities and went to work in the factories. Cities grew larger, and the needs of cities grew, too.

Industrial cultures There was often not enough good housing in the cities. There were not enough ways for people to travel to factories or to office buildings. Which industries do you think grew as a result of people's needs in the cities?

In earlier times, the family provided food, made clothing, and cared for the sick and elderly. Boys and girls learned mainly by working alongside their mothers and fathers. Families were nearly self-sufficient—capable of getting what they needed to live from their land and their work.

After the Industrial Revolution, groups did more of the tasks that families once did. Hospitals cared for the sick. Restaurants prepared food. Schools educated the young. Farmers still produced food, and craftsmen still produced tools and art. But merchants and bankers and transporters became necessary. They were needed to arrange exchanges of money and goods. People were also needed to keep records of what was done.

▶ What do you think happened to the people who made a living by weaving cloth by hand?

▶ How do you think these new inventions affected surpluses?

▶ self′ sə fish′ ənt

45

As cultures became industrialized, methods of selling changed. Stores became more modern. Do both pictures show a specialized society? How do you know?

THE WORLD TODAY

Industrial civilization is spreading throughout the world.

▶ What are two important ways technology has made the world familiar to more people?

▶ med′ ə tə rā′ nē ən

▶ kan′ tl ōp

▶ Persia (per′ zhə) is now called Iran (i ran′).

An American awakens in a bed built on a pattern which came from the Near East . . . he throws back covers made from cotton domesticated in India, or linen domesticated in the Near East, or silk, the use of which was discovered in China. . . . He takes off his pajamas, a garment invented in India, and washes with soap invented by the ancient French. . . . He puts on clothes whose form originally came from the skin clothing of the nomads of Asia, . . . begins breakfast with an orange from the eastern Mediterranean or a cantaloupe from Persia. With this he has coffee, from an African plant. . . . He reads the news of the day imprinted in characters invented by the ancient Middle Easterners upon a material invented in China by a process invented in Germany. But he will say that he is 100 percent American.

Industrial technology has produced many more goods and services throughout the world. But it has also created many problems.

Some of the new problems include the changed ways of life for people. The movement from farms to cities is taking place all over the world. Cities everywhere face housing, health, and transportation problems.

Some of the problems have to do with the earth itself. Everywhere natural resources need protection. Coal, oil, timber, and good water cannot be used carelessly. The whole world must care about pollution.

All people share common problems for the future. All must take care of the earth, our home. The future of mankind depends on all peoples learning to live together through respect for each other's cultures.

1. Why do you think that stone was so important in ancient cultures?
2. What do you think happened when a Stone Age culture came into contact with a Bronze Age culture? What changes do you think the use of bronze brought to Stone Age cultures?
3. Nomad peoples often socialize their children differently from farming peoples. Can you explain why? What kinds of rules and behavior might be better for nomad cultures than for farming cultures?
4. Do you think that there was a connection between the domestication of animals and the growth of cities? Explain.
5. What are the advantages of an industrial culture over a non-industrial culture? What are the disadvantages?

INVESTIGATING THE UNIT

Doing Research

Pretend you are an anthropologist going to live among the people of eastern Africa. What kind of information about their culture would you need before you went? Would you need to learn some of the rules of societies there? Why? Go to your school or town library. What other useful information can you find? After two years in Africa, do you think you could add information to help someone else with the same assignment? How?

Looking at the Evidence

Imagine you are an archaeologist digging up the remains of an ancient city. You find the earliest objects at the very deepest level of your digging. There you find beautiful, well-made pottery. What kind of technology do you think might have produced these things?

The next level up shows things made a little later. There you find more pottery. But the style of decoration is different, and the pottery is not as well made. Along with the pottery, you find metal weapons of a kind that the earlier people did not have.

What hypothesis can you reach from all of this evidence? What do you think might have happened to the earlier people?

Using Maps

Many maps show information other than locations. Find an atlas in your library. What kind of special maps might be useful to a businessman who wants to invest in an area? Would he want to know about transportation and resources? Why or why not? What kind of map might interest a farmer?

Comparing and Contrasting

Compare the way that the Eskimo girl, Raigili, was raised with the way you were brought up. Did your father behave like Raigili's father? What differences do you notice? Do these show basic differences between our culture and Eskimo culture? Explain your answer.

Reading on Your Own

Try reading some books about other cultures. Here are two suggestions: *The Forest People,* by Colin Turnbull (New York, Clarion Books, Simon & Schuster); *Never in Anger,* by Jean Briggs (Cambridge, Mass., Harvard University Press). Look in your school or town library for books about other cultures around the world.

NORTH AFRICA AND THE MIDDLE EAST

Most of the vegetables and fruits we eat began in the Middle East.
Wheat, barley and rye, onions and garlic, figs and olives,
apples and pears, peaches, plums, and apricots, walnuts and
dates, all grew along the rivers and oases of the Middle East.

CARLETON COON

Yesterday and Today

LANDS OF CONTRAST

North Africa and the Middle East are lands where "a cloud gathers, rain falls — people live; the cloud disappears without rain — people and animals die."

These are lands without seasons. Only the temperature changes. Days are hot. Nights are often cold.

Mountains and deserts These are lands of wilderness, rugged mountains, and wide, almost empty deserts. Yet millions of people live in the Middle East and North Africa. They live along the Mediterranean Sea and on green oases in the deserts. And they live along the great rivers, the source of life for much of the region. For it was along the great rivers of the Middle East and North Africa that Western civilization began.

A meeting place The Middle East is often in the news as a battleground and a trouble spot. Throughout its history, it has been a place whose peoples have been conquered by their neighbors from other lands. Look at the map. Try to see why the Middle East is called the meeting place of three continents. What are the three continents? Notice where Asia and Africa join. Why might people moving from one continent to the other come into conflict here?

Think of the sea as a highway. Does the Middle East have a good water highway? Why would the lands around the Mediterranean be a good crossroads for many people?

Throughout the long history of the Middle East, this meeting of peoples has produced

▶ What would it be like to live in a land without seasons? What differences would it make in your life?

▶ med′ ə tə rā′ nē ən

▶ An oasis (ō ā′ sis) is a patch of trees and grass in the desert. It takes water from underground streams. Oases (ō ā′ sēz) is the plural of oasis.

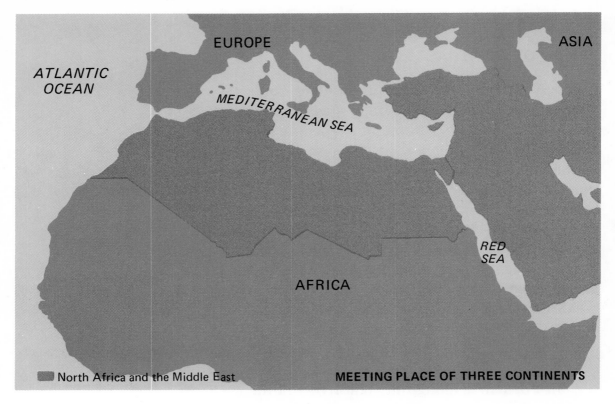

ATLANTIC OCEAN

EUROPE

ASIA

MEDITERRANEAN SEA

RED SEA

AFRICA

North Africa and the Middle East

MEETING PLACE OF THREE CONTINENTS

trouble and warfare. But it has also given the world agriculture, writing, great cities and cultures, and many scientific discoveries. And it has produced three of the world's great religions: Judaism, Christianity, and Islam. In other words, it has given the world **civilization.** The Middle East was the cradle of civilization.

CIVILIZATION

What is this thing called civilization? Everyone has his own idea. But most people agree that it involves a more complicated life than is possible in small tribes or villages. Most archaeologists think that cities are signs of a civilization. Civilization also involves things like writing, trade, complicated manufacturing, and high levels of art and government. These are things that mankind could not produce in primitive villages.

◗ Archaeologists (är′kē ol′ ə-jists) are scientists who study the ruins of ancient cities and villages to learn about the life and culture of a people.

◗ Primitive (prim′ ə tiv) means crude or simple.

52

TIME LINE

	Sumerian cities
	Egyptian pharaohs start rule
3000 B.C.	
	Pyramids built
	Decline of Sumer
2000 B.C.	
	The Babylonians
	Abraham (c. 1800 B.C.)
	Hammurabi (c. 1750 B.C.)
	Moses (c. 1200 B.C.)
	Phoenicians
1000 B.C.	
0	Birth of Christ
	Mohammed (580?–632)
	Moslem kingdoms
1000 A.D.	
	Ottoman Empire (c. 1300–1923)
	Conquest by Europeans
	(c. 1850–c. 1944)
1950 A.D.	Israel created (1948)
	Independence for most
	Middle Eastern nations

Before cities People who lived before there were cities depended on hunting, gathering wild plants, and simple farming. Hunting and gathering took up a lot of time and energy. Almost every adult had to spend most of his time just getting food.

Sometimes very early people developed a simple form of agriculture. They cut down trees and burned them to form small clearings in a forest. Then they dug around the stumps with

▶ Can a society based on hunting do or make many other things? Why or why not?

▶ Contrast these methods of getting food with the ways we get food today. How do city people get their food?

53

simple sticks and hoes and planted their crops. This is called **slash-and-burn** agriculture. Does slash-and-burn farming sound like almost as much work as hunting?

Specialists There are other differences between simple societies and civilizations. It takes **specialists** for a civilization to develop. Specialists are people who can spend much of their time at one particular task, like sewing cloth or making pottery or trading. People who work like this are then able to trade their products for food and other things they need. In that way, food growers and the makers of other products become specialists, too. Why?

Some early people taught themselves to make pottery and tools. They even began to spend part of their time trading the things they had made. But they still had to spend most of their time searching for food. They had become only part-time specialists. Simple cultures were not able to invent writing or the other things that make a civilization.

▶ spesh′ əl ists

▶ Is your father or mother a specialist? Is any adult you know *not* a specialist?

This statue of a woman milling grain is more than 4,000 years old. It is an artifact—something made by human workmanship. What does the statue tell about life 4,000 years ago?

Specialists and cities If a specialist does just one small task—like painting pictures on jars—he must depend on a lot of other specialists to live. The jar painter depends on the man who makes jars. He also depends on the people who buy painted jars from him. He depends on the farmers who trade their food for painted jars. He depends on soldiers to protect him and on teachers to teach his children.

But how did people start living like this? Who invented cities and city life? Archaeologists look for answers to questions like these. They have found answers to many of them in the ruins of the Middle Eastern deserts.

THE CREATIVE SUMERIANS

Land by the rivers The place is the land of Sumer. The ruins date back to 5,000 years ago. They are ruins of the world's first cities. But they present us with a great mystery.

How could civilization have begun in these lands? The desert is dry and hard. There are hundreds of more beautiful and fertile spots

Sometimes archaeologists find buried cities, as well as objects. These ruins are evidence of an ancient civilization.

▶ How many people do you depend on to live? Start counting. Do you think you will ever reach the end? How is our society more complicated than early societies?

▶ sü mer′ē ənz

▶ sü′mər

▶ Find Sumer on the map. What cities are there? What rivers are they near?

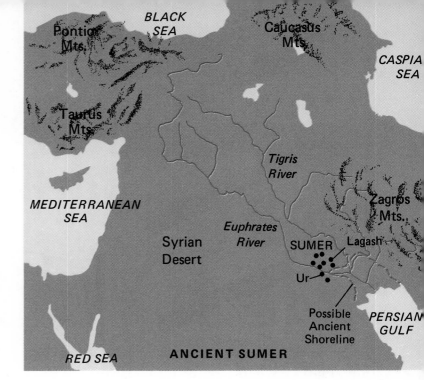

BLACK SEA

Pontic Mts.

Caucasus Mts.

CASPIAN SEA

Taurus Mts.

Tigris River

Zagros Mts.

MEDITERRANEAN SEA

Euphrates River

SUMER

Lagash

Syrian Desert

Ur

Possible Ancient Shoreline

PERSIAN GULF

RED SEA

ANCIENT SUMER

around the earth. Why was this the site of the first cities? Where did these city people get their food?

Archaeologists looking for the answers to these questions found some interesting clues. All around the ruins of the Sumerian cities, they discovered traces of canals, storage basins, and irrigation works. The fields that depended upon these works must have been quite large. Archaeologists believe that Sumerian farmers must have been able to grow more food than they needed. Does that explain why they were able to feed city people who could not grow their own food?

Early traders Archaeologists have also found evidence of another city activity—trade. Many of the tools and other objects found in the Sumerian ruins were made of materials from far-off places. The Sumerians had to trade for gold, tin, copper, and even wood. The things they made from these materials could then be traded for more materials.

▶ Irrigation (ir′ ə gā′ shən) means bringing water to agricultural areas that do not get enough rainfall.

▶ Hundreds of construction men and engineers are needed to build irrigation works today. What do the remains of Sumerian canals and irrigation works tell us about their civilization?

56

Cuneiform Much of what archaeologists know about the Sumerians comes from writing on clay tablets found in the ruins. The marks on the tablets were made by pressing the round end of a stick into clay when it was soft. When the clay hardened, wedge-shaped marks — cuneiform — were left. At first, the marks were small drawings of the ideas they represented. For example, this shape ✳ is the sign for star or heaven. Eventually, the Sumerians changed the sign to ➤⊢ . Try making the two signs. Which would be easier and faster to make with a stick pressed into clay?

Cuneiform was very difficult for scholars to figure out. Suppose you found a slab of clay with strange marks on it. The marks do not look anything like our writing. Can you see why it took years for scholars to translate this language?

Early records Some of the messages seem very ordinary. A few simply record how much wheat or barley a farmer owed a trader or how much one trader owed another.

◗ kū nē′ ə fôrm

Art sometimes tells us about the past. Artists often represented everyday activities in their work. The workers shown below lived almost 5,000 years ago. They were dairy workers.

▶ Why would it be important for traders and farmers to have records like this? Could widespread trade exist without some form of record-keeping?

▶ A shekel (shek′l) is a Sumerian coin.

This man was an important Sumerian governor. How do you think archaeologists found out who he was?

Cuneiform tablets also record how much land or other property each Sumerian had. These records were probably used by tax collectors. Why would tax collectors need such records?

Evidently, Sumerians must have seen quite a lot of tax collectors:

When a citizen brought a sheep to the palace for shearing, he had to pay five shekels. If a man divorced his wife, the tax collector got five shekels and his assistant got a shekel. If a perfumer made perfume, the tax collector got five shekels, his assistant got a shekel, and another assistant got another shekel. From one end of the city to another, there were tax collectors.

Sumerian gods and priests Cuneiform records also tell us about the many gods the Sumerians worshiped. Sumerians believed their gods had the power to control the forces of nature. They could stop the rivers from flowing; they could send insects to destroy a crop.

The Sumerians believed that only a few people could speak to the gods and keep them happy. These were the priests.

Being a priest was an important job in the land of Sumer. The priests collected food and animals to sacrifice to the gods. They were in charge of fields and temples that were set aside for the gods' use.

The priests may have been the first people to invent a way of keeping time. Sumerians believed that each god required certain ceremonies and sacrifices at the proper time. If the priest did not perform these at the right hour, the god might punish the people.

Telling time To tell time, priests kept close watch on the movements of the sun and stars.

They discovered that the stars moved in certain patterns. Once they got to know the patterns, they could tell what time of the year it was. From watching the sun, they learned to divide time into seasons, days, hours, and minutes. All of this took careful measurement by specialists. Would a time system like this be important for planting crops? Why? Would it be useful for city people, too? How?

Think of all the things the Sumerians invented: canals and irrigation, specialization of many different jobs, and a system of writing and of telling time. Would these things have been possible in simple villages? Why or why not? In what ways was Sumerian city life new and different?

THE BABYLONIANS— FIRST OF MANY INVADERS

▶ bab′ ə lo′ nē ənz

Ruined land The Sumerian civilization lasted for hundreds of years. But, despite its brilliance, Sumer slowly declined. No one knows exactly why. We do know that one cause was the ruin of the farmland. What ruined it? A common thing. Something you eat every day. Salt.

Salt makes land infertile. But where did the salt come from? See if you can guess. Do you live near a sea or the Atlantic or Pacific Ocean? Is the water fresh or salty? Suppose that you had to irrigate your land with water from the sea or ocean. Where would the salt go?

▶ Infertile land is land where the soil is too poor to grow crops.

Look at the map. Where did the Sumerians get water to irrigate their land? What do you suppose happened to the salt in the water?

The Babylonian empire A little less than 4,000 years ago, a different people set up some

◗ tī′ gris

◗ ū frā′ tēz

cities on the upper part of the Tigris and Euphrates rivers. The most famous of these cities was Babylon, where the emperor lived. The people were called Babylonians.

The Babylonians lived farther up the river than the Sumerians. The farther up a river, the less salty its water is. The fields of Babylon were fertile. So, as Sumer grew weaker, Babylon became stronger. It did not take the Babylonians long to defeat and take over the land of their neighbors. This invasion was the first of many throughout the history of the area.

From Babylon, the emperor sent his armies to conquer new lands throughout the Middle East. As the Babylonian empire grew larger and more powerful, Babylon itself grew wealthy. It became the center of trade and wealth in that part of the world.

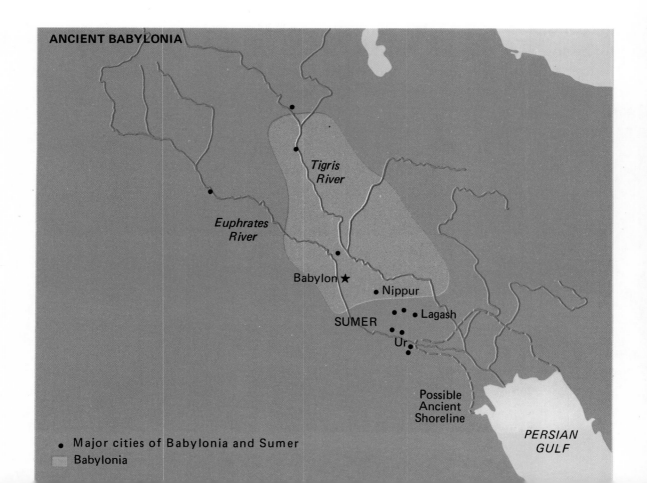

ANCIENT BABYLONIA

Tigris River

Euphrates River

Babylon ★

• Nippur

SUMER

• Lagash

Ur •

Possible Ancient Shoreline

PERSIAN GULF

• Major cities of Babylonia and Sumer

Babylonia

Hammurabi is shown here receiving a scroll from one of the gods. Why would it be appropriate for Hammurabi to be shown with a scroll?

The Babylonian contribution to civilization The Babylonians not only conquered an empire—they developed new ways to run it. The most important of these was their use of law. Many Sumerian cities had had their own laws. The Babylonians brought these laws together into a code. This code became law for the whole empire.

▶ A code is a collection of laws.

Hammurabi's Code The king who ordered these laws to be collected was called Hammurabi. Here are some of the laws of his code:

▶ ham′ ə räb′ ē

If a man has stolen a child, he shall be put to death.

If a son has struck his father, his hands shall be cut off.

If a man is robbed and the robber is not caught, the governor of the city shall give the man the value of his stolen goods.

If a builder makes a house that falls down and kills someone, the builder shall be put to death.

▶ How are these punishments like our punishments for the same crimes? How are they different?

61

Are these good laws? What effect do you think the laws had on the empire? Is it helpful to know what is against the law and what the punishment is? Why? Would the empire be stronger with such a system?

But even with the laws, the Babylonian empire did not last. Babylon and the other cities crumbled. The power of the empire was quickly forgotten. But people still remember the Babylonian laws.

PEOPLE OF THE NILE

As empires rose and fell along the Tigris-Euphrates valley, a different civilization grew up along another great river—the Nile. The Nile lies hundreds of miles to the west, in Africa. The civilization that developed was the Egyptian civilization.

From mountains far to the south, the Nile flows more than 4,000 miles to the Mediterranean Sea. It winds through the African desert like a green, wet snake. Without the water of the Nile, there would be no life. Without the Nile, there would never have been an Egyptian civilization.

The ancient Egyptians knew how vital the Nile was. They believed the river was a gift from their chief god, Re. They wrote a poem of thanks to the river:

> Praise to thee, O Nile,
> River that comes forth from the earth and comes
>   to nourish the dwellers in Egypt.
> That waters the meadows our god Re has created
>   to nourish all the cattle.
> That gives drink to all the desert places which
>   are far from the water.

▶ Look at the time line. How long ago was this?

▶ Why might these first civilizations have begun beside rivers?

▶ Why would the river look green?

▶ Vital means necessary to life.

▶ rā

Flooding of the Nile Each year, in June, the Nile overflows its banks. Water and fertile silt spread over the land of Egypt. The river silt is rich and perfect for farming. The flooding lasts until October. After that, the level of the river drops.

Flooding wipes out boundary markers on the farmers' fields. Because of this, the Egyptians learned to survey the land. Would written records be important for surveying? Why? Surveying also helped the Egyptians to develop arithmetic and geometry.

Hieroglyphics The system of writing that the Egyptians used was called hieroglyphics. Hieroglyphics used picture signs for the things they represented. To say that a man sailed down the river, for example, the Egyptians might draw pictures of a man, a boat, and a river.

▶ Silt is soil carried by a river.

▶ If you had too much water part of the year, and too little the rest of the year, what would you do? What do you think the Egyptians did?

▶ To survey (sər vā′) means to find and mark the boundaries of a plot of land.

▶ hī′ ər ə glif′iks

Here is an example of hieroglyphics. What do you think the picture signs at the top show?

63

The ancient Egyptians buried their dead pharaohs in huge pyramids. The pharaoh's body was carefully preserved and sealed in a beautiful casket like the one at the right. Often, beautiful objects, like those shown on these pages, were placed in the tomb. Do you recognize the objects in the lower picture on the opposite page? They are ancient chess sets. The Egyptians believed that these things would help the pharaoh in the "kingdom of the dead." Much of this treasure was stolen from the pyramids over thousands of years. But enough has survived to give scholars a good idea of ancient Egyptian life.

Try inventing a system of writing like hieroglyphics. What happens to your pictures when you try to write fast? Can you see why the Egyptian signs became less and less like pictures as time went on?

Now try writing about happiness in your picture language. Are there some ideas and emotions that are difficult to say in a picture language?

Hieroglyphics were not written on paper. Most paper is made from wood. The Egyptian desert has few trees. So the Egyptians did not use paper. Instead they used the reeds that grew along the Nile to make a substance called papyrus. When the reeds were split and woven, they made a writing surface that is even stronger than most types of paper.

Reed boats The Egyptians also used the Nile reeds to make boats. You might think that reed boats would not be very strong. But recently, a scientist and explorer named Thor Heyerdahl tried to find out how strong Egyptian boats really were. Using old Egyptian drawings on papyrus as a guide, he had a reed boat built. He sailed that boat thousands of miles across the Atlantic to America. What do you think he proved?

Though the Egyptians may not have gone to America, they did sail to many cities. Look at the map and find out how they went. Would it be easier to sail around, rather than to walk across the desert? Why?

Egyptian traders The Egyptian boats sailed to many lands. They brought food, cloth, and beautiful carvings to Babylon, Phoenicia, and Cyprus.

▶ Papyrus (pə pī′ rəs) is a writing surface something like paper.

▶ thôr hī′ ər däl

▶ fə nish′ ə
▶ sī′ prəs

66

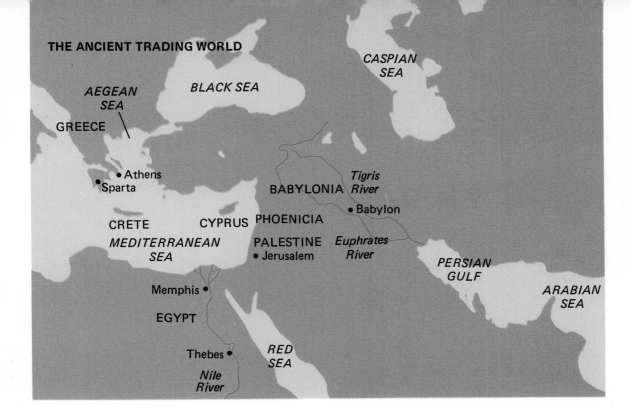

THE ANCIENT TRADING WORLD

In return for their goods, the Egyptians got copper, tin, gold, pottery, and wood. With the copper and tin they made bronze, a much harder metal. The bronze could then be used for picks, hoes, or other farm tools, and for spearheads and swords.

Like the Sumerians and the Babylonians, the Egyptians founded an empire and a civilization built on trade.

▶ Would these things be better because they were made of bronze? Why? Would an army with bronze swords have an advantage over other armies?

The Hebrews One of the things that the Egyptians traded was slaves. At one time the Egyptians were masters of a whole people. These were the Hebrews, an ancient Sumerian tribe. We can learn a great deal about life in those times by studying a famous book—the Bible. The Bible tells us that the Egyptians treated the Hebrews badly:

So they made the people of Israel serve . . . and made their lives bitter with hard service, in mortar and brick and in all kinds of work in the field.

▶ A tribe is a group of related families who live and work as a single society.

▶ "The people of Israel" is another name for the Hebrews.
▶ Mortar and brick are used for building.

THE PHOENICIANS—
SAILORS OF THE ANCIENT WORLD

Find Phoenicia on the map on page 67. Phoenicia was not a rich or fertile land. So the Phoenicians turned to the sea. They built a wealthy and powerful kingdom through trade.

The Phoenicians were a water-loving people. Their ships were smaller than many lifeboats on modern ships. Yet they sailed across the Mediterranean Sea and out into the Atlantic Ocean.

The Phoenician ships carried wood, wine, pottery, and tin to Egypt. In return, the Phoenicians got gold and ivory and finely worked Egyptian handicrafts. They traded these products to other peoples for glasswork and spices. And with each trade, the Phoenicians made a profit.

But the Phoenicians' greatest contribution to civilization was their alphabet. They used a different symbol for each sound, rather than for each word as other early alphabets did. So instead of having hundreds of symbols, the Phoenician alphabet had only 22. The Phoenicians took their simpler way of writing to other lands. Most of today's alphabets are based on the Phoenician idea of using a letter for each sound. The Phoenicians are gone now, but their part in the growth of writing will last.

The Hebrew people revolted and fled from Egypt. After years of wandering, they settled in Palestine. Here they stayed as farmers and shepherds for more than 1,000 years.

RELIGION—ANOTHER GIFT OF THE MIDDLE EAST

Polytheism The Sumerians and Egyptians both believed in many gods. This kind of belief is called **polytheism.** They believed one god controlled the sky. Another might control a river. Another would rule over the kingdom of the dead.

Many gods were pictured as human beings or animals, or mixtures of the two. They were supposed to behave like humans or animals, too. Some gods were jealous, some angry, some strong, some silly.

The Babylonian gods formed families. Of course, some of the family members were stronger than others. Here is a complaint by a

▶ pal′ is tīn
▶ Find Palestine on the map on page 67. Now look at the map on page 77. What nations are there today?

▶ pol′ ē thē′ iz əm

The figures below are statues of Egyptian gods. Do you think these are typical representations? Explain.

♦ ish′tär

♦ Is this how ordinary people talk and complain?

♦ Idols are statues of gods. People would buy these idols and worship them.

♦ Abraham was the founder of the Hebrew people. He and his family moved from the lands of Sumer to Palestine.

young goddess, Ishtar, to one god who had been given the right to give all the other gods their powers:

> The fate of all the great gods is in your hands.
> [The chief god] has given this power to you.
> But me, the woman, why did you treat me differently?
> Me, the holy Ishtar, where are my powers?

A new god Among all the hundreds of Middle Eastern gods, a very different kind of god emerged. He was the God of the Hebrews. Here is a Hebrew children's story that tries to explain how people began believing in this new kind of God.

> Abraham's father, Terah, made idols. When he was a boy, Abraham liked to help him in the shop. One day Abraham asked, "Can these idols eat or talk?"
>
> "Don't ask silly questions like that," Terah replied, "or the gods will get angry with you and beat you with a stick."
>
> Abraham thought about this all morning. When Terah went out in the afternoon, Abraham took a stick and broke all the idols except the chief one. He put a stick in the hands of the chief idol.
>
> When Terah came back he was furious. "Who has broken all these idols?" he thundered.
>
> "It was the chief idol," answered Abraham. "Look, he has a stick in his hands."
>
> "Nonsense!" shouted Terah. "How could something made of wood and stone do that?"
>
> "But if the idols are only wood and stone and can't do anything," asked Abraham, "why do people worship them?"

Why do you think Abraham broke the idols? Do you think he proved anything?

MONOTHEISM—A DIFFERENT WAY OF SEEING EVERYTHING

Abraham stopped believing in the Sumerian gods and started praying to one God. We call the belief in one God **monotheism.** Today, almost 4,000 years later, hundreds of millions of people throughout the world are monotheistic.

Monotheism is a very different way of thinking about the world. In a way, the old gods were quite human. People wrote poems and stories showing that the gods acted with one another just like people do. But a monotheistic God is not thought to be like humans. People believe that He has created everything in the world.

Judaism—the first monotheistic religion Abraham's tribe, the Hebrews, believed that their God had guided them through history. They believed that He rewarded them or punished them when they were good or bad. From that point of view, the Hebrews recorded the laws and history of their people in order to explain the things that happened to them. Do you know what that history is called?

The Hebrews had a small kingdom. In Jerusalem, the capital of the kingdom, was a large temple to their God. The temple was a place to pray, but it contained no idols. While the temple stood, most Hebrews remained in Palestine. But, not long after the time of Christ, the temple was destroyed by the Romans. Many of the Hebrews left Palestine—some on their own and some as slaves—and moved to other parts of the world. They lived away from their homeland for almost 2,000 years.

◗ mon′ ə thē iz′ əm

◗ Can you name the major monotheistic religions?

◗ Would a monotheistic God be more difficult to understand? Do you think people would be more comfortable with one God or with all of the old gods? Why?

Mosaics, like the one on the right, were widely used in early Christian times to portray religious scenes. A mosaic is made by cementing together small pieces of colored glass or stone.

▶ Most people in the world now date time from the birth of Jesus. How long ago was He born? Dates before the birth of Jesus are written with a B.C. after them. 1000 B.C. means 1000 years before the birth of Jesus. How long ago is that?

▶ Universal (ū′ nə vėr′ sl) means belonging to everybody.

Christianity—the second great monotheistic religion The Hebrews, or Jews, created the first of the great religions of the Middle East. And it was a Jew named Jesus Christ who founded the second of the great monotheistic religions—Christianity. Jesus tried to lead his people away from sin and closer to their God. He told them that they could save themselves only if they came to God.

Jesus talked of himself as "the son of God." He talked about himself as a bridge between God and people. What did Jesus' followers do after his death?

The first Christians tried very hard to spread their religion. They thought that many different people could share their beliefs. People who believed the Christian message went out to win more followers. Christianity is often called the first universal religion because many different peoples believed in it.

Christianity spread at a time when uncivilized tribes had overrun the ancient world.

Government and order had broken down. Cities were disappearing. People could not live in peace or safety. Would people be likely to turn to religion in such a time? Why do you think so?

Islam — a new religion While Christianity was spreading throughout the world, another new religion was born in the Middle East. It was also founded by a man who was trying to bring his people closer to God.

Mohammed The founder of Islam was Mohammed, an Arab camel trader. He was born in the small Arabian town of Mecca. When he was about 40 years old, he heard a voice speaking in the name of God — or Allah. Mohammed claimed the voice was the angel Gabriel. Mohammed had a scribe write down everything the angel told him. This record became the Koran — the holy book of Islam. The Koran recognizes Abraham, Moses, Jesus, and others as prophets. But it says that Mohammed was the last and greatest of these.

◗ The word *Islam* means "submission." A Moslem is a believer in Islam, one who submits to God.

◗ mō ham'id

◗ mek'ə

◗ al'ə
◗ gā' brē əl
◗ A scribe's job was to write letters or copy documents.

◗ kô rän'

The illustration below is an example of Middle Eastern art.

Moslems weave beautiful rugs in many colors and patterns. They often dry the rugs on a hillside.

The Moslem world By the time Mohammed died, thousands of Arabs had become Moslems. They also hoped to convert people around the world to their religion. Within a hundred years, they had conquered a large part of the Middle East and Spain. While the European nations became Christian, the Middle Eastern kingdoms became Moslem. Is that still true today?

In Europe at this time, science, learning, and art had died out. The Arab kingdoms became the center of civilization. Arab-speaking scholars and scientists became the most learned in the world.

A new number system Perhaps the most lasting contribution of this Arab culture was the invention of a new system of numbers. It is the same system we use today.

For hundreds of years, people had numbered with Roman numerals. How would you write your age in Roman numerals? If most of you are 11, XI stands for eleven. Can you write the year 1975 in Roman numerals?

But Roman numerals can be difficult. Try multiplying with Roman numerals. Multiply 12 apples × 11¢ apiece. Can you do it? Do you think you could figure out an income tax return with Roman numerals?

Now work out the same problems with the numbers you use. Can you do them? Is it much easier? You are using Arabic numerals — the numbers invented in the Middle East.

▶ Would an easy way of multiplying and dividing be important for trade? Why do you think so?

THE ARAB WORLD DECLINES

The Arabs spread Islam throughout the Middle East. Soon the Middle East became the Arab world. For hundreds of years, the Arabs managed to hold off attacks from other peoples, mainly the Europeans. But they could not stand up to a people who came from Turkey — the Ottomans.

▶ ot′ ə mənz

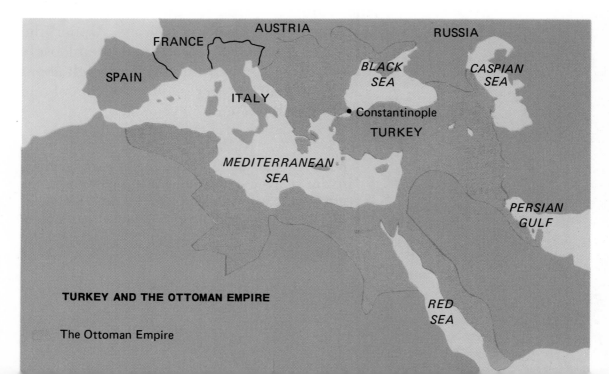

TURKEY AND THE OTTOMAN EMPIRE

The Ottoman Empire

▶ Find Turkey on the map. Why would Turkey be in a good position to attack the Arab world?

▶ Look at the map to see how large the empire was. Do you think it would be easy to govern an empire like that? Why?

The Ottoman Empire The Ottomans made Turkey the center of an empire that stretched most of the way around the Mediterranean, from Italy to Morocco.

Ottoman power lasted for hundreds of years. But they were not able to govern their empire well. The government could not keep up canals and irrigation systems. Crops failed. People got poorer. And soon the government lost its power.

As the Arab world declined, most of its people could not look forward to much. Learning and science all but died out. The few people who could read looked down on all the rest. Improvements were tried. But there were not enough educated leaders to put the improvements into action.

Europeans divide the Arab world As European nations got stronger, they looked across the Mediterranean at a weak Arab world. Can you guess what they decided to do?

Each European nation was jealous of the other. And each wanted to control at least a part of the Middle East. About 100 years ago, the Europeans split up the Middle East into a hodgepodge of many nations. Under the Turks, at least, all the Arabs had been loosely united. How do you think the Arabs felt about European control? Here is the reaction of one man who wrote about 50 years ago:

O Arabs! Are you asleep? When will you open your eyes and see the lightning of swords which are drawn over your heads? When will you know your country has been sold to the foreigner? See how your natural resources have been stolen. Now they belong to England, France, and Germany. You have become their slaves. They take your labor and leave you only the pangs of hunger!

In their eyes you are only a flock of sheep, whose wool is to be clipped, whose milk is to be drunk, and whose meat is to be eaten. Your country they consider a plantation. And you are the slaves on that plantation. Where is your pride? Where is your honor? Take up your swords and cleanse your country of the foreigner!

▶ Why do you think this writer felt this way? How would you react if you were in his position?

INDEPENDENCE BRINGS PROBLEMS

The modern nations of the Middle East developed from the different colonies set up by European nations. In the last 50 years, the people of each nation won their independence from the Europeans.

▶ A colony is a land ruled by another, stronger nation.

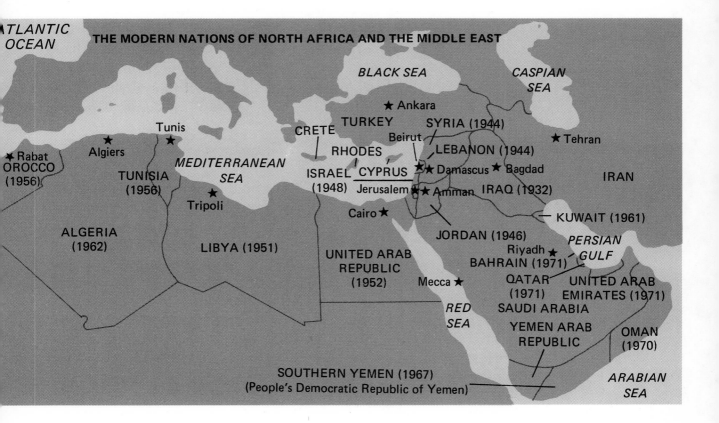

THE MODERN NATIONS OF NORTH AFRICA AND THE MIDDLE EAST

ATLANTIC OCEAN

BLACK SEA

CASPIAN SEA

★ Ankara

Tunis

CRETE   TURKEY   SYRIA (1944)

Beirut   ★ Tehran

Algiers   RHODES   LEBANON (1944)

★ Rabat
MOROCCO (1956)

MEDITERRANEAN SEA

ISRAEL   CYPRUS   ★★ Damascus ★ Bagdad

TUNISIA (1956)

(1948) Jerusalem ★★ Amman IRAQ (1932)

IRAN

Tripoli

Cairo ★

KUWAIT (1961)

ALGERIA (1962)

LIBYA (1951)

JORDAN (1946)

PERSIAN

Riyadh ★   GULF

UNITED ARAB REPUBLIC (1952)

BAHRAIN (1971)

Mecca ★

QATAR (1971)   UNITED ARAB EMIRATES (1971)

RED SEA

SAUDI ARABIA

YEMEN ARAB REPUBLIC

OMAN (1970)

SOUTHERN YEMEN (1967)
(People's Democratic Republic of Yemen)

ARABIAN SEA

Israel One of the new nations of the Middle East is Israel. It was created in 1948 as a homeland for the Jewish people. But the Arab nations surrounding Israel complained that this was not fair to the Arabs who were living there. Why do you think they felt that way?

The Israelis said that they had been promised the land as a refuge for their homeless. They added that there had been Jews living there for many hundreds of years. But the Arab states have refused to recognize Israel's right to exist. They have already fought three wars with Israel since it was established.

Wars and conquest are an ancient problem in the Middle East. Yet people of different religions and cultures have managed to live together in the past. They had helped to make the Middle East the birthplace of some of the world's greatest creations. Think of the discoveries the peoples of the Middle East have made. They are too many to count. Do you think the people of the Middle East will be able to solve their present problems? How?

▶ A refuge (ref′ ūj) is a place of safety and protection.

1. Why is trading necessary for a culture that has specialists? What is the connection between trading, specialists, and cities?
2. Why are reading and writing important for a civilization? What might happen to a culture if its people stopped learning to read and write?
3. Why were priests important in Egypt and Sumer? What did they know that other people there did not know? Do you think that they might have used their knowledge to keep their power? Explain.
4. Do you think that the Egyptians had difficulty living beside the Nile? Why? How did the Nile help Egyptians develop their culture? Why do you think that the Egyptians said, "Egypt is the gift of the Nile"?

The Land and the People

How do you picture North Africa and the Middle East? Swirling sand? Camels and Arab nomads? Well, today, most of the people of the region do not live in the desert. Only 1 person in 10 is a nomad. And the rest of the people are more likely to ride a bus or a bicycle than a camel.

WHERE DO MIDDLE EASTERNERS LIVE?

Some answers to this question can be found in the four maps of the region on pages 82 and 83. Look at the population map on page 82. Are people spread out evenly over the whole region? In what area are most of the people settled? Now look at the landform map on page 82. Are there certain kinds of areas where only a few people live? If so, what land features do you find in those areas?

Water—source of life Now look carefully at the places where people do live. What kinds of land features do they live near? Look at the rainfall map on page 83. How much rainfall do some of the heavily populated areas get? What heavily populated areas do *not* receive much rainfall? What natural features are they near?

People in the United States often take their water for granted. They turn on the tap and use as much water as they wish.

People in the Middle East are not so lucky. Their only sources of fresh water for drinking and farming are wells, rainfall, and rivers. But wells can supply only a small amount of water. Rivers or rainfall must supply the rest. Look again at the landform map. Are there many large rivers in the Middle East?

▶ Imagine having only a few cups of water a day for drinking and washing. Could you survive with only that?

80

Rainfall and landform   In the Middle East and North Africa, rainfall is directly related to land-forms. Rain clouds drift in from the sea. They pile up against the mountains and drop their rain. But the rain falls on only one side of the mountains. Look at the climate map. Which side of the mountains gets the rain? What climate do you find on the other side of the mountains?

Not all of these areas are deserts. Much of these dry areas are called steppelands. Steppelands often have shrubs and grass. Sheep and goats can live by eating this kind of vegetation. But when rain does not come, or when the herds have eaten all the grass in one area, the sheep or goats must be moved. Do you think this leads to a settled kind of life for herders and their families?

Irrigation   With irrigation, grains and fruit can be grown in steppe areas. But such crops need settled farmers to tend them all year round. Yet nomadic knowledge and traditions are centered around the wandering life of herding.

Large areas of the Middle East cannot be irrigated at all. In some desert regions, the soil is too rocky or sandy to be farmed. And sometimes, water is too far away to set up irrigation systems.

▶ How do you think nomads might react to irrigation of their lands? Is it hard to change a people's way of life?

POPULATION DENSITY

Many Middle Eastern countries have large populations and large land areas. Look at the chart below. Density means the number of people living in a certain space. The density of a square block may be 500 people. This means that 500 people live in that block.

▶ den′sə tē

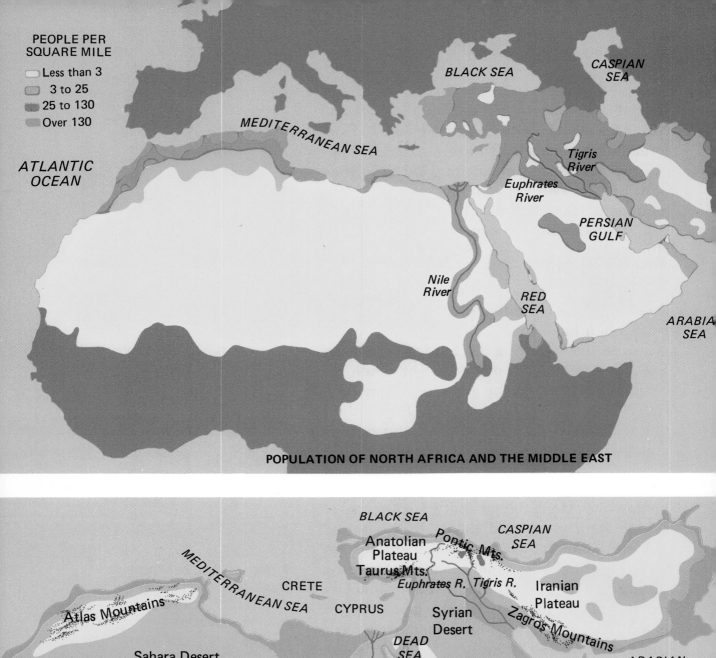

PEOPLE PER
SQUARE MILE

- Less than 3
- 3 to 25
- 25 to 130
- Over 130

ATLANTIC
OCEAN

MEDITERRANEAN SEA

BLACK SEA

CASPIAN
SEA

Tigris
River

Euphrates
River

PERSIAN
GULF

Nile
River

RED
SEA

ARABIA
SEA

POPULATION OF NORTH AFRICA AND THE MIDDLE EAST

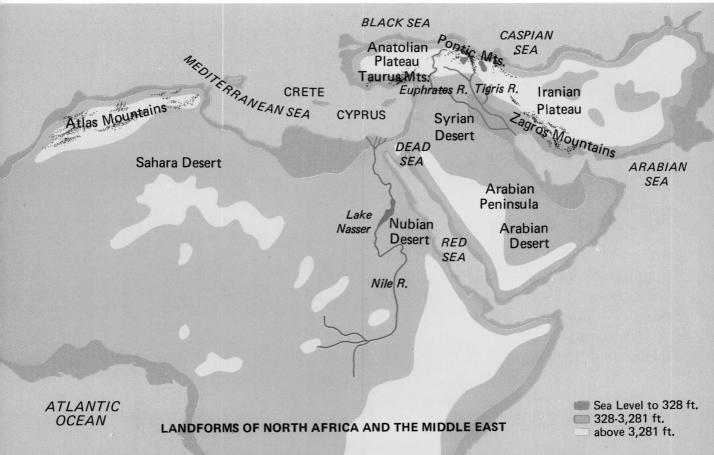

BLACK SEA

CASPIAN
SEA

Anatolian
Plateau
Taurus Mts.

Pontic Mts.

Iranian
Plateau

MEDITERRANEAN SEA

CRETE

Euphrates R.

Tigris R.

Atlas Mountains

CYPRUS

Syrian
Desert

Zagros Mountains

ARABIAN
SEA

Sahara Desert

DEAD
SEA

Arabian
Peninsula

Lake
Nasser

Nubian
Desert

RED
SEA

Arabian
Desert

Nile R.

ATLANTIC
OCEAN

LANDFORMS OF NORTH AFRICA AND THE MIDDLE EAST

- Sea Level to 328 ft.
- 328-3,281 ft.
- above 3,281 ft.

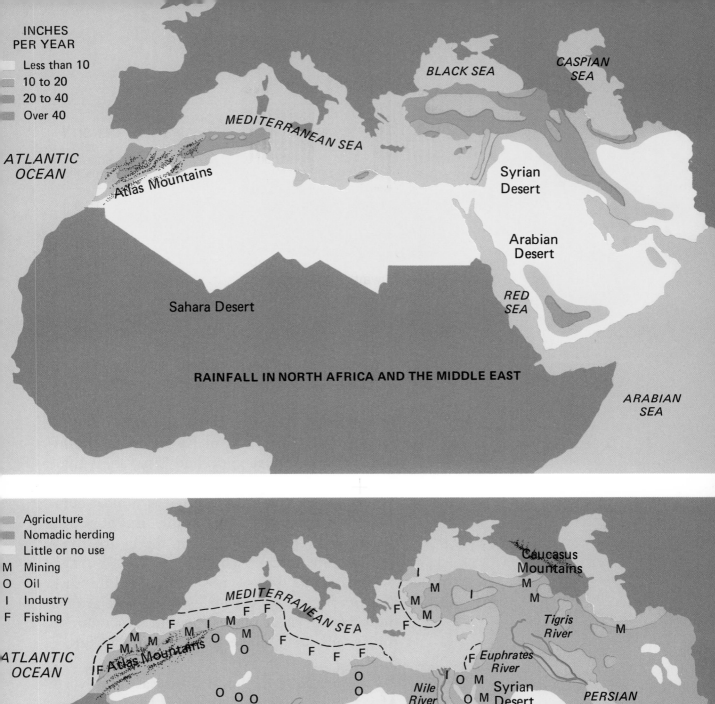

RAINFALL IN NORTH AFRICA AND THE MIDDLE EAST

INCHES
PER YEAR

Less than 10
10 to 20
20 to 40
Over 40

ATLANTIC
OCEAN

MEDITERRANEAN SEA

BLACK SEA

CASPIAN SEA

Atlas Mountains

Syrian
Desert

Arabian
Desert

RED
SEA

Sahara Desert

ARABIAN
SEA

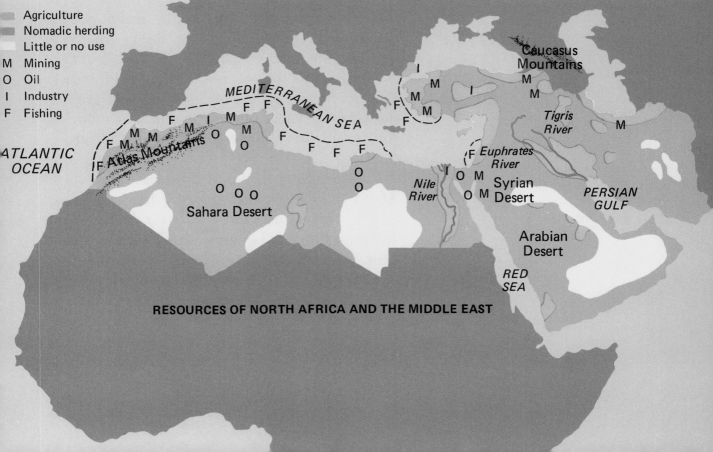

RESOURCES OF NORTH AFRICA AND THE MIDDLE EAST

Agriculture
Nomadic herding
Little or no use
M Mining
O Oil
I Industry
F Fishing

ATLANTIC
OCEAN

MEDITERRANEAN SEA

Caucasus
Mountains

Atlas Mountains

Tigris
River

Euphrates
River

Nile
River

Syrian
Desert

PERSIAN
GULF

Sahara Desert

Arabian
Desert

RED
SEA

	LAND AREA (square miles)	POPULATION (1972 estimate in millions of people)	DENSITY (per square mile)
Algeria	919,590	15.2	15.0
Saudi Arabia	830,000	7.9	8.7
Iran	636,293	30.5	43.8
Egypt	386,662	34.9	86.0
Kuwait	7,780	.9	118.0
Lebanon	4,015	2.9	629.0

1. Which are the largest countries?
2. Which countries have the largest populations?
3. Which countries have the higher densities?

True density Actually, these statistics tell only part of the story. Look at Egypt on the population map. Almost everybody in Egypt lives in a narrow strip of land along the Nile River. Ninety-seven percent of Egypt is almost completely empty. Do you think Egypt's true density is higher or lower than the figure given on the table above? Why?

The same is true of most of the Middle East. Density figures for countries as a whole are not high. But in most places, people are crammed into small areas close to water and to fertile land.

Few peasants in the Middle East and North Africa own even one acre of land. In most cases, peasant farmers—called *fellahin*—rent from landlords. They pay part of their crops as rent. Most farms are small. In Jordan, for example, more than 8 of 10 farms are smaller than 25 acres. In the United States, a farm of 160 acres is not considered large today.

The man at the right is a fisherman with his son. They are making a net. The family below is drawing water from a well. The field above is on an experimental farm run by a Middle Eastern government. The farm tries to find new ways to grow more and better food. Why may these farms be important?

Land reform Some countries, such as Iran, Syria, Iraq, and Egypt, have programs that require rich landowners to sell some of their land to the government. The government then sells or gives the land to small farmers. This is called land reform. But even with land reform, most people in the Middle East remain poor. There are just too many people for too little usable land.

INDUSTRIAL DEVELOPMENT

There are other parts of the world with little land and many people. Japan and Great Britain are islands with many people. Yet the people of both nations have high standards of living. Israel, in the same kind of land as the Arab countries, is also small, but it has a high standard of living.

In these lands and in the United States, most people are not farmers. Most people work in thousands of different industries. Study the resources map on page 83. In which countries is industry very well developed?

How some countries develop industry Some countries are lucky. They have many natural resources. The United States, for example, has great deposits of iron ore, coal, gas, and oil.

Some countries, however, have few raw materials. Great Britain, The Netherlands, and Japan are three examples. How do they build industry? They trade for raw materials. The people of these countries are skilled and well-educated. They make the raw materials into products that people in other countries will buy. That way, they bring in money to help build industry. Do you think this can be done in the Middle East?

▶ Japan has no iron or coal for steel. Yet television sets, radios, cameras, and cars are made there. How do you think Japan pays for the steel it buys from other countries?

86

Oil is wealth Most of the wealth of the Middle East and North Africa comes from oil. The region has a large part of the world's supply. But even this great resource is not enough for most countries. Oil is not evenly distributed. Kuwait has a lot, but Egypt has little. Some countries have wasted their oil income. Yet to the Middle East, oil is black gold.

THE WAYS PEOPLE LIVE

Though land reform and oil are bringing a better way of life to some people of the Middle East, new problems have been created. For many, a better way of life means changing the ways in which they have always lived.

There are three distinct ways of life in the Middle East and North Africa. One is found in cities. Another is found in small farming

Often, very different ways of life must exist side by side. What contrasts do you see here?

▶ How do you think oil could be used to develop other industries?

▶ Distinct means separate or not alike.

87

villages, where most people of the region live. The third is that of desert nomads who move from place to place seeking water and grass for their animals.

NOMADS OF THE DESERT

The desert nomads' way of life is like no other in the world. Nomads have no government as we know it. They have no schools, no churches, no policemen. Yet their way of life is very well organized and regular.

▶ bed′u inz

The Bedouins The Bedouins are nomads found in parts of North Africa and the Middle East. Bedouins keep flocks of sheep and goats and herds of camels. Their herds supply Bedouin people with food and a means of travel.

Traveling between oases and water holes, Bedouins follow set routes with their herds and flocks. Sometimes they stop at farm settlements. They are very dependent on oases for water and on town dwellers for grain, dates, fruits, and sugar. In exchange for these goods, Bedouins give meat, wool, and camel hair.

▶ A clan is a group of families related by blood.

Nomad groups A person alone in the desert could not survive long. As a result, each Bedouin knows how important the group is. He is first loyal to his family, then to his clan, then to his tribe. These groups are responsible for training the young and looking after each person's behavior.

▶ Do boys and girls in the United States receive training in male and female tasks? If so, how would you describe the training?

Bedouin men are camel herders and warriors. Women attend to the flocks, to housework, and to children. Children enjoy great freedom until they are about seven. Then boys begin to learn

the roles of men, and girls begin to learn the roles of women.

Related families form clans which are led by nobles. Several clans make up a tribe. A tribe is led by a sheik who rules with the aid of a council of elders. A sheik inherits his position from his father. Among Bedouins, decisions about routes to follow on the desert and relations with other groups are made by tribal leaders.

Generous hosts The Bedouins used to be tough warriors who attacked and robbed caravans and towns. Yet a reporter found that they have always been generous and hospitable, too.

".. . Providing hospitality is an honor for us," the sheik said, "and a sacred duty. Even if an enemy appears at this tent, I am bound to feast him and protect him with my life."

Bedouin nomads travel by camel. Do you think their clothes are practical? Why?

▶ shēk

▶ Are the Bedouin ways of making a decision especially suited to nomad life? Would the Bedouin system of making decisions work in the United States? Explain.

▶ Hospitable (hos′pi tə bl) means enjoying feeding and housing guests or strangers.

▶ Sacred (sā′crəd) means holy.

Water on wheels Today the way of life is changing rapidly for all nomads. Here is what another reporter recently wrote from a Bedouin camp.

Before dawn I awoke to the shouts of herdsmen and the braying of camels. We could hear a sound approaching in the far-off sand dunes. Finally, at sunrise, a big, wide truck pulled up. The driver got out and rolled out some oil barrels cut in half. Then, as fast as he could fill them with water, the camels gulped them dry.

"When I began driving, eight years ago, the animals were terrified," the driver said. "Now they flock around the truck like it's their mother."

Today there are few caravans either to guide across the desert or to rob. Some nomads herd animals for villages. Some have become soldiers or policemen. Some work for oil companies. Nomads had always looked down on farming as a way of life. But thousands are now becoming farmers and living in houses instead of in tents.

Perhaps the time will soon come when settled Bedouins will look back to their old ways in the same way Americans remember the old West—as a wild, free time that is gone.

FARMING VILLAGES

The old life of the nomads meant constant movement. If a tribe saw rain clouds far off, they would break camp and ride toward the rain. But most Middle Eastern villagers have never gone more than a few miles from the place where they were born.

In most farming villages, life goes on with little change. Parents joyously celebrate the

▶ Do you think it will be possible for some Bedouins to keep living as they once did? Why or why not? How do you think the Bedouins feel when they settle down to a village life?

▶ Why would they ride toward rain?

90

birth of a son. They raise their children in the same way they were brought up. Girls learn from their mothers to cook, sew, and do other household tasks. Boys learn to farm or herd or are trained in a craft, such as sandal-making.

Here is a description of a farming village:

One village is called the village of watermelons. It was so named because it came into existence a century and a half ago to grow watermelons. Now it also grows cantaloupes, rice, tomatoes, oranges, and limes. . . .

▶ Why do you suppose farming families are so happy to have sons?

Animals and machines cannot always do the work of people. Here men use backstraps to pull their boat.

The pictures here show scenes of village life. The men at the left are setting up their place in the market. The man above is shaping a bowl from copper. The Iranian boys below are learning to keep the village herd. Can you see scenes like this in the United States? Explain.

Recently the villagers came up with the idea of digging a long, deep ditch to trap the sand. They empty the ditch once a week. It is a hard, unpaid job, but the village never has lacked volunteers.

The population of 20,000 lives in brick houses or tiny huts, except for some 200 Bedouins living in tents.

The oldest villager, who is 90, said he could remember when the village had only 500 persons, mostly women and children. . . .

A century ago, the village had no mosque and no schools. Now it has one mosque, a kindergarten, and two primary schools. Apart from that, little has changed. . . .

The village has no movie theater, no electricity, no piped water. . . .

The people now take pride in their village and have hope for the future. Without losing their simplicity, they have stopped being servile.

The average family has seven children. The village has one grocer and one government medical unit. . . . There are no paved roads and no public transportation.

Whether villages are changing or not, farmers love their land. They are deeply attached to the soil. One observer spoke of the Egyptian *fellah*, or peasant, in this way.

The earth itself seemed to him a symbol of strength, of that which will last forever, and of honor. . . . He knew every inch of it, every detail. This land was his own life and his own history. When a boy, [he] had been given a little hoe, the same tool that his father had carried before him. . . . He knew the history of this land, of its crops, of its beasts. . . . The land never let you down. His father had planted [clover]. He had changed to cotton, then to beans, or perhaps sugar cane, and always the land was generous. If you were faithful to the land, if you tended it . . . , it would care for you.

▶ Why do you suppose removing sand from the trench is such a hard job?

◗ A mosque (mosk) is a building where Moslems worship.

◗ Servile (ser'vl) means being obedient without question.

◗ fel'ə

CITIES—PLACES OF CHANGE

Cities everywhere are busier and noisier than villages or small towns. But Middle Eastern cities seem even busier than most. There are the usual traffic and construction noises of a large city. But there are also bazaars—streets or markets of small stalls and stores. Sometimes store owners will call out to get the attention of customers. When a customer comes over, the two usually bargain in loud voices until the price of the article is decided.

The Old City Bazaars are usually located in the old section of Middle Eastern cities. Here is how a traveler described one of these old sections.

> The Old City was built for people, not machines. The streets are too narrow, crooked, and uneven for cars or even horse-drawn carts. The streets follow the natural curves of age-old needs, much like a riverbed.
>
> In some sections you feel you are not outdoors at all, but in the hallway of a large, rambling house. The streets are no wider than a hallway. Many of them are roofed over. Sometimes the area becomes a roomlike square with a roof supported by green and red pillars.
>
> At the crossroads of the main streets, a huge nail-studded door is hung, rusting on its hinges. It was designed to close the area off at night and to ward off the dangers of long ago.

There is often a mosque at the very center of an old city. Sometimes mosques are the tallest buildings in the old area. You can see them towering over the jumble of low, white buildings. These old sections are often surrounded by walls.

▶ bə zärz'

▶ Why does shopping sometimes take a long time in the Middle East?

▶ Would American cities be practical with streets like this? Why or why not?

▶ How would you feel in a city like this? Do you think you would feel closed in? Why?

▶ Is there a church at the center of your town? Why do you think towns often grow up around places of prayer?

The new cities The new parts of Middle Eastern and North African cities are different. Streets are wide and tree-lined. There are tall office and apartment buildings. Crowded streetcars and buses make their way down the streets. Cars made in Europe mix with bicycles, pedestrians, and even donkeys and camels. There are beggars and street merchants shouting and calling.

The suburbs Outside the cities, there are two kinds of suburbs. One kind has middle-class homes. The other kind is crowded with shacks

This Middle Eastern market is a jumble of people, stalls, and goods for sale.

▶ How is this different from your city?

Crowded shacks contrast with the modern high-rise buildings in the background. What problems might result from this mixture of housing?

▶ What kinds of specialists live and work in American cities? Why do you suppose there are so many different kinds of specialists in this country? Why would you expect to find fewer specialists in a farming village—even with a large population—than in a city?

and shelters made of mud, tin sheets, or anything at hand. This is where the jobless people and those with low-paying jobs live. Wages for these people may be a dollar a day or even less.

Jobs and half-jobs One of the reasons for low wages is the system of dividing jobs into small parts. For example, there are several kinds of messengers in Middle Eastern cities. Messengers of one kind carry messages only for banks. Others specialize in messages for department stores. Still other messengers work only for office buildings.

Beauty parlors and barber shops offer many kinds of services, each performed by a different specialist. In a barber shop, for example, there will be a barber who cuts hair in one style only, and another who cuts it in a different style. On crowded streets, there are men who help drivers find parking spaces for their cars, and get paid for it. And those helpers have helpers, too. They get part of the driver's pay.

Middle Eastern women There is much, like job specialization, that is old and traditional about cities in North Africa and the Middle East. But these cities are also places of important change. In traditional Moslem society, for example, women have always been treated as less important than men.

Women are supposed to obey their fathers and husbands without question. In some countries, they cover their faces (except for the eyes) with veils. Girls usually marry the man their parents choose for them. In some forms of Moslem marriage, the man is the center of the ceremony. The bride stays behind a closed door.

A veiled Moslem woman shops in a spice market. Her culture requires that she wear a veil.

97

A man can divorce his wife simply by saying three times, "I divorce you." Traditional Moslem girls do not go to school. Women cannot own property or vote.

But in several cities, especially in countries like Egypt and Turkey, the position of women has been changing. Women can vote in Egypt. In Turkey, they can own property and they can go to college. They no longer need to wear veils. Algerian women are even becoming stewardesses.

CHANGING LANDS, CHANGING PEOPLES

All through the Middle East and North Africa, change and tradition go together. Men in flowing white robes stand next to towers of oil wells. Camels hump across the desert carrying food, woven goods, and salt. Jet planes streak across the sky, carrying people and sometimes bombs.

Some things change very little. For a long time to come, there will be people with too little to eat and too many children who cannot read and write.

In the Middle East and North Africa, a slow revolution is occurring. Tradition is slowly giving way to change.

1. How does the geography of the Middle East affect where and how people make their living?
2. Does the condition of the land in the Middle East help explain the poverty of the people? If so, how?
3. What are some advantages and disadvantages of the nomadic way of life? Would you like to be a nomad? Do you think this way of life will be possible much longer in the modern world? Explain.

Case Study:
Immigrants Make a Nation

LOOKING FOR A BETTER LIFE

▶ An immigrant is one who comes to a new country to live.

Millions of immigrants came to the United States during the 1800s and the early 1900s. They came from nearly every country in the world. In the United States, they hoped to find jobs, new homes, and a better life. Because the United States became a country with many different peoples, it was called the "melting pot" of nations. But many people say that the United States is more like a stew than a melting pot. Here many kinds of people keep their differences, rather than "melting" together.

▶ What is a stew? Could you pick out the separate things that are in a stew—carrots, potatoes, meat, or tomatoes? Could you pick out the different things in a melting pot? Do you think a stew is a good comparison to use? Explain.

A new nation Today there is another melting pot, or stew, in the world. This is the nation of Israel.

When Israel became a nation in 1948, it opened its doors to Jews from everywhere. A special law called the *Law of Return* granted all Jews the right to move to Israel if they wished. And they came from all over the world. They came to Israel for many of the same reasons people had come to the United States.

▶ What happened in the 1940s to make many Jews leave Europe?

Jews came to Israel from all the countries of Europe—Germany, Austria, Rumania, Italy, and many others. They came from India and from Indochina. They arrived from Iraq and from Iran, and from Morocco, Algeria, and Libya in North Africa. Some came from Great Britain, and some from the United States. Still others came from Latin American countries. In 1961, the millionth immigrant arrived. By 1971, almost 2 million had come. Altogether, 79 countries were represented in the tiny new nation.

▶ rü mā′ nē ə

▶ mə räk′ ō
▶ lib′ ē ə

All of these people joined together to build a new land and a new culture. But the new culture will have customs from many lands.

DIFFERENCES IN IMMIGRANT GROUPS

Westerners and Orientals The population mixture of Israel is important and interesting. Sociologists sometimes explore such subjects. They study differences in groups making up a society. They look for clues to the values or beliefs of people in that society. They study how people affect each other. They want to know how distinct each group is from others and how each preserves its differences. A sociologist interested in Israeli society might

Some of the people who fled when the state of Israel was created still live in camps like this.

◗ sō′ sē ol′ ə jists

101

ON THE WINGS OF EAGLES

For thousands of years, Jews have lived in Yemen. Yemen is a small, mountainous country at the tip of the Arabian peninsula. The Yemenites lived by themselves among Arabs, cut off from other Jews. But they kept alive their religion, their language, and their traditions. They remembered the words of an ancient Hebrew prophet who said, "They that keep the way of the Lord . . . shall mount up on the wings of eagles."

The Yemenite Jews had kept the way of the Lord for many centuries. When the nation of Israel was born, it welcomed Jews from Yemen. The Israeli government sent planes to fetch the Yemenites. None of these people had ever seen a plane before. But each waited quietly for his turn to climb aboard. In a few weeks, more than 45,000 Yemenites were carried "on the wings of eagles" to Israel.

investigate the differences between two Israeli groups—immigrants from Europe and America and immigrants from Asia and Africa. Those from Europe and the United States are usually called Westerners. Those from Africa and Asia are called Orientals.

When people from the two groups first came to Israel, their differences were obvious. Europeans and Americans were used to the ways of life of their former countries. Most believed strongly in education. Their families were usually small. Standards of health and cleanliness were usually good.

Jews who came from Africa and Asia, on the other hand, sometimes had different values. Many of these immigrants were illiterate. They were not used to education in schools. Their families were large, but the death rate was high. The people had poor living conditions, and could catch diseases quite easily. In general, the standard of living was low.

Problems of the immigrants Both groups of the immigrants faced difficult problems when they arrived. Israel was poor and barren. The most urgent need was food. People who had been doctors or craftsmen had to learn how to farm. There was little housing. Hundreds of thousands of immigrants had to live in tents— sometimes for years. Though everyone got enough to eat, there were no luxuries for many people for years.

STATUS

Now things have changed. Most people have apartments and many appliances. Yet there are important differences between Oriental and Western Jews. In all societies, some groups are

◗ Oriental (ô′rē en′ tl) means eastern. The Orient refers to the eastern countries of the world. In the United States, Oriental usually refers to people from Asia rather than Africa.

◗ Illiterate (i lit′ ə rit) means unable to read or write.

◗ Barren (bar′ ən) means that the soil does not produce much food.

◗ How would you and your family adjust to living like this? Would you go through this just to live among your own people?

▶ Status (stā′təs) is the degree of importance of people or groups in a society.

more powerful than others. Sociologists say that these more powerful groups have a higher **status** than other groups. But how do they find this out? How do they measure status?

There is no single way of measuring status. Sociologists may study several different sets of statistics about various groups. Sometimes a pattern will develop that shows which group is most powerful and important.

Only modern construction methods can supply all the housing that is needed in the Middle East.

104

Status depends on the values of a culture. Some cultures give high status to wealth. In other cultures, education or birth determine status. Sociologists must learn the values of a particular culture.

Income One of the most common measurements of status is the income of the family. Look at the following table of family incomes of groups in Israel. See if a pattern emerges from the statistics.

♦ stə tis′ tiks

	ORIENTAL IMMIGRANTS	WESTERN IMMIGRANTS	ISRAELI-BORN	OTHER
Percent of families living in Israel	40.3	41.4	15.5	2.8
Average annual income in 1971	$2,549	$3,419	$3,452	$2,045
Average family size	4.8	3.1	3.7	6.4

1. Which are the two largest groups in Israel?
2. Which are the smallest groups?
3. Which groups have the most people in their families?
4. Which groups make the least money?

When immigrants arrive The Western Jews had come to Israel first. By Independence Day, May 15, 1948, almost 90 percent of the Jewish immigrants were Westerners. After Independence Day, the pattern of immigration changed. Westerners still came to Israel. But the majority of immigrants after Independence Day were Oriental.

In immigrant societies, the people who arrive first usually have more status and money than people who arrive later. Look at the following table to see if this is true in Israel.

TIME OF IMMIGRATION	ORIENTAL IMMIGRANTS	WESTERN IMMIGRANTS
Before 1947	$2,833	$3,833
1948–1954	$2,738	$3,309
1954–1960	$2,333	$3,071
1961–1971	$2,024	$2,619

1. Which groups make the most money?
2. Does every group make more than the group that arrived after them?
3. Do Orientals and Westerners who arrived at the same time make the same amount of money?
4. Does any group of Orientals make more money than a group of Westerners who arrived later?
5. What can you conclude about status and income? Do they depend on time of arrival? Why might this be?

What families own The number of things owned by a family is another indicator of status used by sociologists. Look at the following table to determine which groups of Israeli families own more than others.

	ORIENTAL IMMIGRANTS (percent)	WESTERN IMMIGRANTS (percent)	ISRAELI-BORN FAMILIES (percent)
Telephone	17.9	54.0	55.1
Television	59.1	66.1	65.2
Vacuum cleaner	7.3	33.8	25.4
Car	9.2	22.1	34.9

1. Which group has the greatest number of the goods listed?
2. Which group has the fewest number of the goods?

NUMBER CLUES

Hebrew is the official language of Israel. Most immigrants have learned to speak it. But even so, many people cling to habits from their old way of life. One visitor learned to tell where an Israeli was from.

The visitor quoted a newspaper article about David Ben-Gurion (ben gür' ē ən), the head of the government at the time. It seems that Ben Gurion used Yiddish when he wanted to count things. Yiddish is a language taken from an old form of German and written in Hebrew letters.

The visitor began to listen to people as they counted. He learned that one man he knew counted in Serbian (ser' bē ən). A girl at a supermarket check-out station counted in Rumanian. In a restaurant where he often ate, the visitor heard the waiter add up the bill in Persian, the language of Iran. A gas station attendant, he noticed, counted in Arabic. This system, the man wrote, had only one drawback. "To be good at it," he said, "you had better learn to count in at least 40 or 50 different languages."

The status of jobs Another way that sociologists measure status is to analyze jobs of wage earners. In Israel, professional workers (like doctors and architects) and administrative workers (like government workers) have a higher status than factory workers. Study these charts:

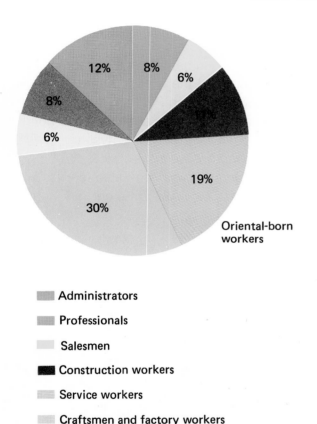

Oriental-born
workers

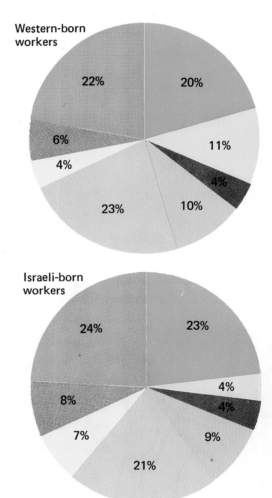

Western-born
workers

Israeli-born
workers

Administrators

Professionals

Salesmen

Construction workers

Service workers

Craftsmen and factory workers

Transportation workers

Farmers and fishermen

1. Which groups have the highest percentage of workers in high-status jobs?
2. Which group has the lowest percentage of workers in lower-status jobs?
3. What conclusions can you draw about the status of Oriental workers?

You might suggest that this situation applies only to the immigrants, not to their children. Look at the chart to see if this is true:

▶ Notice the change in the percentage of Oriental workers in administrative positions.
Is this a sign that the status of groups is beginning to change in Israel?

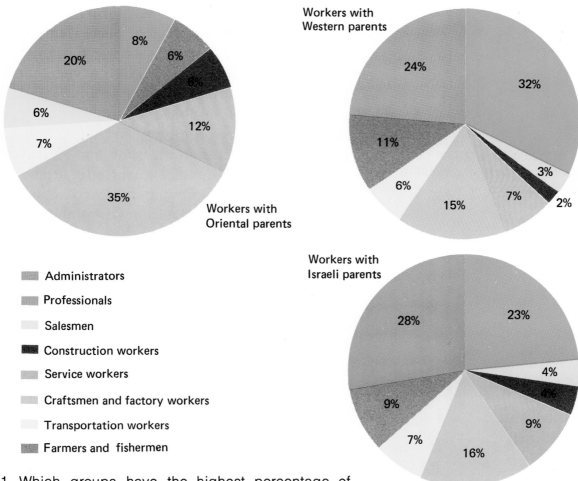

Workers with Western parents

24%
32%
11%
3%
6%
7%
15%
2%

8%
6%
6%
20%
6%
7%
12%
35%

Workers with Oriental parents

Workers with Israeli parents

28%
23%
4%
4%
9%
9%
7%
16%

- Administrators
- Professionals
- Salesmen
- Construction workers
- Service workers
- Craftsmen and factory workers
- Transportation workers
- Farmers and fishermen

1. Which groups have the highest percentage of workers in high-status jobs?
2. Which group has the lowest percentage in high-status jobs?
3. Which group has the highest percentage of workers in low-status jobs?
4. Which groups have the lowest percentage of workers in those categories?
5. How similar is this pattern to the preceding chart?

▶ Why would sociologists call this kind of gap a "social gap"?

▶ A retraining program is a course of study that helps a person learn a new job.

The social gap Sociologists at Israel's universities have been gathering statistics like those on the previous pages. They worried that too large a gap was developing between their people. Oriental people seemed to be making less money, working at lower-status jobs, and owning fewer goods than Westerners.

The Oriental population is becoming aware of this gap, too. They are asking the government for more help. In the last few years there has been an addition to this problem. Immigrants from Russia have been pouring into Israel. They are being given help such as apartments and retraining programs. How do you think most Orientals react to the programs to help the Russian immigrants?

Read these statements from Oriental leaders:

"If the government spends $35,000 to help a Russian family," asked one, "why does it not spend the same amount to help our people? We were immigrants ourselves 20 years ago and never got what the Russians are getting." Said another, "I don't mind if the Russian Jews come, but I don't want them coming at the expense of us Orientals."

Warnings heeded The Israeli government responded quickly to the warnings of the Orientals and the sociologists. It set aside $250 million to build new housing for the Oriental population. It began to clear slums. It developed new school programs to prepare Orientals for better-paying jobs of higher status.

Sociologists in Israel and elsewhere are watching these programs carefully. Already there have been great increases in the number of Oriental young people staying in school. The number of Oriental officers in the army has gone up, too. In a few years, sociologists will be trying to tell if the status of Oriental Jews in Israel has changed. How can the sociologists determine this?

People all over the world will be watching Israel to see how these problems are settled. Equality for all is a problem in every society. If this young country can solve its problems, then people all over the world can benefit from the solutions.

1. In what way is Israel similar to the United States?
2. What reasons can you give for sociologists to study the differences between social groups?
3. What problems might arise when one group in a society has much less status than another?
4. Do you know which group of immigrants was the first to come to the United States? How could you find out which immigrant groups had the highest and lowest status in the United States?
5. What do you think your status among your friends at school depends on? How could a sociologist studying your school find out?
6. Are there "social gaps" in the United States? How do we know?

INVESTIGATING THE UNIT

Doing Research

Look in some of the stores in your neighborhood. Try to find at least three products from the Middle East. Did you have any trouble finding them? Were the items that you found things that everyone in your area might buy? Can you tell anything about the economic problems of the Middle East from what you found?

Looking at the Evidence

Imagine that you are on vacation in the Middle East, by the Red Sea. While skin diving, you have come across an old, sunken boat. It is made of some kind of reed, rather than of wood. The boat contains pottery, jewelry, and some sculptures with hieroglyphics on them. Where do you think the boat could have been made? How old do you think it might be? What do you think it might have been doing when it sank? Where might it have been going? Explain how you would find the answers to these questions.

Compare and Contrast

Compare and contrast the positions of women in the United States and in the Middle East. Do women have the same rights in both places? Are they treated the same in both places? Do they have the same kind of opportunities as men in either place? Would you like to be a woman in the Middle East? Why or why not?

Using Maps

In 1967, Israel won a piece of territory called the Sinai (sī′nī) Peninsula in a war with Egypt. Since then, Israel has administered the territory, claiming that the region is vital for its defense. Find the Sinai Peninsula on the map. Why do you think that Israel makes its claim? What claim do you think Egypt makes in return? What important trade route is located in the Sinai region? Can you find out what has happened to that trade route because of the war? Look at the map. Where must the trade go now?

Reading on Your Own

The pharaohs were among the most interesting people of the ancient world. You can find out more about them in a book called *The Pharaohs of Ancient Egypt* by Elizabeth Payne (New York, Random House). One of the monarchs of Egypt was a woman. She is considered one of the most beautiful women who ever lived. You can read about her in *Cleopatra of Egypt* by Leonora Hornblow (New York, Random House).

WESTERN EUROPE

For 400 years the nations of Europe had led the world in technology and warfare. Now their day seemed to be ending. The question was asked: what if the leaders and peoples of Europe recognized at last that their common interests were greater than their differences?

J. ALEXANDER, F. G. MURPHY

Two thousand years ago, about the time when Christ was born, most people knew very little about the world in which they lived. Most people believed the world was flat. What we call Western Europe was one end of that flat world. Find Western Europe on the map on page 147. What modern countries does it include?

Think about this land long ago, before it was divided up into the nations of today. Only a few parts of it were crowded. There were a few busy cities — in what are today Italy and Greece. But the cities of Paris and London were just small towns.

Most people were farmers. Some were members of warlike tribes who lived by robbing and stealing from peaceful farms and towns. Some people, then as now, were traders or weavers or shepherds.

THE EARLIEST EUROPEANS

Cave paintings We know very little about the earliest Europeans. We have some information about them from paintings found on the walls of deep caves. Look at the picture of these cave paintings on this page. What do cave paintings tell modern scholars about the way of life of these ancient people?

The beginning of villages About 5,000 years ago, invaders moved into the lands of the cave dwellers. These invaders brought a new way of life to Europe. Archaeologists who have studied the remains of the villages say that many of the new people were farmers. Instead of hunting animals or following them from place to place, many of the new people stayed in one place. The cave dwellers, who hunted, often

Cave paintings often give modern archaeologists important information about the lives of the people who drew them.

◗ Archaeologists (är′ kē ol′ ə-jists) are scientists who learn about past cultures by studying the remains of those cultures — houses, tools, art.

115

▶ Which way of life do you think is a more settled one—that of farmers or hunters?

▶ Bronze (bränz) is a yellowish-brown metal made from copper and tin.

▶ Do you think archaeologists can tell how long ago a people lived by the kinds of tools they left? Can they tell how advanced a people were?

went hungry in the winter when they could not find animals. But the farmers were able to store the extra foods and grains that they grew. They began to build permanent villages.

Tools and weapons   For a long time, these farming peoples used stone tools. But gradually, they learned to use tools and weapons made of metals like bronze and iron. Metal tools were harder and lasted longer than stone. The knowledge of metal came originally from old cultures in the Middle East. Egypt was one of the oldest of these Middle Eastern cultures. Look at the historical map on page 117. What part of Europe is closest to Egypt? This part of Europe was the first to trade with Egypt.

THE RISE OF GREECE

A seafaring people   There is a good reason why the Greeks learned so much from Middle Eastern cultures. The Greeks were the greatest sailors of their time. The soil of Greece was too thin and poor for good farming, and the land was too mountainous for large farms. But Greece has one excellent natural feature. Look at the map of Greece on page 117. Describe the coastline of Greece. This coastline is blessed with many good harbors. Can you see why many of the Greeks left the mountains and took to the sea?

Ideas they have given us   The ancient Greeks have given the world many ideas about life and how to live it. The idea of democracy started in Greece. So did many ideas of science, religion, and government. But these ideas did not come out of Greece as a whole. Instead, they grew up in different cities spread throughout the Greek empire.

City-states The cities of Greece grew up in valleys near the sea. Each city was separated from the others by mountains. The roads connecting the cities were narrow and winding. Robbers camped alongside these roads.

Each city had its own vineyards, olive groves, and pastureland. Each city governed itself in its own way. And the citizens of each city were very proud of their city and its way of life. In fact, each city was really an independent state. Political scientists call such places **city-states.**

Two of the most famous Greek city-states were Athens and Sparta. Their ways of life were very different from each other. Yet both

◗ A vineyard (vin′yərd) is a place planted with grapevines.

◗ ath′ənz
◗ spär′tə

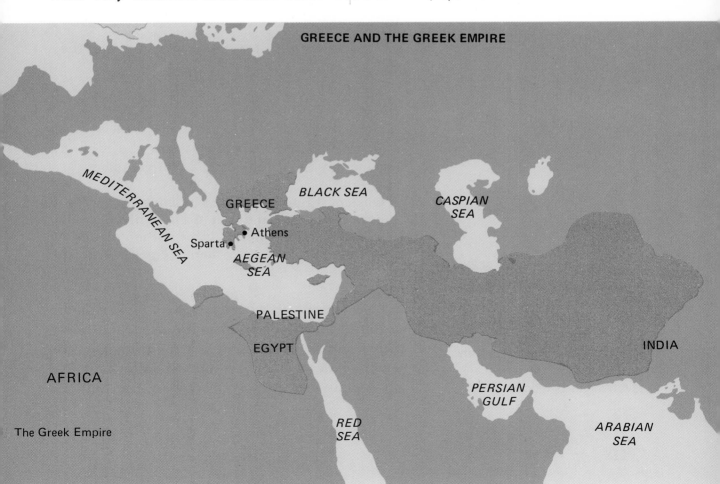

GREECE AND THE GREEK EMPIRE

MEDITERRANEAN SEA

GREECE

BLACK SEA

CASPIAN SEA

Sparta • Athens

AEGEAN SEA

PALESTINE

EGYPT

INDIA

AFRICA

PERSIAN GULF

ARABIAN SEA

RED SEA

The Greek Empire

The Greeks believed that a healthy body was as important as a sound mind. They invented the Olympic games and honored the victors with parades and garlands.

are remembered for the styles of life they developed.

Athens The most famous leader of Athens was named Pericles. Pericles lived from around 490 to 429 B.C. Here is how he defined democracy in Athens over 2,000 years ago:

> Our constitution is called a democracy because power is in the hands not of a minority, but of the whole people. When it is a question of settling private disputes, everyone is equal before the law.

Yet, despite its constitution, Athens was not a perfect democracy. Women and slaves were not regarded as citizens. Do you think a nation can be a democracy if it does not allow some of its people to participate? Why do you think so?

▶ per′ ə klēz

▶ Do you agree with what he said? Can you think of a better definition of democracy? Do you think American democracy is like this? If not, how do you think Athenian democracy differs from American democracy?

Sparta Find the word *Spartan* in your dictionary. What does it mean? Where do you think it might have come from? Try to imagine what life in such a place might be like.

Now find the ancient Greek city of Sparta on the map on page 117. Can you see any reason from its location why it should be very different from Athens?

Unlike Athens, Sparta was a military state. Twenty-five thousand Spartans conquered and ruled nearly a half million of their neighbors. These neighbors were forced to accept the Spartan way of life. They learned very quickly that the Spartan man was a warrior first. Seven-year-old boys were taken from home to be raised as soldiers. Spartan girls were raised to be the mothers of soldiers. Travel to other cities or lands was forbidden.

▶ Why might a very strict state forbid its citizens to travel to other lands?

In modern Athens, ruins of ancient buildings are an impressive monument to Greek culture.

Ancient Athens and Sparta did not last forever. For a time, the Greek city-states joined together to fight off outside attackers. But the Greeks began to fight among themselves. The city-states paired off. Some supported Sparta, some Athens. The wars went on and on. Finally, Athens surrendered.

Science The most important idea that the Greeks developed was that of reason. By reason, the Greeks meant using one's intelligence to figure out the way things work. Until the Greeks, people thought the world was controlled by strange and unseen powers. Believing in reason leads people to study their world so they can learn how it works. That is what scientists do. It is not surprising that the study of mathematics and medicine, of geography and of plants and animals, all grew into important sciences in the time of the Greeks.

▶ Do you recognize this idea of government? What do English-speaking people call this idea of government?

Government The Greeks used reason in other ways, too. They wanted to govern themselves so that people would be happy and able to work well. In most cultures until that time, governments controlled people. The Greeks thought that people should control government.

ROME—CITY AND EMPIRE

▶ lat'nz

In the center of Italy, there is a city called Rome. About 1500 B.C., a tribe of people called Latins settled there. Rome was in a good location. It had seven hills in it, which provided protection from attacking neighbors. It was built near a large river. Find the river on the map on page 121. Do you think Rome's river also helped it become a great city? How?

▶ How would a position on a hilltop be an advantage in battle?

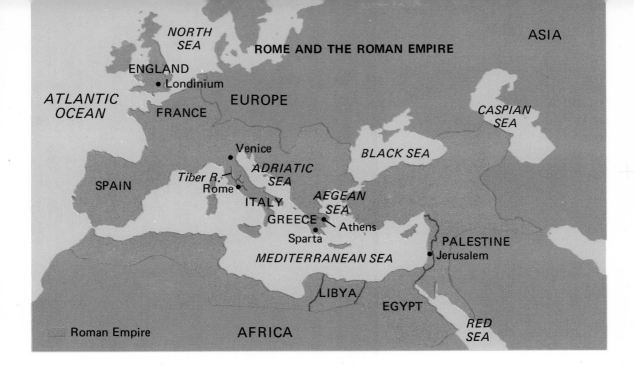

Look at the map and find Rome and Greece. Do you think it would be easy for ideas to travel between these two places? Early in the history of Rome, people from an island near Greece settled in Rome. These people had learned writing from Greek traders. They taught this writing to the Romans. They also taught Roman farmers the Greek way of making tools from bronze and other metals.

Romans at war   In time, the city of Rome grew stronger. Its soldiers went out and conquered all of Italy. But trained Roman warriors went even further. Look again at the map above. What regions of the world did Roman soldiers conquer?

One place the Romans conquered was Greece. But somehow, Roman ideas did not conquer Greek ideas. In a way, Greece conquered Rome. Rich Romans spoke Greek. They sent their children to schools where Greek subjects were taught. They built buildings that looked like the buildings in Greece. Greek culture became a large part of Roman life.

Hunting was considered a man's activity in many ancient cultures. But the Greek goddess Artemis was often pictured as a hunter.

Like the Greeks, the Romans built an empire. They began by developing a large and skillful army. Roman soldiers trained longer and harder than those of other lands. They learned the best ways of warfare. Their empire kept on growing.

Roman laws The Romans used laws to keep their empire together. The laws were based upon Greek laws, which were based upon the idea of reason. According to this idea, something was lawful if it was reasonable. A law was not made simply to prevent people from doing things. A Roman law was made only if sensible people believed it was fair.

Roman roads A road called the Appian Way leads out of the busy city of Rome today. It is narrow and crowded, but it has been there for more than 2,000 years. And it has been busy every day since it was built.

One of the first things the Romans did when they captured a city was to build a road linking it with Rome. Roman soldiers used the roads to reach all parts of the empire. But traders and government officials and ordinary people also used the roads. The roads were like a rope that connected the empire.

New towns Whenever Rome conquered a new area, soldiers were given part of the land. They were encouraged to build new towns on the land. These towns grew up all over the empire. Because the soldiers were Roman, the towns were set up like small Romes. Because the soldiers spoke Latin, the people who lived in the region learned to speak Latin. They built Roman-looking buildings, wore Roman clothes, and brought up their children in Roman fashion. Because of the new towns, Roman soldiers were within easy reach of disturbances. And the people of the empire felt protected by their presence.

▶ ap′ē ən wā′

▶ Who settled the new towns? Do you think they helped to keep order throughout the whole empire?

The people in this engraving are bakers. They are shown weighing their loaves of bread. Why would weighing be important to business?

123

Beyond the borders   Few Romans ever traveled beyond the borders of the empire. Tribes of wild barbarians lived beyond these borders. In fact, the tribes often attacked the settlements along the borders. For a few hundred years, the Roman Empire was able to protect its borders from these barbarians. But after the first century A.D., the empire became weaker. Towns and cities were not as prosperous. Traders found it hard to carry on their businesses. The empire found it harder to raise the money to pay for soldiers. The barbarians got bolder and bolder. They attacked and destroyed one Roman city after another. Finally, in A.D. 410, Rome itself was attacked and conquered.

The end of Rome   When the city of Rome fell, government in Europe fell almost completely apart. It became impossible to govern large areas. Barbarians continued to attack. Without Roman soldiers to defend them, roads became unsafe. Robbers attacked travelers and traders. Villages and towns became isolated from one another. Each area could only depend on itself for food, clothing, and other goods. And each area could only depend on its own people for defense.

THE MIDDLE AGES

When historians talk about Western Europe, they divide its history into parts. The end of the Roman Empire is the end of what they call Western Europe's ancient history. The Roman Empire ended around the year A.D. 400. Historians call the period from around A.D. 1500 to the present, modern history. The period between A.D. 400 and A.D. 1500 in Western Europe is called the Middle Ages.

This scene was originally painted on a medieval calendar. What could future historians learn about our culture from our calendars?

After the barbarian attacks, Europe was split up into many different lands. The rulers of these territories were not able to protect their lands from attacks. So, again, they divided their lands among their followers. The followers promised to be loyal to the landowner. The landowner was called a **lord.** The people who served him were called **vassals.**

◗ vas′ lz

Knights A vassal could serve his lord in different ways. Some became **knights.** It was a knight's duty to protect his lord's lands from attacks by knights of a neighboring lord. In return for his service, a knight lived in his

Medieval knights wore heavy steel armor when they went into battle. What does this tell you about the weapons of the Middle Ages?

lord's mighty stone castle and enjoyed a good life. The lord, the women of his family (called ladies), and the knights ate in large banquet halls and were entertained by wandering musicians and poets.

Lords, vassals, and serfs Not all vassals were knights. Most spent their time ruling over the lands their lord had given them. Sometimes vassals owned so much land that they were

THE CATHOLIC CHURCH

When the Roman Empire crumbled, there was little left to hold Europe together. Trade stopped. Governments could not protect their citizens. The Europeans no longer had one government, as in Roman times. But they did have one Church. It was called the Church of Rome. That was where the leader of the Church, the Pope, lived. It was the Church that kept Europeans together.

Priests really took the place of government leaders. They owned land, collected taxes, worked farms, carried on trade, and even protected their people with armies. The money they collected went into the church treasury.

Some people became monks or nuns. Men entered monasteries (män ə ster ēz) and women went to convents. These were places where men or women could live quietly. Some monks and nuns farmed; some became craftsmen. Others spent their lives meditating (med′ ə tā ting), or thinking about God.

But many monasteries were also places of deep study. Libraries with the books of ancient writers were kept there. The monasteries collected many of the old books written by the Greeks and Romans. If the books were falling apart, the monks copied them by hand. So the monks and nuns kept alive a great deal that might have been lost forever.

In many ways, the Church worked to keep Europe united. It helped Europeans feel that they had something to belong to as a group. It gave them a feeling of protection. It kept their ancient culture alive.

▶ Peasants (pez′ənts) are people who own small farms or who work for other farmers.

able to divide it up among other vassals. In this way, a vassal could also become a lord.

The people who worked the lands of a lord were called **peasants.** Some peasants were **serfs.** Serfs were peasants who gave up their freedom to work for a lord. The lord, in return, protected his serfs from attacks. Peasants did not *have* to become serfs. But if they did not, they might have no way of getting land to grow food, and no place to find protection during attack.

▶ Feudal (fū′dl) comes from a Latin word. A fief or feud means the piece of land a landlord gives in exchange for military service.

The feudal system This system of lords, vassals, and serfs is called a feudal system. The people of Western Europe lived under this system for much of the Middle Ages. Because of barbarian attacks, town life almost died.

The life of a serf European peasants had a very hard life. Though they were not slaves, serfs' lives depended completely on their lord. And, just as a lord's children also became lords, so a serf's children remained serfs.

Serfs had to work on the lord's land three or four days a week. On Sundays, the Church would not allow anyone to work. The rest of the serfs' days were spent in growing food for themselves. Serfs could not leave their lord's estates or marry without his permission. They were not allowed to complain about the way they were treated. They could not own land, and it was almost impossible for them to gain freedom.

The lord did have some duties to his serfs. He had to protect them during attacks and

The pictures on these pages come from a medieval calendar. Each picture represents the activities of different months.

feed them when the crops failed. Were there advantages to all people in the feudal system? Were the advantages equal?

The world of Bodo What was life like for the people of the Middle Ages? For some, it was very hard. Bodo was a free peasant who lived over a thousand years ago in what is now eastern France. The story of Bodo and his wife, Ermentrude, was written by a woman who was both an economist and a historian. She was interested in how people earned their living and spent their lives long ago.

Let us try and imagine a day in Bodo's life. Bodo gets up early, because it is his day to go and work on the monk's farm. He does not dare to be late. It is Bodo's day to plow, so he takes his big ox with him and little Wido, his son, to run by its side and poke it with a stick. Bodo joins his friends from some of the farms nearby, who are going to work at the monk's big house.

Let us go back and see what Bodo's wife, Ermentrude, is doing. She is busy, too. She has been busy all morning gathering eggs and vegetables to bring up to the hall. Now she leaves her second son, age nine, to look after the baby and calls on one of her neighbors, who has to go up to the big house, too. Ermentrude and her neighbor go up together to the house. All is busy there.

She goes back to her own farm and sets to work in the little vineyard. After an hour or two, she goes back to get the children's meal and to spend the rest of the day weaving warm woolen clothes for them.

. . . At last, Bodo comes back for his supper, and as soon as the sun goes down they go to bed; for their handmade candle gives only a flicker of light, and they both have to be up early in the morning.

◗ er′ mən trūd

◗ wē′ dō

◗ Think of the way you spend your evenings. Do you watch television or listen to your stereo? Are the lights on every night? If you had no lights, would it be sensible to go to sleep early and get up early?

Town fairs But there was a bright side to life in the Middle Ages. On some days of the year, towns held fairs where thousands of people could enjoy themselves. These were days of singing and dancing and games. There was business at the fairs, too. There were foods and clothes from other parts of Europe for the wealthier people to buy. Spices came from thousands of miles away. Meat did not stay fresh very long, and spices made spoiled meat taste better.

Some fairs specialized in certain products like cloth and spices. Some fairs attracted traders from all over Europe; some were held every week for nearby farmers.

THE CRUSADES

For many hundreds of years, life changed little. Most people farmed. Some traded. A few lived in cities. In monasteries all over Europe, the

Medieval people did not have television, movies, or concert halls. They looked on town fairs as social events. But the people conducted business there, too.

▶ Why do you think spices were so much in demand in Europe for hundreds of years? What modern way do we have for preserving meat?

This shield shows Philip of France and Richard the Lion-Hearted of England as they leave on a Crusade.

▶ Jerusalem is also a holy place for two other famous religions. Can you name them?

great writings of the past were copied and stored for the future.

During this time, many religious Christians made long trips to Jerusalem. Jerusalem was the chief city in Palestine, the Christian Holy Land. It was occupied by Moslems, but the Moslems allowed Christians to travel to the Holy Land.

Wars of religion Nearly a thousand years ago, a new group of Moslems captured Jerusalem. These people were cruel to Christian visitors. The Pope urged the people of Europe to free Jerusalem and return it to the Church. Thousands of people agreed to go.

These trips were called Crusades. *Crusade* comes from the Latin word *crux,* which means cross.

Altogether, there were eight Crusades. One is called the Children's Crusade, for many of the crusaders were children. None of the

Crusades were successful for the Christians. Thousands of people had been killed. And, by the end of the last Crusade, Jerusalem was still in Moslem hands. Yet something had happened. And it changed Western Europe forever.

How culture changes Before the Crusades, most Europeans spent their lives in the neighborhood where they were born. Each day was like the last, and year faded into year. Few strangers ever came to a village. Children learned their roles from their parents. Boys farmed; girls spun thread and sewed clothes.

What each family could not make, it traded for. Money was not used because it was not needed.

During the Crusades, all of this began to change. Thousands of people traveled thousands of miles. In each place, these new travelers heard different languages. They found that even in neighboring areas, people spoke the same language differently. They met people who ate different foods.

The Crusaders came back to Europe and told their friends and relatives. People all over Western Europe wanted to see the exciting new things.

THE GROWTH OF TRADE

During most of the Middle Ages, there had been towns in Western Europe. You have read about some of the fairs that were held in towns. But during the Middle Ages, towns did not grow. People seldom traveled the dangerous roads from farm village to town. But the Crusades had made travel safer. The Christian

Medieval craftsmen often belonged to groups called guilds. The guilds set wages and standards. The guild members marked their products with designs like the one at right. Why do you think they did that? Can you see where our word trademark *comes from?*

▶ How would this help the cities to grow?

▶ Which people do you think escaped to cities?

▶ ə prent′ əs iz

soldiers had removed most of the enemies from the roads.

So after the Crusades, towns began to grow again. In addition, people who escaped to some big towns or cities could be free. Landowners could not control the law in big towns and cities.

Because travel was safer, farmers could bring their food to sell in towns and cities. Sometimes, with the money they earned, serfs could buy their freedom. Instead of service, they might offer the landowner money. If the landowner needed the money, he would free the serf.

City people could set up bigger businesses; they could afford to hire young people to learn their business. Such people received very low wages, but they did receive careful training. They were called **apprentices.**

The beginning of modern Europe About 600 years ago, a new spirit came to European life. Historians call this period the **Renaissance.** It comes from a word meaning rebirth. Artists and scholars studied the old cultures of Greece and Rome. The artists of the Renaissance did not want to create the same sculptures, buildings, and poetry that had been created in ancient Greece and Rome. But they wanted to make works of art that were as beautiful as the ancient works.

▶ ren′ə säns

Gutenberg invented a system of printing which used wooden blocks. The blocks could be put together to print one book, then used again later. This invention was called movable type.

Renaissance artists worked out new ways of painting that made their art seem more lifelike than anything that had been done before. Many artists, like Raphael and Fra Angelico, whose paintings are shown here, used the new techniques to portray religious scenes. These artists were part of the new spirit of discovery in Europe.

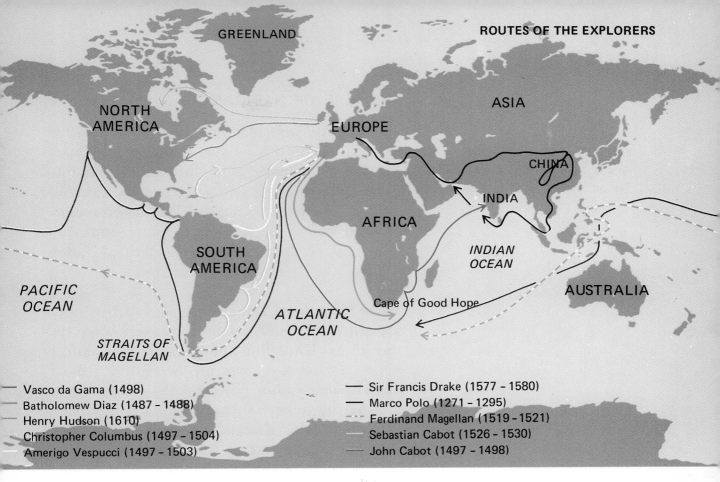

GREENLAND

NORTH AMERICA

ASIA

EUROPE

CHINA

INDIA

AFRICA

INDIAN OCEAN

SOUTH AMERICA

PACIFIC OCEAN

Cape of Good Hope

AUSTRALIA

ATLANTIC OCEAN

STRAITS OF MAGELLAN

Vasco da Gama (1498)
Batholomew Diaz (1487 – 1488)
Henry Hudson (1610)
Christopher Columbus (1497 – 1504)
Amerigo Vespucci (1497 – 1503)

Sir Francis Drake (1577 – 1580)
Marco Polo (1271 – 1295)
Ferdinand Magellan (1519 – 1521)
Sebastian Cabot (1526 – 1530)
John Cabot (1497 – 1498)

The new styles of building, art, and literature soon spread to France, Spain, and most of the other European countries. Cities in all parts of Europe were becoming homes for artists and scholars.

Science But the Renaissance was not limited to art, building, and literature. It was also expressed in new inventions like movable type and guns and cannons. It was shown in the new interest Europeans took in the world around them. European astronomers started to question old beliefs, like the one that said the earth was the center of the universe.

New lands Europeans invented new ways of sailing and set out to explore the rest of the world. Can you name any famous explorers of the fifteenth and sixteenth centuries?

▶ Is it possible for two different styles of art or music or writing to be beautiful? Can you name two different styles you like?

▶ An astronomer (əs tron′ ə mər) is a scientist who studies stars, planets and other heavenly bodies to see how they move and affect each other.

137

THE RISE OF NATIONS

▶ Do you think the Greeks would have approved of the Renaissance?

In the Renaissance, the idea of belonging to a nation grew stronger. People who spoke the same language and who came from the same culture began to consider themselves citizens of the same nation. The governments of each nation became much more powerful than any of the small rulers of the Middle Ages.

When kings were kings One sign of this new growth of nations was the increased power of the kings. Until the Renaissance, most kings were not very powerful. Sometimes their vassals were more powerful than they were. During the Renaissance, though, the power of the kings grew. Traders and people in towns and cities agreed to pay taxes to the king if he would keep peace and protect them. Kings began to build strong armies and governments. And their nations grew more unified and very strong.

▶ Do you think traveling would be safer in one big nation or many tiny states? Why do you think so? Do you think the ability to travel helps people gain knowledge?

The increased power and importance of the king was shown in the new courts and palaces of Europe. The courts were the centers of society and of the arts. Scholars, writers, artists, and friends of the king began to make up a new kind of European life. These people spent their lives around the court.

The common people Had the life of ordinary people changed since the times of the Middle Ages? In some ways it had. Most of the serfs were now free. They were not owned by one lord and did not have to stay in one place.

How did serfs become free? Historians have many different answers. But they know it was a process that went on for many centuries.

Some lords realized quickly that they could farm better with hired help. So they usually let their serfs buy their freedom.

Often, former serfs would continue farming the same land after they were freed. They would rent the land from the lord or hire themselves out.

Still, many European peasants did not have the rights of a modern citizen. They had no say in government. They were still at the bottom level of society. They had to pay taxes on the simple things that everybody needed—like bread and salt. Noblemen paid very little in taxes.

The French Revolution Little was done about this situation for many years. But about 200 years ago, the people of France could stand no more. And what was to happen in France changed almost all of Western Europe.

Louis XIV of France and other kings had beautiful palaces built for themselves. Does the room above give you an idea of Louis' wealth and power?

▶ American slaves were freed in a different way. Do you remember how? Which way of becoming free is better? Why do you think so?

▶ What happened in North America in 1776? Do you think news of this event could have influenced the French people? Why or why not? How might the French people have found out?

▶ Do you know of another declaration that uses some of the same words?

The middle-class people wanted a voice in their government. They wanted freedom of speech. A political protest against the king began in Paris. When nothing was done, people began rioting. In time, all of France became involved in the revolution.

The peasants in the countryside stormed the great country houses of the nobles. They destroyed the hated tax records. Some drove the noblemen off their huge estates.

But the city people had different ideas. They wanted to make this a revolution for equality and liberty. In 1789, the new government in Paris drew up a "Declaration of the Rights of Man and Citizen." The first article read: "Men are born and remain free and equal in rights." The Declaration then went on to say that people's rights included "liberty, property, and security." It said all citizens could take part in government. It said laws were to be made by representatives of all citizens. And the laws made were to apply equally to everyone.

THE INDUSTRIAL REVOLUTION

How do you picture a revolution? Guns blasting? People rioting in the streets? The French Revolution was probably as loud and bloody as that. But in the eighteenth century, there was another, much quieter revolution. The quieter revolution began in England. And it changed the world.

Machines and people The word *revolution* means turning something around completely —a complete change in ways of doing things. The revolution in England is called the

Industrial Revolution. It changed the way people made things and the ways they spent their time. It changed the ways nations traded with each other throughout the world. It changed the ways these nations grew powerful. And it changed the ways people became rich or poor in modern societies.

For a long time in the history of the world, people made whatever they needed by hand. Sometimes they invented tools to help them. The invention of tools and the knowledge of how to use them is called **technology.** In the past 300 years, technology has become more complicated and more productive.

Power and the revolution An important part of technology is the way machines are powered. Before the Industrial Revolution, there were only three ways to keep machines moving — muscles, wind, and running water.

There were problems with these kinds of power. A spinning wheel, turned by muscle power, turned only as fast and as long as the hand turned the wheel. When the arm got tired, the machine stopped. All human beings —from babies to powerful men—get tired.

There were problems with wind and water, too. On some days, wind does not blow. On others, it blows in the wrong direction. During some parts of the year, rivers dry up. In other times, they freeze over. Can you see some of the disadvantages of these kinds of power?

Steam and the modern world The Industrial Revolution brought the first power source that could always be depended on—steam. Does steam have the power to drive heavy machines?

▶ From what you already know, how much do you think technology has changed? Could our nation exist as we know it if our technology were simpler?

▶ Can you name some of the new ways of technology that started in different ages? in the Iron Age? in the Bronze Age?

141

Sometimes people who were put out of work by the first machines reacted by smashing those machines.

Changes Most of the new machines were made of iron. All used coal to create the steam. So large amounts of both iron and coal were needed. New mines had to be found. Many more workers had to be brought to the mines. Roads, canals, ships, and railroads were built to transport the coal and iron — and the products that the machines made. Machine shops with skilled workers grew up to make the machines. Millions of unskilled workers were trained to run the machines. Even new farming methods had to be found to feed all these people.

The machines very quickly changed the lives of ordinary Europeans. Europeans now had more products available than ever before. Often these products were cheaper than hand-made products. This was good for the people who could afford new things.

Disadvantages of machines But the machines also produced bad effects. One machine could make cloth more quickly and cheaply than hundreds of handweavers. This meant that thousands of village handweavers were thrown

142

JAMES WATT

People had known about steam power for hundreds of years. But they did not know how to apply it to machines. About 300 years ago, some mining engineers discovered that they could use steam power to force water out of deep mines. This helped miners dig deeper than they ever had. But little more was done with steam power until one man, James Watt, discovered how to make steam turn a wheel.

When he was a boy, James Watt's parents had scolded him for playing with mechanical things. There were few complicated machines then. And almost nobody could make a living by fixing them. So Watt's parents thought that fooling around with machines was a waste of time. But someone asked Watt to repair a steam coalmine pump. Watt fixed the pump and then began to build models of other pumps.

Once Watt had built his first steam engine, the new machine could do many things. Machines were built that could weave, spin, grind flour, drive a boat or a train, and even make other machines. Nearly anything that needed pushing or turning could be powered by steam. Within 50 years of Watt's invention, steam engines were producing and transporting things in ways that were impossible with muscle, wind, or water power.

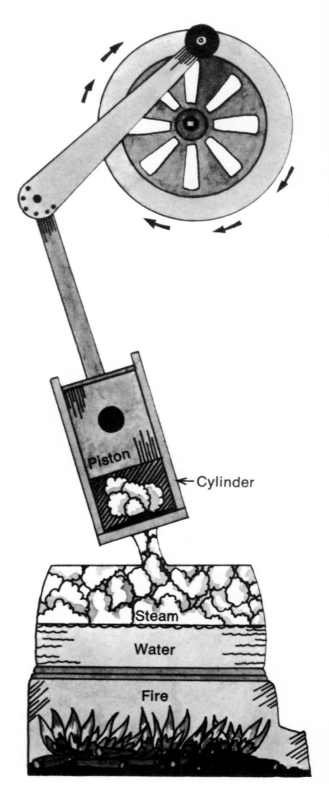

out of work. They were forced out of their villages into the new industrial cities. If they were lucky, they might find jobs working 14 hours a day in the new factories.

Here is a description of one of the early factories.

▶ Do you think workers could go elsewhere and find a job with better conditions?

> Once inside the factory, the worker had to stay by his machine for 14 hours. As long as the machine kept running, the worker had to stay with it. Lighting was very bad and the worker had to do his job in near darkness. There was little fresh air, so the place was unbearably hot and bad smelling. Many of the older workers were deformed from tending their machines. Quite a number had lost fingers or other limbs.

▶ Deformed (di fôrmd′) means out of correct shape.

Child labor Often the workers in conditions like these were children. In the early days of the Industrial Revolution, children as young as five or six years old were sent out to work. Most did not go to school. Many became sick, and some died young.

▶ Why do you think parents allowed their children to work at such a very young age? Why do you think child labor was permitted?

▶ If you worked 14 hours a day, would you want to go to school or would you be too tired to care?

Living conditions Wages at this time were so low that workers often could not afford a decent place to live. Thousands of families in London thought they were lucky to live in cellars like this:

> The home has only two rooms, both underground. The front room is used as a kitchen. Even though it is always wet and smells bad, it is usually better than the back room.
>
> In this back room the whole family of eight people make their beds. The floor of the room is packed earth and is always damp. Many families in homes like this do not even own beds. They simply put down straw for everyone, even sick people, to sleep on.

These children are carrying clay to make bricks. Factory owners often preferred to use child labor. Can you explain why?

The Industrial Revolution spreads The Industrial Revolution spread quickly. In the early nineteenth century, an English worker memorized the plans for textile machinery and carried them to the United States in his head. Soon, giant machines and factories were as much a part of the United States as of Great Britain. The Industrial Revolution wakened people's curiosity. With new machines, people began thinking about manufacturing new things. And with so many new things to be sold, people began thinking of new ways to make and sell products for a profit.

A CHANGING WAY OF LIFE

Think about the American way of life today. Do you know people who work in factories? Do they work 14 hours a day, six days a week? Or do they work 8 hours a day, five days a week? Do they live in poor housing? Or do they live in pleasant houses and apartments? Do their children work in factories, or do they go to school and play in the afternoon?

For a long time, working conditions were very poor. But then workers began to organize. Sometimes they went on strike for higher wages. Sometimes they worked to change the laws. In time, factories *had* to be safer. Children were not allowed to work at machines. And owners had to pay their workers a certain amount of money. Higher wages meant that factory workers could afford to buy more things. This, in turn, meant that more factories, more stores, and more banks were needed. And all of these meant still more jobs and even higher wages.

European empires in Asia and Africa The Industrial Revolution raised the standard of living of the European countries. By the middle of the last century, many Europeans were proud that they were more powerful and lived better than any other people in the world.

This pride had some bad results. It made European people think that they were better than other people. So European nations competed with each other for trade and power. Since they needed raw materials for their factories, they conquered parts of Asia and Africa and used the resources of these places. Europeans did not feel guilty about this. They believed that God had given them the task of civilizing the rest of the world.

War and a new Europe But many things happened in this century to change Europeans' ideas about themselves and others in the world. The European nations fought two major wars with each other—World War I and World War II. Both were fought on European soil. Millions of lives were lost.

▶ Europeans thought that they were the only people with an advanced civilization. Does this explain why they went out to "civilize" other places? Do you think other places had advanced civilizations too?

146

THE NATIONS OF WESTERN EUROPE

ATLANTIC OCEAN

ICELAND

SWEDEN

FINLAND

NORWAY

GREAT BRITAIN

Oslo

Helsinki

IRELAND

Stockholm

Dublin

DENMARK

THE NETHERLANDS

Copenhagen

London

Brussels

Berlin

BELGIUM

Bonn

LUXEMBOURG

WEST GERMANY

Paris

EAST GERMANY

FRANCE

Geneva

Vienna

AUSTRIA

PORTUGAL

SWITZERLAND

Madrid

Belgrade

ITALY

YUGOSLAVIA

Lisbon

SPAIN

Rome

MEDITERRANEAN SEA

GREECE

Athens

People starved. Factories were destroyed, and people had no work.

After World War II, the European powers were forced to give up their empires. Great Britain, France, and Belgium no longer have colonies in Asia and Africa. Today, European nations have few sources of raw materials for their factories. They must trade for their raw materials.

Europeans are still proud that they were the people who made the breakthrough to the modern world. With the United States, they led the way to a new industrial society.

1. For hundreds of years, educated Europeans spent most of their time in school studying the cultures of Greece and Rome. Why do you think Europeans thought these cultures so important?

2. What might happen to a society when its people are no longer safe and secure?

3. In what ways did the Industrial Revolution change the lives of Europeans?

The Land and the People

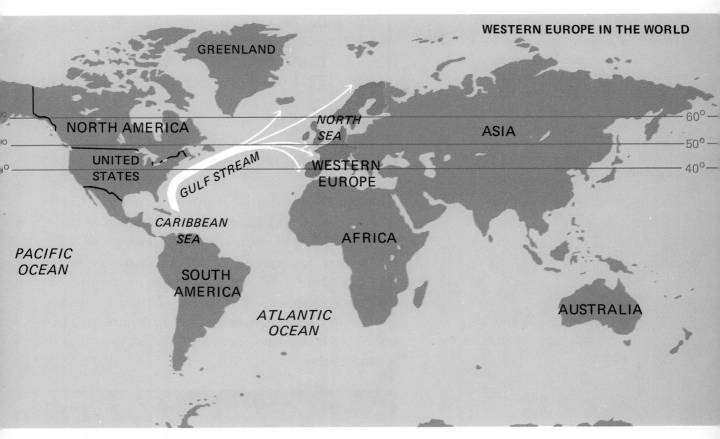

Map labels: GREENLAND · NORTH AMERICA · UNITED STATES · NORTH SEA · ASIA · WESTERN EUROPE · GULF STREAM · CARIBBEAN SEA · AFRICA · PACIFIC OCEAN · SOUTH AMERICA · ATLANTIC OCEAN · AUSTRALIA · 60° · 50° · 40°

THE GEOGRAPHY OF SUCCESS

Some of the reasons for Western European success in trade and industry can be found in the geography of Western Europe. Look at the map on this page. How big is Europe compared with the other continents? Read ahead to see how the size and other features of its geography helped Western Europe to become the world's first capital of industry.

A small continent Western Europe is small, but being small has many advantages. The many different peoples of Western Europe have always lived close to each other. This has made it easy for them to borrow ideas and new ways of doing things from each other.

▶ Try this experiment. Read through a copy of a newspaper from a small town or small city and one from a large city. Which paper do you think tells you more about all the events happening in that town or city? Does this help explain how size might affect the spread of new ideas and inventions?

▶ A geographic feature is the shape the land takes in a certain area. Mountains, rivers, plains, and lakes are all examples of geographic features.

▶ A peninsula is land surrounded on three sides by water.

Although the western section of Europe is small, it has many different kinds of geographic features. Look at the map of Western Europe on page 152. Find two major mountain regions. Find the Great European Plain. Can you name three large rivers and two lakes? All of these features provide different conditions for the people who live in the areas.

Seacoasts Western European countries share one very helpful geographic advantage—their seacoasts. Look again at the map on page 152. Only two countries in Western Europe have no coastline. Which countries are these? Which countries of Western Europe are islands? Which are **peninsulas** or share peninsulas with another country? Is Europe itself a peninsula?

Here a fisherman carefully mends his nets. Fishing is an old way of life in Europe.

Why is seacoast such an advantage to Europeans? One reason is that fish comes from the sea. Fish is good food. Even before refrigeration had been invented, all Western Europeans could eat fish.

The seacoast is useful for another reason — trade. Trade by water is often cheaper and more efficient than other forms of transportation. In the past, water was the best way in which heavy goods could be transported. Does this help explain why the countries of Western Europe have long been powerful? Today, one ship can carry as much as hundreds of trucks or several long trains. Do you think this helps Western Europe remain a leader in world trade?

The geography of Western Europe has other advantages for trade. Notice the long rivers on the map on page 152. Europe has over a dozen large rivers. Ships can travel a long way up many of these rivers. How many of the rivers can you find? Why would they be important for trade?

An ideal climate The geography of Western Europe is also ideal for people to work and farm in. Look at the rainfall map of Europe on page 152. Twenty inches of rainfall is needed for many kinds of farming. Is there any place in Western Europe that does not receive that much? Large parts of other continents do not get much rain. What problems might this cause?

Some places in the world get so much water that needed minerals are washed out of the soil. But Europe is lucky. It has no heavy rainy seasons, and it rarely has floods. The rain falls fairly evenly all year around. So there are no dry seasons, either.

▶ How does refrigeration make it possible for people far away from seacoasts to eat fish?

▶ Efficient (ə fish′ ənt) means doing things without wasting time or energy.

151

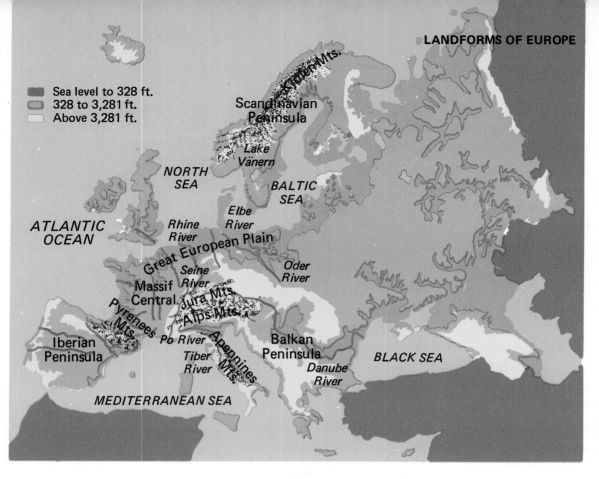

LANDFORMS OF EUROPE

Sea level to 328 ft.
328 to 3,281 ft.
Above 3,281 ft.

Kjölen Mts.

Scandinavian
Peninsula

Lake
Vänern

NORTH
SEA

BALTIC
SEA

ATLANTIC
OCEAN

Elbe
River

Rhine
River

Great European Plain

Oder
River

Seine
River

Massif
Central

Jura Mts.

Alps Mts.

Pyrenees
Mts.

Po River

Apennines
Mts.

Balkan
Peninsula

BLACK SEA

Iberian
Peninsula

Tiber
River

Danube
River

MEDITERRANEAN SEA

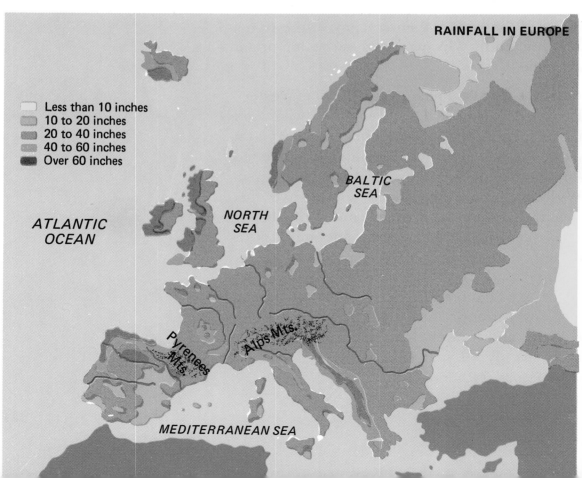

RAINFALL IN EUROPE

Less than 10 inches
10 to 20 inches
20 to 40 inches
40 to 60 inches
Over 60 inches

BALTIC
SEA

NORTH
SEA

ATLANTIC
OCEAN

Pyrenees
Mts.

Alps Mts.

MEDITERRANEAN SEA

The temperature of Europe, like the rainfall, is moderate. Do you feel like working outdoors when it is very cold outside? Do you feel like working hard when it is very hot?

The Gulf Stream Look at the map on page 149. Why is the climate of Western Europe so mild? How far north is the northern part of Europe? How far north is the northern part of the United States? Why is Western Europe warmer than the United States then? The reason is a large ocean current called the Gulf Stream.

The Gulf Stream is like a huge river in the Atlantic Ocean. It brings warm water thousands of miles from the Caribbean Sea across the whole Atlantic Ocean and up the coast of Western Europe. It warms the coast of Western Europe as far as northern Norway. And it keeps the climate of Western Europe moderate all year round.

Climate and farming This moderate climate is especially good for farmers. Too much heat or cold makes it hard to raise many farm animals. Most farm animals cannot survive the heat and dryness of the desert. And they could not survive in rain forests where insects would damage crops and cause disease in cattle. But Western Europe has no rain forests or deserts. Its climate is very good for farm animals.

Soil is also important for agriculture. Deserts, mountains, and many other places in the world have soils that are too rocky or sandy for farming. Again, Western Europe is lucky. Most of its land is good for farming.

Geography and industry The geography of their continent helped Western Europeans to

▶ Moderate (mod′ər it) means not too much and not too little.

▶ Find the Caribbean Sea on the map. What do you think the climate is in that part of the world?

European farming is a mixture of old and new methods. Find the contrasts in the picture above. The man on the left is hauling soil on his back. Do you think his way of life will survive in Europe?

build the first modern industrial societies the world had known. When one area put up a factory, others sprang up in neighboring places.

Western Europe was the first area in the world to be industrialized. But what is so different about Western Europe today?

HOW IS EUROPE DIFFERENT?

Look at the map of Western Europe. Now look at the map of the United States. Is any country in Western Europe as big as the United States? Size is one big difference between Western Europe and other industrial areas of the world.

A different language is spoken in almost every Western European nation. In Switzerland, four languages are spoken. So one clue that you were in Western Europe would be the many languages you would hear.

Population density   There are some differences between Western Europe and other countries that are more basic. Look at the following chart. The figures on the chart refer to **population**

▶ Early factories were always built near rivers or waterfalls. Do you know why? Can you see how the many rivers of Western Europe helped industry to grow there?

▶ How many European languages can you name? Take a poll in your class. Can anybody in your class speak these languages?

▶ Find Switzerland on the map. What countries surround it? Can you guess three of the languages that are spoken there?

Venice is a city with canals instead of streets. Instead of trucks, the city uses barges to collect garbage.

density. Population density means the average number of people who live in a certain area.

How many Americans are there per square mile? Population density figures are an average, of course. There are many more people per square mile in Chicago than there are in Nevada or New Mexico. Which is higher—the population density of a city or of a farming area? Why?

COMPARATIVE POPULATION DENSITIES
(people per sq. mi.)

India	426
Ghana	96
* Europe	492
United States	58
Canada	6

* France, Germany, Great Britain, Italy

AVERAGE ANNUAL INCOME PER PERSON

* Belgium	$2,372
* Denmark	2,702
* France	2,783
* Germany	2,520
* Great Britain	1,660
* Ireland	953
* Italy	1,525
* Luxembourg	2,210
* Netherlands	1,797
India	73
Ghana	262
United States	4,400

* European countries

1. Look at the chart again. What is the population density of the listed Western European countries?
2. Compare the following information. Which countries have the highest personal income? Is any country in Western Europe really poor? Population density often tells something about the wealth of an area.
3. Do you think an area with a high density would be richer than one with a low density?

Population density does not always tell the whole story about wealth. India has fewer people per square mile than Western Europe. Yet India is a poor country, while Western Europe is rich.

How can Western Europe have such a high population density yet be so rich? Part of the answer lies in its geography. You have already read about its fertile land and good waterways. Yet there are other reasons for its wealth, too.

LIFE IN INDUSTRIAL COUNTRIES

An American visitor asked an Englishman about life in Western Europe. As you read, ask yourself how geography is responsible for what he describes.

"Many Europeans do not have the large appliances—big refrigerators or freezers—that Americans take for granted. We are getting these things slowly. But our countries are not as rich as yours.

"The United States is one of the richest countries in the world in raw materials. You have plenty of iron, silver, copper, coal, oil—and food.

"We have enough coal here in England. And we have just discovered some natural gas a few miles off our coast. But we have used up most of our iron. Our forests have been cut for 2,000 years. But with conservation and replanting we can still get wood from them.

"The skills of our people are our wealth. The more people we have, the more brains, technical knowledge, and experience we have to the square mile. We bring in raw iron ore, but our people turn it into high quality machine tools.

"We import raw cotton and turn out high quality cloth or finished clothes. We can sell the finished products for more than we paid for the raw materials. Our profit makes up for our lack of resources. . . . That makes sense, doesn't it?

▶ What do you think would happen if every country ran out of things like iron and copper? Do you think this could ever happen? Why or why not?

▶ Many years ago, cotton picked in the South of the United States would be sent to England to be made into cloth. Then the cloth would be shipped back and sold in the United States. Do countries in Western Europe still make profits from trade in this way?

▶ What does the Englishman think is a geographical disadvantage of the size and the geography of the United States?

Think of all the things that are made of steel. Can you see why this steelworker is contributing to Europe's industrial success?

"But," said the American, "every other nation, including the United States, wants to do the same thing. How can you compete with us?

"Sometimes we have trouble," the Englishman admitted. "But often we can haul things halfway around the world by sea just as cheaply as you can haul them across your country by land. We have a lot of skilled labor in this country. And often it is cheaper than your labor."

Great Britain has been an industrialized nation for a long time. But other parts of Western Europe have also built up industries over the last few years. One example is Italy.

Italy exported nearly 100 million dollars worth of faucets last year. Most of these were put together in a small valley in the north of Italy. This valley of faucets is located about 40 miles from Milan, one of Italy's largest cities.

Most of the faucets are put together in small workshops in people's homes. But the people are so skillful that they can produce nearly all of Italy's needs for watertaps, bathroom equipment, and industrial faucets, as well as the 100 million dollars worth of faucets that were exported. This production started more than 50 years ago. In the last few years, the industry has been so profitable that it has brought prosperity to the whole valley.

PROBLEMS IN INDUSTRY

Western Europe has had problems in being the world's first center of industry. Many of the early factories have had trouble changing to meet the needs of the modern world. This problem is especially true of Great Britain.

About a hundred years ago, Great Britain was called "the workshop of the world." It was the first country to build factories. But later it had to pay for its early success.

The price of success Suppose that somebody built a factory to make pipes and tubes in Great Britain a hundred years ago. It cost him a lot of money to design all the machinery. He spent even more to lay out the factory and give jobs to the workmen. But once the factory was started, it made pipes that were sold all over the world.

As time went on, the owner of the factory might have seen many ways the factory could be improved. New machines were being designed. New methods were invented to turn

◗ mə lan′

◗ Would the valley of faucets be as prosperous if manufacturers sold only in their own area?

◗ What must the manufacturers do to make a large profit? How do you suppose they get the raw materials they make into faucets?

159

▶ Do you live in New England? Do you know of any factories that have closed down? If so, find out why. Was it because the machines were no longer modern? If so, did the factory move elsewhere?

out more pipe and tubes in less time. But the owner could not afford to buy new machines and start all over. So he continued with his old factory.

The old British factory was still turning out pipes. But the pipes were old-fashioned and more expensive to make. The owner found it harder and harder to compete against newer factories. Finally the British owner had to modernize or go out of business. That was the price Great Britain had to pay for its success.

Staying ahead All European industries are trying to be as modern as possible. Nevertheless, not all Western European countries have the same problem as Great Britain. Some countries, like Sweden and Denmark and Italy, built their factory systems long after Great Britain. Their factories are more modern. Industry in some countries, like Germany, was destroyed by war. New, modern factories were built to replace them. Such factories produce goods quickly and cheaply. Yet they must make sure that their industries stay up-to-date.

COMMON MARKET

For years, Western European businessmen were worried. They knew they could not compete against businesses from the United States. The United States is a much larger country and has many more resources than any Western European country.

Some European people realized that the European nations needed to join together to help each other. If they could forget their language differences and the differences in

Cheese making began as a farm activity in
Europe. Now it is a large industry.
European cheeses are still made by hand
and aged for as long as four years. But
many cheeses are now made by machines in
modern factories. Whatever way they are
made, the best cheeses still find their
way to markets like the one below.

customs, they might become strong competition against other countries.

In 1958, six of the European countries—Belgium, the Netherlands, Luxembourg, France, Germany, and Italy—got together and decided to cooperate. They called their group the European Economic Community, or the Common Market.

These countries agreed to join their resources together. France had plenty of iron. But it did not have as much coal as it needed. Germany had the opposite situation—not enough iron but lots of extra coal. By sharing their resources, they could produce more goods.

Within a few years, the European Economic Community had worked so well that its members were more prosperous than many other European nations. Soon, other nations began to realize the advantages of the Common Market. Today the Common Market includes most of the important countries of Western Europe. It is helping Western Europe to again take its place as a leader among the industrial nations of the world.

▶ Economic (ē′kə nom′ik) means having to do with money and trade.

▶ Do you think that there were many people in different Western European countries who did not want to join together? Explain your answer.

▶ Can you guess why the economic plan is called the Common Market? What do the countries share in common?

1. What does the phrase "geography of success" mean? How does the phrase apply to Europe?
2. Why is the education of Europe's people necessary for its success?
3. In what ways has Europe paid the "price of success"?
4. Europe is divided into many small countries. What kinds of problems has this caused?

Case Study: Migrant Workers in Europe

AN OPPORTUNITY

Juan Morales is 19 years old. He has left his father and mother on their small farm in Spain. Juan now works in a huge automobile plant in Germany. Every 30 seconds, a car rolls past Juan on a long conveyor belt. Juan must dive into the open trunk of the car and tighten two bolts that help to hold on the gas tank. Two times a minute, Juan must tighten these same two bolts on every car that comes by on the belt. Juan's job is hard and boring. How many times does he have to tighten the bolts in one hour? How many cars will he work on in eight hours on the job?

▶ A conveyor (kən vā′ ər) belt is an endless moving platform that carries things from one place to another. It is especially useful in automobile plants where new parts are added to each car as it passes by different workers.

The car bodies move slowly along an overhead belt in an automobile factory. Each worker adds a part to the car as it passes.

164

A tiring job Juan has done this job on every working day for six months. When he goes back to his rented room at the end of each day, he is very tired. Sometimes he will go out for supper with other Spanish people who are also working in Germany. But supper in a restaurant costs money, and Juan is trying to save money. Often he just cooks supper in his room and eats alone.

Why is Juan so many miles away from home? Why is he working at a hard and boring job in a strange land?

A chance to save Juan is there because there is plenty of work in Germany—more work, in fact, than there are workers to fill the jobs. Because of this, few German workers have to take a job like Juan's. But people from poorer countries are eager to do the work. This is because wages are high in Germany—maybe 10 times higher than they are in Juan's village.

Juan does not spend all his money. Every payday, he goes to the post office and puts half his pay in the savings bank. Then he sends about a quarter of the money home to his family. The rest is enough to live on—if he is careful.

In two and a half more years, Juan will have saved enough money to buy a store near his parents' village. Then he will have enough money to get married and set up a home. But first, he faces two and a half years of tightening bolts on the cars that roll past him on the conveyor belt.

Juan is one of almost 10 million Europeans who have left their homes, friends, and families to go to work in a strange land. These Europeans are called **migrant workers**. They have

▶ Juan does his banking at a post office. Do you think he works in a small town in Germany or in a large one? Explain your answer.

▶ Migrant (mī′grənt) workers in Europe are people who move from their native countries to find higher-paying jobs.

165

European migrant workers often come from poor countries in Southern Europe. This is a slum in Portugal. The young men from this neighborhood often seek opportunities in the industrial areas of Northern Europe.

gone to countries where people speak foreign languages and live by different customs. Some bring their families to their new homes and settle there. Others work alone for many years and then return to their homeland to retire. Still others, like Juan, work hard, save money, and hope to go into business when they return to their own countries.

The money that is sent back will help these countries grow. Some families will be able to start stores or small factories with the money. Then they will be able to hire other people in their communities. These employees will have more money to spend. So the other storeowners and factories in the area will be able to sell more. Can you see how the money sent back can help a country to grow? What kind of countries do you think need this help?

Income from the migrants No one is really sure how much money migrant workers have sent back to their countries. The money is usually sent directly to their families. So the government only knows about the part of the money that the migrants' families report. In one year, 1962, the governments of the Southern European countries reported that the following amounts were sent back by migrants.

	AMOUNT OF MONEY SENT BACK (millions of dollars)	PERCENTAGE OF TOTAL NATIONAL INCOME
Italy	638.1	2
Greece	153.3	5
Portugal	51.1	2
Spain	156.9	2

1. Which countries had the largest amount of money sent back?
2. In which country was this money the largest percentage of total national income?

DIFFERENT ECONOMIES

Push forces Most migrant workers leave their homes because of the higher wages paid in another country. For many of them, this is the best opportunity they will ever have to get ahead. But economists and sociologists try to understand all the reasons why this is so. They look at the conditions in the migrants' home countries to see why so many people are willing to leave. Most people do not want to leave their homes and familiar cultures to go to strange places. There must be strong forces around them to *push* people into migrating. The conditions that cause people to leave their homelands are called **push forces.**

▶ Why do you think these forces are given this name?

Pull forces Economists and sociologists also look at the conditions in the countries that accept migrants. They want to find out what these countries have to offer people from other lands. Why are there extra jobs in these countries? If these jobs pay well, why do the citizens of these countries not take these jobs for themselves? Why are wages better in some countries than others? The sociologists and economists want to understand the conditions

There are slums in some cities of Northern Europe, too. Here, French politicians examine a neighborhood of poor migrants from Africa and Southern Europe.

168

that work as **pull forces** in countries that receive migrants.

Which countries push—which pull? Economists and sociologists are anxious to find out which countries have these push and pull forces. They study charts like the one that follows to reach some conclusions. Study the chart. See if you can figure out which countries have pull forces and which have push forces.

	PEOPLE IN AGRICULTURE (percentage)	INCOME PER PERSON (annual)	NUMBER OF CARS (per 1,000 people)
Great Britain	4	$1,660	167
Belgium	6	2,372	132
Switzerland	9	2,020	144
Netherlands	10	1,797	103
Germany	11	2,520	164
Sweden	12	3,553	231
France	18	2,783	197
Italy	26	1,525	106
Ireland	32	953	99
Spain	35	818	25
Portugal	42	423	25
Greece	55	811	11

1. What are the four countries with the highest percentage of people employed in agriculture?
2. What are the seven countries with the smallest percentage of people in agriculture?
3. Which countries have the highest incomes and the most cars?
4. Now compare these figures with those of the countries that have the most people in agriculture. Do the countries with the most people in agriculture also have the highest incomes and most number of cars? Or is the opposite true?

Now look at the next chart. It shows the countries that gained workers and the countries that lost workers. The countries that lost workers have minus signs in front of their numbers. The countries that gained workers have plus signs in front of their numbers.

NUMBER OF MIGRANT WORKERS	
Belgium	+ 24,000
England	+ 66,000
France	+296,000
Germany	+318,000
Greece	− 40,000
Ireland	− 26,000
Italy	− 86,000
Netherlands	+ 9,000
Portugal	− 52,000
Spain	−135,000
Sweden	+ 17,000
Switzerland	+ 74,000

1. Which are the countries that gained migrant workers?
2. Which countries lost these workers?
3. Compare these results with the information in the chart on page 169. Do the countries that took in migrants have many workers in agriculture?
4. Are these the same countries that have the highest incomes and the most cars?

Industry and agriculture Stop to analyze these results. Countries that have many people doing agricultural work have many people who are willing to migrate. These are also the countries that are just starting to develop modern industries. Why should this be true?

In countries with little industry, most people are farmers. Often these farms are very small.

▶ From these charts, can you guess whether farm workers get high wages? Do you think that the countries with the most farm workers also have many industries? Do you think workers in industry get higher wages than farm workers?

They supply only enough food for the farmers and their families. But when modern farming methods are introduced into the country, small farms are no longer needed. Modern ways make it possible for just a few farmers to feed a great many people. For example, only 4 percent of the people of Great Britain are farmers, but they are able to supply more than half of all the food that Great Britain needs. The other 96 percent of workers can work at other kinds of jobs.

▶ How do you think Great Britain gets the rest of the food it needs?

But in countries that have little industry, there are not many other kinds of jobs available. Farmers who do not produce very much food cannot make much money. They cannot live very well. But there are few other jobs available for them to work at. Do you think that many of them would want to leave their homes to find work somewhere else?

Now analyze the countries that accept migrant workers. Why do these countries have jobs available? Most of them have few people working on their farms. People who used to be farmers have already gone to work in factories.

▶ Sixty to a hundred years ago, some workers in countries like Great Britain and Germany also migrated. Where do you think they went?

When new jobs are created in these countries, there are not enough people at home to fill them. This is the cause of the pull forces that attract migrant workers to these countries.

A MELTING POT?

European sociologists have asked if these push and pull forces bring Europeans closer together. They want to know if migrant workers can break down the differences between European countries and make Europe more of a melting pot.

▶ The United States is the home of people who came from many different cultures. Can you guess why it has often been called a melting pot?

Cristobal Martin was born in Granada, Spain, 38 years ago. "Granada is the most beautiful city in the world," says Mr. Martin. "Its sun is warm and its air is clear." Today, Mr. Martin works in Germany, where the weather is often cold and rainy. But in Germany, he works in a factory and makes about $500 a month. "In Granada, there is very little industry. I was only a farm worker. When the German company came and offered me a job, I took it right away." Mr. Martin works in a chemical factory where he measures out chemicals, pours them into packages, and prepares them for shipping. He works from 7:00 A.M. to 4:00 P.M.. From 10:00 P.M. to 1:00 A.M., he has another job cleaning out the office of a doctor in his neighborhood.

Mr. Martin does not speak much German. "I wish I had time to go to school and learn more. It would be easier to live here. I have sat with the same men at lunch every day for four years, and we never talk to each other. They think of me as a 'foreigner,'" he says.

After work, Mr. Martin rides home on the bicycle he brought with him from Spain. "I live in a small room that I don't like very much," he says. "But there is no reason for me to live like a gran señor. That is not why I came to Germany." Cristobal hopes that in two more years he will have enough money to return home to Granada. "I want to open up a small shop, find a wife, and have a decent life for me and my family."

Mr. Martin lives in a neighborhood with Italians and other Spaniards. "We think alike," he says, "and we don't mind the noise of the wives and children that the Germans complain about. I do not hate Germany. I am thankful for the jobs it has given me. But Germany is not the proper place for me. It is not my home."

172

▶ Do you think that working in another country changes a person's outlook?

▶ In many countries, including the United States, only a small number of immigrants are allowed to enter every year. Can you think of any reasons why countries do not welcome too many newcomers to share their land?

▶ Why is it bad for a country to have unemployed workers? How might it make the unemployed feel about their country? Does it cost governments money when they have unemployed workers?

The movement of workers has not gone on long enough to give an answer yet. But there are some signs that have already shown up. Unlike Juan, many of the migrants do settle in the countries they move to. But most of them have not been successful. Can you guess why they have had so many problems resettling?

In some countries, like Switzerland and Germany, migrants are not allowed to stay for more than three years. Some countries will not allow migrants to bring their families with them. Yet other countries, like France and Sweden, have welcomed migrants and allowed them to become citizens. Even in these countries, though, most migrants have not become citizens.

Geography of the migrants What are the three push countries that provide most of the migrant workers? Find them on the map on page 147. What part of Europe are all these countries in?

This region has a different way of life from many of the other countries of Europe. The languages — Italian, Spanish, and Portuguese — are closely related. The customs and attitudes of people of this region are similar. But they are quite different from those in Sweden, Germany, Great Britain, the Netherlands, and other countries with pull forces. Even the foods of these countries are different. These differences lead to complaints.

Advantages for push and pull countries Countries that lose workers do have some advantages. They do not have as many unemployed people as they might. The money that migrants send back home helps their countries to prosper and to develop industry. When migrants return, they bring still more money with them. They also bring back training and skills that can be important for developing business or industry in their home countries.

The countries that accept migrants also receive many benefits. The migrants do necessary jobs that otherwise might not be done. Many migrants work very hard in these jobs. Since most of the workers do not bring their families along, the pull countries do not have to provide schools or health services.

For the migrants, too, there are many advantages to staying only a few years. When they return, they have the experience of being educated through travel. They have money. They have new skills and languages. Their status—their position in their home communities—is higher.

Many people feel that there are still great differences between the many countries of Europe. Do you think this is a fair conclusion to draw from the experiences of the migrant workers? Why or why not? Are the push and pull forces drawing European people closer to each other or further apart?

▶ If a Spaniard working in Germany sent his family in Spain some money and his wife bought groceries with it, how could this help the country of Spain? As a hint, try to trace where the money might go after it was first spent for groceries.

▶ stā′təs

▶ Can people from different parts of the United States move to other regions and settle down? Do you think that they have as hard a time fitting in to their new homes as the European migrants do?

---

1. What do you think were some of the problems, differences, and complaints that arose when new immigrant groups entered the United States? Were any of these problems or differences solved?
2. Do people from the same areas of the world have more in common with each other than people from different areas of the world? Explain.
3. What can traveling to other countries teach you about people and the world?

INVESTIGATING THE UNIT

Doing Research

Are there any products from Europe in your house? Are these products also made in the United States? Do the European products have any advantages? If so, try to find out why the European products have those advantages. Is it because of the geography of Europe?

Looking at the Evidence

Talk to a local antique dealer about furniture made over 200 years ago in Europe. What kind of furniture was made then? For whom was it mainly built? Do those kinds of people live in America today? How much would you have to pay for a chair made 200 years ago in France? Why do you think it would cost that much?

Compare and Contrast

Find some books on England and Italy in your library. What differences are there in the way people live in the two countries? How are the traditions and history of the two countries different? In what ways can people of both countries consider themselves Europeans? How does this compare with people from New York and California?

Using Maps

Compare a map of Europe 200 years ago with a map of Europe today. What nations or empires existed then that do not exist now? What nations exist now that did not exist then? What nations have "put themselves together" out of smaller nations? What countries have not changed much?

Reading on Your Own

Several great European leaders were women. You can find out about Queen Elizabeth of England in Elizabeth Jenkins' *Elizabeth the Great* (New York, Coward, McCann and Geoghegan). The story of another Queen whose reign did not go so well is told in Marguerite Vance's *Marie Antoinette: Daughter of an Empress* (New York, E. P. Dutton).

EASTERN EUROPE: THE SOVIET UNION

More than fifty years ago, a train crossed Germany. The doors and
windows of the train were sealed shut. No one could enter or leave.
Inside the train were food, supplies, and men. The train would
not be opened until it reached Russia. The men who traveled in this
sealed train would change history.

Yesterday and Today

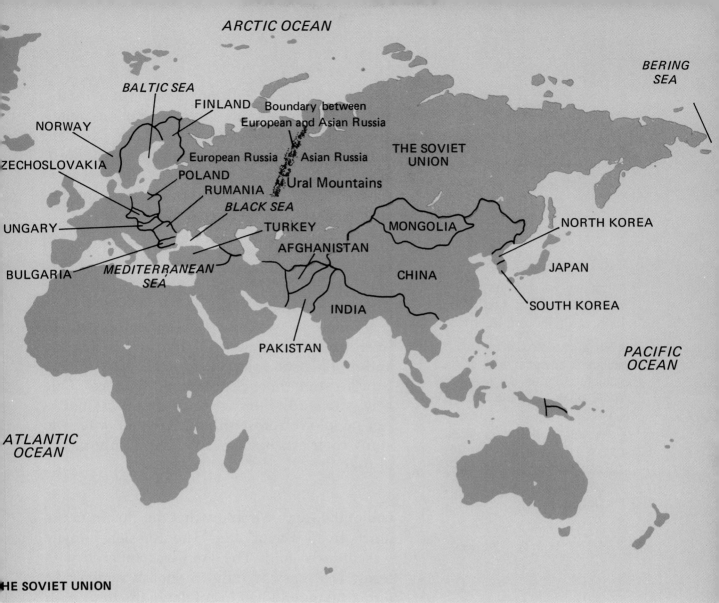

ARCTIC OCEAN

BERING SEA

BALTIC SEA

FINLAND   Boundary between
European and Asian Russia

NORWAY

ZECHOSLOVAKIA

European Russia   Asian Russia

THE SOVIET UNION

POLAND

RUMANIA

Ural Mountains

BLACK SEA

UNGARY

TURKEY

MONGOLIA

NORTH KOREA

AFGHANISTAN

BULGARIA

MEDITERRANEAN SEA

JAPAN

CHINA

SOUTH KOREA

INDIA

PACIFIC OCEAN

PAKISTAN

ATLANTIC OCEAN

HE SOVIET UNION

The Soviet Union, or Russia, is a widespread country. It stretches from the Pacific Ocean on the east to the Baltic Sea on the west; from the Arctic Circle on the north to the Middle and Far East on the south. Find the Soviet Union on the map on this page. Name the countries that border it. Name the big bodies of water that border it. Look at your classroom globe. Are there any other countries in the world that are bigger than the Soviet Union?

▶ The population of the United States is close to 209 million people. Are there as many differences among Americans as among Russians? Why or why not?

▶ Usually we call the time before Christ, B.C. After the birth of Christ, we call A.D.

▶ An archaeologist (ar′ kē ol′ ə-jist) is a scientist who studies ancient cultures by examining such things as tools, ruins, and art.

▶ An anthropologist (an′ thrə-päl′ ə jist) is a scientist who studies the remains of man to see how man has changed throughout history.

▶ What part of the United States do you live in? Are these crops like the ones grown where you live?

▶ To smelt means to melt ore in order to purify the metal.

More than 250 million people live in the Soviet Union. Among them there are many different races of people speaking different languages and having different histories. More than 25 major, and many minor, languages are spoken there. How did such a big country, with so many different peoples, develop?

Early times For historians, Russian history begins about A.D. 970—when a people called the Rus came to trade in Russia.

No one knows exactly how these people lived back then. Scientists, like archaeologists, anthropologists, and historians, have many ways to study how people lived long ago. One way is to study their writings. But these northern people left no writings. Another way is to study their art. But we have found only a little of their art.

Life of the Rus We know that the Rus from the north lived a hard life. The Russian climate was bitterly cold. The land was covered with trees. Is it easy to farm in such a region? To farm, the people had to cut down the trees with axes. Then they would burn the trees and use the ashes to fertilize the land.

They grew barley, wheat, apples, and pears on this land. But after a few years, the land lost its fertility, and the people had to move on.

We know that the people knew how to smelt iron and that they knew how to weave and to make pots. But life was hard.

In the forest, however, there were many valuable things for the people to use. There were furs from animals, and honey and wax from bees. The people discovered that they

WHY DO NATIONS CHANGE THEIR NAMES?

Below are two lists of names. See if you can match the correct name in column A with the correct name in column B. Sometimes even experts are confused.

A	B
Egypt	The United Kingdom
Persia	The U.S.S.R.
Russia	The United Arab Republic
England	Iran

Did you match them all? If so, you might grow up to be a map maker. Most map makers complain when a nation changes its name. Why, then, do nations change their names?

Sometimes they do it to seem more modern. Once there was a very old nation named Persia. Today, that nation is named Iran. The king of Iran thought a new name would seem more modern, and he wanted his nation to be more modern. But people from Iran still speak Persian.

Long ago, the nation of England conquered the nations of Scotland and Ireland. After that, the combined country was called the United Kingdom. Can you see why they made this change?

Not long before you were born, the very old nation of Egypt joined with a neigh-bor to form a bigger nation. They called themselves the United Arab Republic. In time, the other nation left the union. But Egypt still calls itself the United Arab Republic. On many maps, both names appear. Do you think people from Egypt call themselves Egyptians or United Arab Republicans?

The Soviet Union is a country with three names. How can one country have three names? Its first name was Russia. Can you make a guess as to where that name came from? Today, however, Russia is only one of 15 states in the Soviet Union. In a way, it is what New York and California are to the United States.

Many states in the Soviet Union were once independent nations. Some people still think of themselves as members of those nations. A person from Latvia (lat'-vē ə), for instance, may think of himself as Latvian, not Russian. People still use the name Russia, however, because that name is so old. Also, Russia is probably the most important state in the Soviet Union.

Russia's other two names are the Soviet Union and the Union of Soviet Socialist Republics—the U.S.S.R. They both stand for that huge country made up of the 15 different states.

could trade these products for grain, woven fabrics, and manufactured items from the south.

The founding of Kiev In time, the people from the north started a town. The town was Kiev. Find Kiev on the map opposite. Would it be a good place for trade? Remember that trains, planes, and trucks had not been invented yet.

Kiev eventually became a great city. Many people came there to trade. The more people who came, the more trade there was. Kiev grew and prospered.

The rise of Kiev Every fall, the leaders of Kiev built boats and traveled to nearby lands. There they collected taxes throughout the winter. In the spring, when the rivers melted, the princes of Kiev returned. In this way, a kingdom grew up in the area around the city. This small kingdom was called Russia.

◗ kē′ ef

A twelfth-century book illustrates the early history of Russia. The picture here shows Kiev warriors.

The people of the kingdom were of many classes. Some were rich and lived in luxury. Others were traders. Most of the rest were farmers or hunters or woodsmen. Almost all of these were free. If they wanted to live on another farm or in Kiev itself, they were free to move.

Religion For a long time, the people of Russia had been pagans. That is, they did not believe in one God. Instead, they worshiped the spirits of their ancestors and the gods of nature. For example, they believed in a god of thunder. But, in 988, the Grand Prince of Kiev suddenly converted to Christianity.

The prince's name was Vladimir. Vladimir was an excellent soldier and a very good ruler. But he is most famous for being the man who changed Russia to a Christian nation. The day after Vladimir converted, he angrily grabbed an idol of the thunder-god, with its silver head and gold moustache, and threw it into a river of Kiev. Then he ordered all the people of Russia to become Christians. The great nobles of Kiev converted immediately.

But most of the poorer people continued to believe in the old gods, as they had for hundreds of years. Today, however, Vladimir is honored as a saint of the Russian Church.

Kiev declines Kiev did not remain strong. When a king died, his sons and brothers fought over who would succeed him. In time, the kingdom around Kiev was split by warring princes.

And then another, and even greater, danger appeared. A frightening enemy came out of the east.

♦ vlad' i mir

*Russian Christians painted icons—religious pictures—
on wooden panels. What events do you think this icon
shows?*

THE MONGOLS—WARRIORS ON HORSEBACK

The Mongols were a fierce, strong, and warlike people. They were expert horsemen who rode small, shaggy ponies into battle. They were even able to eat and sleep on horseback. What were the advantages of expert horsemanship in that time? Look at the map on page 179. Where did the Mongols come from?

In the 1200s, one group of Mongols spread out to the south and conquered China. At about the same time, another group moved west and conquered many lands, including much of Russia.

Mongol chiefs ruled the lands they conquered with an iron hand. They expected, and received, instant obedience from everyone. They forced everyone they ruled to pay them taxes.

Muscovy For hundreds of years, the Mongols ruled most of Russia in this manner. But there was one part of Russia, in the north, that they

◗ məs′ kə vē

This is a picture of a Mongol camp in 1807. Compare what you see here with what you know about the early Mongols. Had their life changed much by 1807?

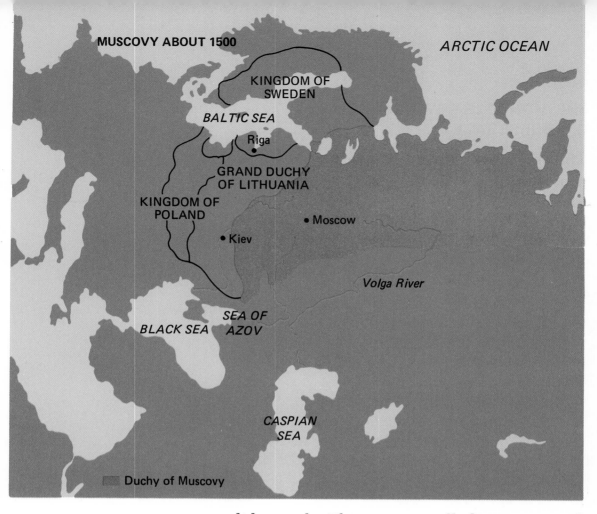

Map labels:
ARCTIC OCEAN
KINGDOM OF SWEDEN
BALTIC SEA
Riga
GRAND DUCHY OF LITHUANIA
KINGDOM OF POLAND
Kiev
Moscow
Volga River
BLACK SEA
SEA OF AZOV
CASPIAN SEA

▨ Duchy of Muscovy

did not rule. This part was called Muscovy, and its chief town was Moscow. At first, Muscovy was a poor land. Like Kiev, it, too, was divided among many princes. These princes fought with each other for a long time. Gradually, some princes became stronger and took over the lands of weaker princes. The rulers of Moscow grew stronger. By 1500, the Mongols were driven completely out of Russia, and the rulers of Muscovy became the rulers of all Russia.

One strong Mongol influence remained, however. Most of the Russian people had lived under the iron rule of the Mongols for more than 200 years. They were used to strong rulers who commanded strict and instant obedience. They would have many more such rulers.

▶ Do you think that a people might grow used to having a strong leader make decisions? Might people forget how to make decisions for themselves?

186

THE ROMANOVS

By the early 1600s, Russia had begun to take the same shape it has today. It stretched from the Baltic Sea on the north to the Caspian Sea on the south. East and west, the country ran from near the Ural Mountains to Poland.

But the country was still divided. Russian nobles and wealthy landowners were fighting fierce battles among themselves. Things got so bad that they stopped the battles and met to set up a strong central government. They chose Michael Romanov, a young noble of only 16, to be their tsar, or king. The Romanov family would rule the Russian people for the next 300 years.

▶ Tsar (zär) comes from the name of Caesar, a great Roman general.

The first Romanov   The tsars were never elected by the people. Michael Romanov was selected by other nobles only because he was too young to have made any enemies. When he took office, there was no code of laws.

What kind of nation do you think might have developed in a situation like this? Do you think the people could learn to be free by themselves? Do you think the rulers would allow the people to govern themselves? As you read, ask yourself how freedom develops.

▶ When the United States became a nation, it drew up a code of laws. Do you know what it is called?

THE GROWTH OF SERFDOM

A new Russia   The new, united Russia needed workers. The tsar wanted them to start farms. He wanted them to settle in towns. This way, Russia could grow into a strong country. Until then, few Russian people had ever stayed in one place. They were used to running away to new places to escape landowners and rulers.

Life for the Russian peasant was never easy. Whether he had a master or worked for himself, the peasant struggled to feed his family. What chore is the man behind the horse doing?

But the tsar wanted the people to settle down. He wanted some people to live in towns, some to work on lands of rich landowners, and some to become soldiers in the army.

Russia wanted another thing from its people —money. It sent men to collect taxes from the workers. If the workers and farmers could not pay, they were punished. If they did not join the army, they were tortured.

Slavery As a result, people sometimes sold themselves into slavery. They were then considered "nonpersons." As nonpersons, they did not have to pay taxes or fight. But they had now become slaves—the personal property of their owners.

Other people just ran away. On one estate owned by the tsar, more than two out of every three workers simply left. The government passed laws against runaways, but still the people ran away. Some rich landlords paid workers extra money, but still they left.

Finally, the government grew angry. It made a law forbidding peasants to leave the land they worked on. Furthermore, their sons and grandsons could no longer leave the land. Town dwellers could not go to another town or even change their jobs. Finally, custom said that the peasant belonged to his landlord. Free peasants had now become serfs.

▶ Serfs are unfree peasants.

Serfs Serfs had to do the work landowners told them to do. For example, a story is told of a lady who had a serf for a hairdresser. When he was not working for her, she kept him in a cage. She did this because the serf knew that she was bald and wore a wig. She did not want him to tell anyone.

Russian serfs received food, clothing, and shelter from their masters, but little else. Russian serfs were really no better than slaves.

Most Russian villages were small and far away from the cities. Villagers were mostly peasants who lived in small huts. Only the milkman (shown here) and the few rich men of each village owned horses. Do you think these people knew much about the world outside their village?

Middle class The next-highest class of people in Russia was the middle class. This included shopkeepers, merchants, lawyers, doctors, and other city dwellers. They had to pay many taxes and were forced to serve in the army.

Nobles Nobles formed the upper class. Some of them were landowners, some were army officers, and others did not work at all. At the top of all these classes was the tsar, "autocrat of all the Russians." The Russian people called the tsar "Little Father." They were told that they owed him their loyalty and their lives.

An isolated nation Romanov rule began at a time when exciting and important events were happening in other parts of the world. The Age of Discovery was at its peak. Men were sailing on a direct route from Europe to the East Indies and returning with ships full of silks, spices, and other rich cargo.

▶ An autocrat is a ruler with unlimited power.

▶ What new places do you know of that were being explored or colonized?

RUSSIA UNDER PETER THE GREAT

But, in Russia, few people were aware of this change. Russian eyes were turned inward. The people had problems of their own and wanted nothing to do with the outside world. One man alone did much to change this attitude. His name was Peter the Great.

PETER THE GREAT

In 1696, Peter Romanov became Russia's tsar. Peter is called "the Great" for two reasons. One reason is that he was an enormous man—six feet, eight inches tall. But a more important reason is that he was the person most responsible for making Russia into a powerful nation.

A disguised tsar Peter the Great's curiosity about the world led him to visit Europe in 1696. He was the first tsar ever to leave Russia. With 250 men, he traveled in disguise and, in some places, even worked as a common laborer to learn about Europe's modern ways.

Peter visited Germany, England, and Sweden and learned new things in each place. He found out how Europeans made cannons, how they printed books, and how they studied the stars. He was especially interested in learning how to build ships and how to sail them.

While Peter was away, a revolt broke out in Russia. He quickly returned home. He put down the revolt and captured many of the rebels.

Modernizing Russia When the revolt was over, Peter went to work on the ideas he had gained in Europe. He printed newspapers and improved the system of collecting taxes. Peter forced Russian men to shave off their beards,

Peter the Great liked to spend his quiet moments in deep thought. What game is he playing?

▶ Why do you think Peter disguised himself?

♦ nē′ və

▶ Why do you think Peter built himself a new capital?

▶ A sovereign (sov′rən) is a ruler who is usually a king or queen.

♦ zär ē′ nə

because men in Europe were not wearing beards at that time. But most important for the future of Russia, Peter built large factories which would supply his army with modern guns and cannons. He also began to build the navy which he had always dreamed of.

In 1700, Peter the Great sent his armies to attack Sweden. Sweden was then the most powerful country in northern Europe, and the Russians were defeated. But Peter rebuilt his army and, in 1709, attacked again. This time he won. Russia took land from Sweden along the Baltic Sea. On part of this land, along the Neva River, Peter built the city of St. Petersburg—now called Leningrad. St. Petersburg would remain one of the world's great capitals for the next 200 years.

Peter the Great died in 1725. Behind him he left a large and powerful Russia.

CATHERINE THE GREAT

For 37 years after Peter's death, Russia had six rulers. All of them were weak. Finally, in 1762, a sovereign nearly as strong as Peter took the throne. Her name was Catherine II.

A time of freedom Catherine II was tsarina during a time when people were talking about freedom and about their rights to govern themselves. Soon they were fighting for those rights. While Catherine ruled Russia, the American colonists revolted and formed the new nation of the United States. In France, the people revolted against their king and queen and set up their own government.

Like other European rulers, Catherine II was frightened by the French Revolution. So

Most early Russian art was used in churches. In the eighteenth century, Peter the Great and Catherine II sent Russian artists to Europe to learn Western styles. Why do you think these rulers did this?

she claimed that she, too, believed in the rights of man. She gave her people a new system of laws, but these laws did not really give them more rights. In fact, they gave landowners even more rights over the serfs. Serfs were again like slaves.

▶ Why did Catherine pretend that she was for the rights of man?

Why Catherine the Great? Catherine II is better known as Catherine the Great. This is because Russia conquered much land during her rule.

In war, Russia won a part of Poland and much land around the Black Sea. The Black Sea is warm all year round. This is especially important to the Russians because their seaports on the Baltic Sea freeze up in winter.

By 1825, Russia had become about as huge as it is today. Russia's armies had conquered

▶ What effect do you think this would have on trade?

193

all of Siberia. They had extended Russian control over the areas we now call Finland, Poland, and eastern Germany. On the south, Russia bordered Iran and Afghanistan. Russia had become a giant of a nation which the rulers of European nations respected and often feared.

A police state Life inside Russia, however, had hardly changed. While people in other countries were receiving more rights, the Russians were losing the few they had. They were forbidden to travel to other countries. Their activities were closely watched by the secret police. They could not have public meetings.

KARL MARX

A German thinker and writer did much to end the rule of the tsars. His name was Karl Marx.

Karl Marx was born in 1818. He spent years studying history and law. His studies convinced him that before the world could improve, the poor would have to take part in a revolution. They would have to revolt against the rich and against governments that robbed them of their rights.

Communism In many countries, individuals privately own land, stores, and often, means of production like factories and railroads. Marx believed that the private ownership of land and other property such as factories had helped many people. Workers had earned wages, businessmen had received profits, and people in general had many products to enjoy. But Marx believed this system, called **capitalism**, would fail. He said that factory owners, or capitalists, always wanted to make

▶ A country where no one is free to act on his own is known as a police state. Why did the tsar forbid these activities? What was he afraid of?

These two pictures show a great difference between the way Russian people spent their time. What do the pictures tell you about the differences between rich and poor in tsarist Russia? Would poor people in a country like this be more likely to accept the ideas of Marx? Why or why not?

▶ In the United States, many people work for stores and manufacturers. Do you know anyone who works for a big store or a big manufacturing company? Do they work long hours, or do they have nights and weekends off? Do they live in a nice house or apartment?

▶ Look at the word *communism*. What words do you know that begin with the same letters? How is the word *communism* like the word *common*?

▶ Why did the people want a written constitution in addition to better working conditions?

larger and larger profits. To do this, he said, they had to keep expenses down. One way to do this was to keep workers' wages low. As profits increased, the rich would grow richer and the poor would grow poorer.

In most countries, wages were very low. Workers labored as long as 12 hours a day, six days a week. They worked with dangerous machinery. They lived in wretched slums. And a worker might lose his job at any time.

There was, Karl Marx believed, only one solution—do away with private property. Let the people, through their government, own everything. Then everyone could share what factories produced. Each person would contribute according to his own ability. Each person would receive according to his needs. No longer would there be rich people or poor people. Everyone would be equal. At first, Marx said, the government would control all of this. But in time, there would be no need for government, and it would wither away.

The system Marx argued for is called **communism.** He called for a revolt of the masses of people against governments and capitalists.

People in many countries read the many articles, pamphlets, and books Marx wrote. Some people became Marxists, or Communists. They talked, thought, and wrote of revolution.

THE RUSSIAN REVOLUTION

In Russia, many uprisings occurred. One of the most famous ones took place on a January day in 1905. A huge crowd of people gathered in St. Petersburg and angrily marched to the Winter Palace of the tsar. They had planned to ask the tsar, now Nicholas II, for a constitution and for better working conditions.

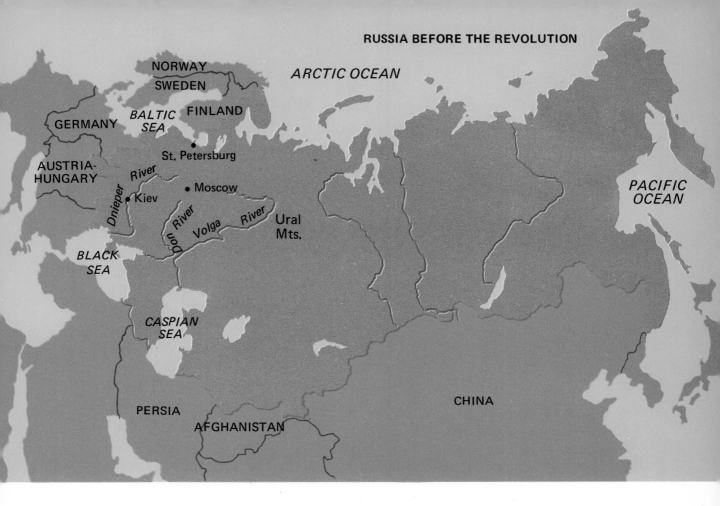

Strike The tsar never came out to answer the people. Instead, he sent out soldiers to gun down the people. They killed nearly 100 people. Workers protested by going out on strike. Schools, factories, banks, and businesses were forced to close down.

Frightened by the strike, Tsar Nicholas II began to see that change was necessary. He gave Russia a constitution. The constitution allowed the people to choose representatives and to meet as a *Duma*. The Russian Duma was something like the United States Congress. The Duma met several times, but it accomplished little.

♦ dü′mə

World War I For many years, there had been unease among the nations of Europe. Some were building great armies. Some were taking

197

◗ A colony is a country that is ruled by another country.

colonies in Africa and Asia. In 1914, a great war broke out. Great Britain and France were allied on one side. Germany and other nations fought on the other.

Late in 1914, Russia joined the world war on the side of France and Great Britain. The United States joined France, Britain, and Russia in 1915.

For Russia, the war was a disaster. The German army marched deep into Russia. The Russian army suffered badly, and citizens did too.

◗ To abdicate means to resign from the monarchy.

Each year the Russian people celebrate the anniversary of the Russian Revolution here in Moscow's Red Square.

Revolution begins In March 1917, a revolution began in St. Petersburg. There were no real leaders. But there were mobs of desperate, hungry people running through the streets. Nicholas II abdicated and turned the government over to the Duma.

Nikolai Lenin Many people had been working for a Communist revolution in Russia. Some had devoted their entire lives to that cause. One of these was Vladimir Ilich Ulyanov. He was better known as Nikolai Lenin.

Lenin was in exile in Switzerland when the revolution broke out. Lenin believed he had to get back to Russia to lead his people to Communism. The Germans offered to send him back in a sealed train. Lenin accepted the offer to take him through the war zone to Russia in the sealed train.

Here are three of the Russian Revolution's most famous leaders—Lenin, Joseph Stalin, and (with glasses) Leon Trotsky.

◗ ē′ lēch ül yän′ əf
◗ ni′ kō lī len′ ən

▶ bōl′ shə vəsts

▶ Which Russians would have been against the Communists? Why?

After the revolution was won, a large wheat crop was harvested. Can you see where the extra wheat was stored?

Lenin and a group of fellow Communists, called Bolshevists, arrived in St. Petersburg in April 1917.

In the summer and fall of 1917, Lenin and his followers went to work. By November, they were ready. Armed workers and soldiers, under their command, seized government buildings. The nobles and government officers fled in terror. The Duma fell. Soon, Lenin was at the head of a new kind of Russian government—a Communist government.

Lenin's first step was to take Russia out of the war. His government signed a peace agreement with Germany. In exchange for peace, Russia gave up large areas of its territory.

But a new kind of war ended any hopes of peace for Russia. Many Russians were against the new government. Communist armies spent the next few years fighting people within Russia. And Britain, France, and the United States sent soldiers to help these people overthrow the Communists. Lenin was afraid that the monarchy would be brought back. He had Tsar Nicholas II, his wife, and his children

killed. It was not until 1920 that peace finally came to Russia.

Communism in action Now the Communist government was in complete control. It took over factories, banks, businesses, and farms. It gave land to the peasants. It assigned workers to jobs in factories. Things were almost as Karl Marx had pictured them.

Stalin Lenin died in 1924, and Joseph Stalin became the leader of Russia. Russia's name was changed to the Union of Soviet Socialist Republics. Soviet was the name given to the groups of workers, peasants, and soldiers who joined together to set up a Communist government in 1917.

Stalin took all control of the government and of the people into his own hands. Workers, scientists, and artists were told what jobs they had to take and what wages the government would pay them. Peasants were forced to work on large farms which the government owned. Those who refused—and thousands did—were killed or sent into exile. Under Stalin, the secret police became even more powerful than they had been under the tsars. People lived in fear.

WORLD WAR II AND AFTER

By the 1930s, Europe was moving toward another world war. Remembering what happened in World War I, Joseph Stalin signed a treaty of friendship with Adolf Hitler, the German dictator. But in 1941, Hitler ignored the treaty and sent his armies to invade the Soviet Union. Russia, under a new name, was again fighting on the side of Britain, France, and the United States.

◗ Stalin (stäl′in) means "man of steel" in Russian. The early Russian Communists made up new names for themselves to confuse the tsar and his army.

◗ A treaty (trēt′ē) is a written agreement between nations.

And once again, the Soviet people suffered terrible hardships during a world war. Many of their cities were bombed by German planes and suffered great damage. At least 20 million Russian people died from disease, starvation, or bullets during those four years of war.

Stalin the conqueror Joseph Stalin decided he must try to prevent any future invasion. What do you think he did to prevent more invasions?

Stalin's answer was this: He wanted friendly, Communist governments in all the countries bordering the Soviet Union on the west. With Stalin's help, Communists took over the governments of Poland, Hungary, Rumania, Bulgaria, and Czechoslovakia. The eastern part of Germany was also under Communist control. West Germany was controlled by Britain, France, and the United States.

▶ Find these places on the map on page 179.

Russia after Stalin The Russian government watched its neighbors very closely. If Russia did not like what a country was doing, it sent orders for them to stop. When the Hungarian people tried to change their government in 1956, Russia sent in troops to put down the uprising. In 1968, the government of Czechoslovakia wanted to become a little more independent of Russia. Once again, Russian troops invaded.

Today, the Soviet Union is becoming friendlier with nations around the world. The United States and the Soviet Union have signed important treaties with each other.

But the Soviet government still does not like its people to criticize its decisions. It has jailed many persons, including writers and scientists,

▶ Do you know of any group of people who have not been allowed to leave the Soviet Union?

who have spoken against Soviet policies. It forbids many of its people to leave the U.S.S.R.

But there is a certain strong spirit in the Russian people that has fought back against all harsh rule.

Many Russian writers have tried to put these feelings into words and share them with the world. One of these writers, Alexander Solzhenitsyn, has written so well of the Russian spirit that in 1970 he was awarded the Nobel Prize for Literature—one of the world's greatest honors.

▶ äl eks änd′ ėr sōl zhen ēt′ sən

In the speech he wrote to accept the prize, Solzhenitsyn said, ". . . on our crowded earth . . . mankind's sole salvation lies in everyone making everything his business. In the people of the East being vitally concerned with what is thought in the West, the people of the West vitally concerned with what goes on in the East."

▶ Why do you think Solzhenitsyn warned everybody to mind everybody's business? Do you think the words "our crowded earth" give a hint? How?

The Soviet government did not approve of Solzhenitsyn's comments. It told him that if he went to receive the prize in Sweden, he would not be allowed back into his own country. Solzhenitsyn, who is not allowed to publish any books in the Soviet Union or to speak to the public, decided to stay.

▶ What comments do you think the government disliked? Why?

1. What was the name of the town the Rus settled? How did it grow?
2. What kind of rulers were the Mongols? What part of Russia did they *not* control?
3. Why did some Russian peasants sell themselves into slavery?
4. Do you think the building of factories under Peter the Great made life easier for the serfs? Who do you think worked in the factories?
5. Explain why Karl Marx was against capitalism.

The Land and the People

"If you spent a week in Russia," the man said, "you could write a book about it. If you spent a month there, you could write a magazine article. But, if you spent a year there and saw all the different peoples, their ways of life, and the different regions in which they lived, you would be too confused to write a letter home about what you saw."

It is easy, of course, to say this about any country. The more you learn about a place, often the harder it is to make a decision about that place. But it is especially easy to say this about the largest country on earth.

THE LAND AND CLIMATE

Climate regions   Geographers divide land areas around the world into climate regions. The kind of climate region an area is depends on two things — weather (temperature, rainfall, and moisture in the air) and vegetation (the plants and grasses that grow in the area).

There are many kinds of climate regions in the world. Look at the climate region map on the following page. What is its major climate region? On your classroom globe, find the boundary line between the United States and Canada. Now follow this line around to the Soviet Union. Is most of the Soviet Union north or south of the United States? Look again at the climate map. Can you find any tundra? taiga? Where are they? Does the United States have any areas of land like these? Do you think you could find a warm climate in the Soviet Union?

Flatland and highland   There are four major kinds of landforms in the world: mountains, hills, plains, and plateaus. Plains are flat and

▶ Tundra (tən'drə) is a treeless plain that is found in very cold regions.

▶ Taiga (tī gä') is a swampy forest of evergreen trees that begins where the tundra ends.

▶ pla tōz'

205

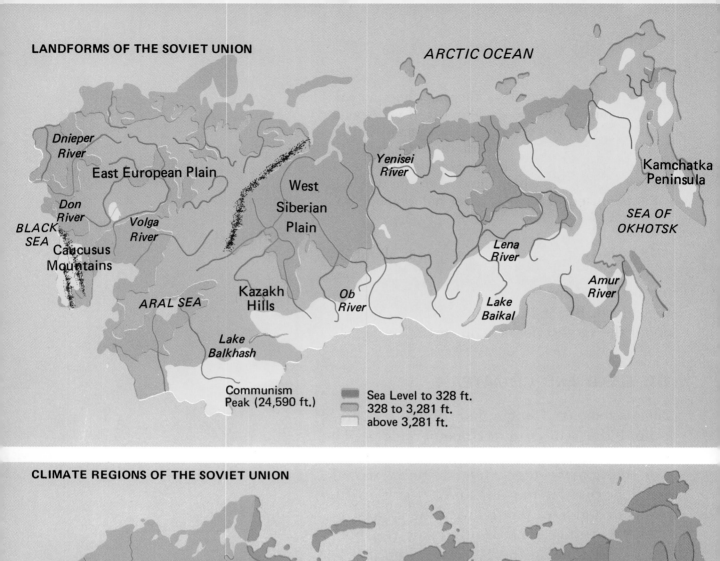

LANDFORMS OF THE SOVIET UNION

ARCTIC OCEAN

Dnieper River

East European Plain

Yenisei River

Kamchatka Peninsula

Don River

Volga River

West Siberian Plain

SEA OF OKHOTSK

BLACK SEA

Caucusus Mountains

Lena River

Amur River

ARAL SEA

Kazakh Hills

Ob River

Lake Baikal

Lake Balkhash

Communism Peak (24,590 ft.)

Sea Level to 328 ft.
328 to 3,281 ft.
above 3,281 ft.

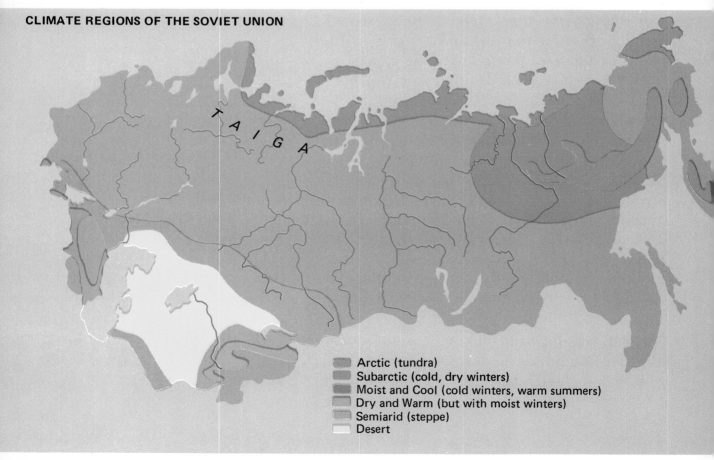

CLIMATE REGIONS OF THE SOVIET UNION

T A I G A

Arctic (tundra)
Subarctic (cold, dry winters)
Moist and Cool (cold winters, warm summers)
Dry and Warm (but with moist winters)
Semiarid (steppe)
Desert

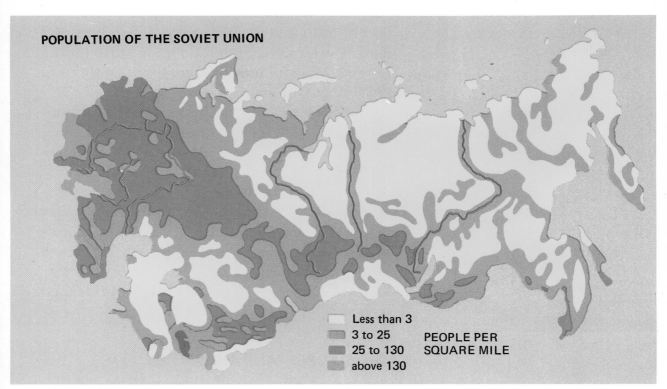

POPULATION OF THE SOVIET UNION

Less than 3
3 to 25
25 to 130
above 130

PEOPLE PER SQUARE MILE

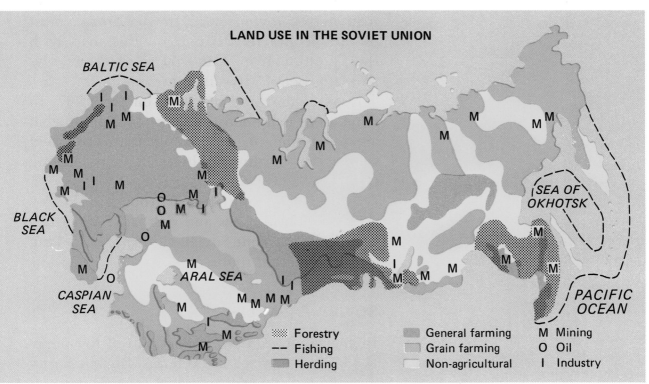

LAND USE IN THE SOVIET UNION

BALTIC SEA

BLACK SEA

CASPIAN SEA

ARAL SEA

SEA OF OKHOTSK

PACIFIC OCEAN

Forestry
Fishing
Herding
General farming
Grain farming
Non-agricultural
M Mining
O Oil
I Industry

▶ What kind of landform do you live on or near?

▶ Are there many farms where you live, or do you live in an urbanized area?

gently rolling land. Plateaus are also long and flat but are raised higher than the surrounding ground. Which kinds of landforms are there in the Soviet Union?

The Soviet Union stretches across two continents. What are they? What mountains separate European Russia from Asiatic Russia? Name two other major mountain ranges in the Soviet Union. Name six rivers.

Can you guess which of the four landforms is best suited to farming? Which landforms would be best for roads and railroads? Which kinds of landforms are best for large factories? Does the Soviet Union have much of this kind of land?

THE PEOPLE AND HOW THEY LIVE

Where people live Look at the population map on the previous page. In what area do most of the people live? Compare this map with the landform map. Can you see reasons why so many people live in these regions?

Look at the land use map on page 207. In what areas is the most industry found? In what areas are the oil fields? What area is used mainly for herding? Where is grain farming the major activity?

Study the transportation map opposite. Where are most of the roads and railroads? What can you find out about Soviet industry by looking at transportation routes?

SOVIET FARM LIFE

In the Soviet Union, almost half of the population lives and works on farms. But the farms, and indeed the entire way of life on a farm, is

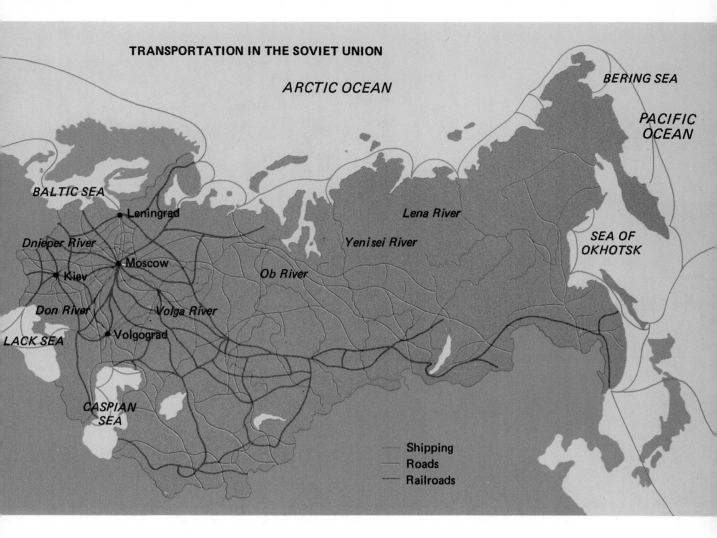

TRANSPORTATION IN THE SOVIET UNION

ARCTIC OCEAN

BERING SEA

PACIFIC OCEAN

BALTIC SEA

Leningrad

Lena River

Dnieper River

Yenisei River

Moscow

SEA OF OKHOTSK

Kiev

Ob River

Don River

Volga River

LACK SEA

Volgograd

CASPIAN SEA

Shipping
Roads
Railroads

different from farm life in our country. Most differences are due to the way land is owned in the Soviet Union.

The government as farmer In the Soviet Union, a farmer does not own his own piece of land. Instead he works on either a **collective farm** or a state farm. A collective farm is made up of many farmers who own the land all together. The farmers sell their crops together and share the profits. Every year they must sell a certain amount of crops to the government. The government can then sell food to the people at a low price.

▶ Why do you think farms in the Soviet Union are so much larger than farms in the United States?

209

According to an old saying, "Russia is not a country, but a world." The Soviet Union covers more than half of Europe and nearly two-fifths of Asia. It has over 250 million people. How might the lives of the Soviet citizens in these pictures differ from that of a resident of Moscow?

Some farmers work on state farms. State farms are huge. Some are as large as 75,000 acres. All land on a state farm is owned by the government. On such farms, everyone is a specialist. Everyone has his own particular job to do.

Soviet farm workers use modern farm machinery. They receive a salary for their work. What they raise is decided by the government. When the crops are picked, the government selects where they will be sold.

The backyard farmer Most Russian farmers live in villages. Every day they travel to the fields, much as your parents go to work. Many have their own private backyard farms. These are small plots of ground behind the houses that line both sides of village streets. Farmers can grow whatever they wish on their small plots. They can eat the food or sell it and keep the money. Here is how one farm village looks.

The moment I drove into the village . . . I found a scene I had never witnessed anywhere in the Soviet Union. No pigs and chickens wandered the streets. No chained dogs barked at passersby. There were no slimy mudholes anywhere. The streets and sidewalks were paved. . . . Mud . . . was no longer a problem here, even in the wet season.

There were none of the whitewashed adobe houses with thatched roofs, found everywhere in the Ukraine. Instead, there were one-story, one-family homes newly built out of sandstone rock. They were roofed with tile or sheet iron. Each had a living room, one or two bedrooms, a kitchen and a storeroom. All were equipped with gas and electricity. A huge, black water tank towered over the village, just as in the towns of America's Midwest. . . .

▶ Adobe (ə dō′ bē) is a brick made out of sun-dried earth and straw.

▶ The Ukraine (ū krān′) is a republic of the Soviet Union.

▶ Does this farming village seem prosperous to you? According to the writer, are all villages as prosperous?

Coffee break or exercise break? Which would you choose?

▶ A quota (kwōt′ ə) is a fixed amount of work that a factory unit must produce.

▶ How long a week do most people in the United States work?

▶ Are United States factory workers paid in the same way? Are they paid by the same people as the Soviet workers?

CITIES AND FACTORIES

The Soviet Union, like the United States, has become a nation of large cities. More than two dozen cities have populations of over 500,000 each! And several, such as Moscow, the Soviet capital; Leningrad; and Kiev have over a million residents. Just as in the United States, people have moved to the cities because they prefer life there, and they can find jobs there.

Life is crowded in the city, however. There is a shortage of housing. Many families have to live in small, cramped apartments. Some even have to share their small apartments with other families.

City jobs In the cities are the factories that produce steel, chemicals, and other industrial goods. These factories have made the Soviet Union the second-largest industrial nation in the world. It ranks just behind the United States in terms of manufactured goods produced.

The production of machinery, autos, steel, chemicals, and all other factory goods is planned by the government. Government officials consult with factory managers and other factory officials to decide how much of any good will be produced in a year. Each factory has a quota of so many autos, or so much steel, to fill within a certain time.

Soviet factory workers work a 40-hour week. They are paid by the government according to their ability and the amount of work they produce. There is a major difference between workers in the Soviet Union and the United States, however. Soviet workers all work for the same boss — the government.

Industry is spread throughout the Soviet Union. But all workers have one thing in common—their employer is the Soviet government. The man above is canning caviar. The woman below works in a carpet factory. The factory is named after a worker who became the first woman in space. In what ways are American factories different?

Could this be the palace of a tsar, a museum, or a concert hall? Look carefully at the right side of the picture. What do you see? Do you think a rush hour would be more comfortable here?

Here is how one writer describes the life of a Soviet city dweller who works in a factory:

Try, for a moment, to put yourself in Russian shoes. You work as a mechanic in a tool plant in Moscow. You know that you are better off than you were only ten years ago. Still, there are problems.

You get up in the morning in your apartment, the one you share with two other families. The apartment has three rooms, only one of which is your family's. The sink, the toilet, the bathtub, and the kitchen, however, are shared with the others. It is around six o'clock, and your wife begins to get breakfast. . . .

At seven o'clock, you and your wife leave for

your jobs. Your son goes off to school. You work a five-day week now, so each work day is a little longer than it used to be. You might have to stay at work longer to help meet the production quota. Or you might have to go to a political meeting after work. . . .

You have eaten your lunch at the factory canteen. Now you are ready for home and a nice hot meal. When you arrive home, the kitchen is jammed with people. But you are used to this. You have been sharing this apartment for some time now. The others, too, must make their supper. Long ago you learned to live with the smells of other people's cabbage, tobacco smoke, and newly washed clothes. You dream, though, about the new apartment buildings going up, and hope that you can someday have an apartment for your family alone. . . .

Escape from the cities Like Americans, Soviet city dwellers like to get out of the city on weekends. They like to get away from city crowds to live for a day or two in the open.

Things have changed in the Soviet Union, as everywhere else on earth. But perhaps the changes have been greater there than any place else.

▶ Did Soviet workers always work a five-day week? How do you know?

◗ A canteen is a cafeteria.

Soviet children learn to enjoy sports in their cities' main squares.

1. How has geography—landforms and climate—affected the growth of Soviet agriculture and industry?
2. In 1973, United States housewives protested against the high price of meat and the large profits cattle ranchers were making. Why would Soviet housewives never protest against a rancher's profits?
3. What is the difference between a state farm and a collective farm?
4. Name three large Soviet cities. Are there large cities spread throughout the Soviet Union? Are most of the large cities located in one section of the country?

215

Case Study: Political Tradition

The Soviet Union became a truly modern nation under Communist rule. It built up its industry and developed new farmland. It made great advances in science. For example, it was the first nation to send a satellite and then a manned satellite into orbit around the earth. Under the tsars, most Russian people could not read or write. Under the Communists, most people can. The Russian system of education encourages people to learn and to advance as far as their ability will allow them.

But the Russian people have little political freedom. In elections, they *can* often choose between several candidates. But all candidates belong to the same political party. The people are not free to give their opinions about the government, its officials, or the only political party—the Communist party.

But the government does have an answer for its critics. It says that it is responsible to its people. It gives all its citizens jobs and places to live. Therefore, it says, all Soviet people are free. They all have an *equal* chance to have a job that suits their ability, to earn an equal salary, and to improve their lives.

The Soviet government works according to a written constitution. The constitution spells out how the government will be run. It also grants the people certain rights.

▶ What kind of freedom does the Soviet government say it gives its people? Explain. Is this the same kind of freedom that the United States gives its citizens?

THE COMMUNIST PARTY

The Communist party is the only political party allowed in the Soviet Union. Though it is a Communist nation, not all Soviet citizens are members of the Communist party. Only about 13 million out of the total population of 250 million are members. A person can join the party when he or she becomes 18 years old. But first, a person must pass a long period of study and examination.

Members of the party Schools, factories, farms, and government offices all have Communist party clubs. Members of these clubs elect representatives to larger district organizations. Their members, in turn, elect representatives to regional organizations. The Soviet Union is divided into republics. Each republic has its own Communist party organization, too.

At the top of all is a party Congress made up of 5,000 members elected by lower party organizations. The Congress has a Central Committee of about 350 members. This group conducts party business and decides what issues the Congress will vote on. The committee elects a Politburo which has 11 members. The Politburo makes all important party decisions.

The government itself is headed by a premier, or first minister. There are other ministers who are responsible for different parts of government and Soviet life. The government also has a legislature, or law-making group. It is called the Supreme Soviet of the Union of Soviet Socialist Republics. All members of the government are members of the Communist party.

How the Soviet Union is governed. Look at the chart on page 219. In the United States, the President is the only chief executive. But in the Soviet Union there are three such chiefs: the Secretary of the Communist party, the Chairman of the Supreme Soviet, and the Premier of the Council of Ministers. Under

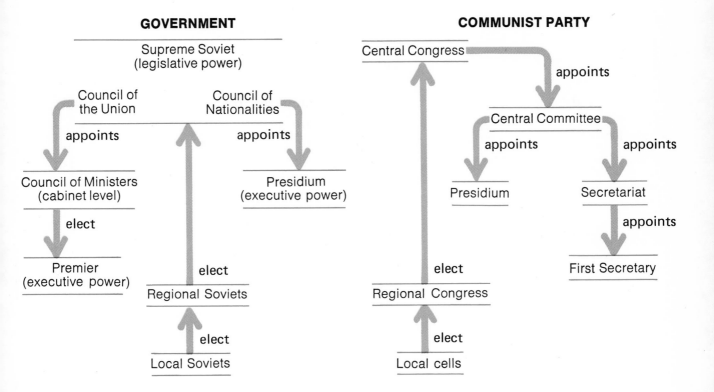

GOVERNMENT

Supreme Soviet
(legislative power)

Council of
the Union

Council of
Nationalities

appoints

appoints

Council of Ministers
(cabinet level)

Presidium
(executive power)

elect

Premier
(executive power)

elect

Regional Soviets

elect

Local Soviets

COMMUNIST PARTY

Central Congress

appoints

Central Committee

appoints

appoints

Presidium

Secretariat

appoints

elect

First Secretary

Regional Congress

elect

Local cells

the United States Constitution, the President and the Congress share power between them. But in the Soviet Union, the power really belongs to the three chief executives and the small group of people closest to each of these leaders. Study the chart on this page again. What are the names of the small groups closest to the three leaders of the Soviet Union?

The Supreme Soviet is supposed to be like the Congress of the United States. But the Supreme Soviet meets only once or twice a year for only a few days. In the Supreme Soviet, there is no debate over the laws passed. Most of the time, the Supreme Soviet just approves the decisions already made by the Presidium or the Council of Ministers.

▶ Do you think 23 is old enough to run for political office? Why or why not?

▶ Do you think the Soviet government cares if people protest? Why or why not?

▶ If there is only one candidate for an office, why do you think candidates campaign? Why do you think the government cares whether or not people vote?

ELECTIONS IN THE SOVIET UNION

The United States Constitution permits almost anyone who is old enough (25 years old for the House of Representatives, 30 for the Senate) to run for Congress. According to the Soviet Constitution, anyone over 23 years old can be nominated by any "popular organization" (such as a labor union or a social club) for election to the Supreme Soviet. But in more than 50 years, no one has run for election except Communist party candidates.

Is there a choice? The instructions on the election ballots in the Soviet Union tell voters to cross off the names of all candidates but the one they choose. But there are never any other candidates on the ballot. Still, in the last election, more than 350,000 people crossed out the name of the Communist party candidate. In effect, these people voted against the Communist party, even though they could not vote for anyone else.

Campaigning for office Elections to the Supreme Soviet are held every four years. There are campaigns. Some of the candidates make speeches promising more to the voters. And signs are put up everywhere telling people to get out and vote for the candidates.

The Soviet government goes to great lengths to make sure everyone votes. It puts ballot boxes in trains, airports, hospitals, and vacation resorts. Once it even sent ballot boxes to a large group of mountain climbers who were halfway up the side of a mountain!

How many candidates? Look at the chart on the next page to see how many people were running for national office.

	UNITED STATES (1972)	SOVIET UNION (1970)
Number of offices up for election	470	1,517
Number of candidates running	1,300	1,517

1. How many national offices come up for election in the United States?
2. Was there more than one candidate per office?
3. Compare the United States statistics with the statistics given for the Soviet Union.
4. What conclusions can you draw from the chart?

Who can vote? In the United States, almost anyone over the age of 18 can register to vote. The same is true in the Soviet Union. But look at the chart below to see how many people vote in elections in both countries.

	UNITED STATES (1972)	SOVIET UNION (1970)
Number of people of voting age	139 million	144.2 million
Number of voters	77.8 million	144 million
Percentage of voters	55.9	99.9

1. How does the percentage of voters in the Soviet Union compare with that of the United States?
2. How can you explain this?

Portraits of Lenin are still displayed in Russia.

Election Day Here is an American newspaper account of one election day in Russia:

▶ A polling place is a place where votes are cast.

Today was Election Day in the Soviet Union. A single list of Communist-approved candidates was placed before the voters. Election Day began at 6 A.M., and it was snowy and overcast in Moscow. The gloom caused by the weather was brightened a little by red flags and banners and by music blasting from loudspeakers. The Premier cast his ballot in midmorning at a polling place a block from the government buildings where he has his office. Other Russian officials were also seen voting here.

Other Moscow voters went to the city's 2,600 polling places singly or in family groups. Before voting, the citizens identified themselves to election workers. They received printed ballots. They dropped the ballots into wooden boxes.

Some voters dropped the ballots in the slot with scarcely a glance at them. Others stopped briefly and looked at them. Still others went with their ballots into curtained booths.

The reason for the booths was explained:

"Voters who know their candidates drop the ballots directly into the boxes. Others use the booths to study the names of the people for whom they are casting votes."

"Some use the booths to vote against a candidate by crossing out a name and writing in another. Others use them to write messages or greetings to the Communist party and the government."

Whatever the reasons, it seemed that the booths were being used by voters without fear.

By 2 P.M., according to election officials, more than 90 percent of Moscow voters had voted.

Each polling place was a little different from the others. Some were quiet places. Others were noisy and crowded.

One polling place was a social club. Voters there cast their ballots in a room that was almost bare, except for a large statue of Lenin.

Both the head and the ballot boxes were guarded by schoolchildren in uniforms.

After the closing of the polls, election officials were to meet to open the ballot boxes and count the votes. . . .

Results of the election were announced two days later. All candidates were elected. Russian citizens must be 18 years old or older to be able to vote. In this election, 99.95 percent of the nearly 140 million Russian citizens who had the right to vote cast their ballots. Only 2 million voters showed their disapproval of candidates by spoiling ballots or in some other way.

1. Ask your parents if they have ever written in the name of a candidate for office. If so, why?
2. Would you vote in an election if there were only one candidate to consider? Why or why not?
3. Do you think more people might vote against the Communist party candidates if they had another choice?

INVESTIGATING THE UNIT

Doing Research

Using encyclopedias and old newspapers and magazines, gather information for a political study of recent Soviet leaders. First, find out the difference between the Premier of the Soviet Union and the Chairman of the Communist party. Now make a list of the top Soviet leaders since the death of Stalin. Have any of these leaders been both Premier and Chairman? Find out how long each leader remained in power. How did each lose power? Have any Soviet leaders visited the United States while they were in power? If so, try to find newspaper accounts of their visits.

Looking at the Evidence

Imagine you are an American reporter in Russia in 1916. You are spending a vacation with some wealthy Russian friends at the Black Sea resort pictured on page 195. Two weeks before, you had been staying with a villager who agreed with the writings of Marx and Lenin. Explain to your friends the villager's feelings about the way the poor of Russia live. Describe what his village is like. Tell about his hopes for the overthrow of capitalism and the future of Russia. Now have one of your classmates take the position of a rich Russian and give his feelings about the villager's ideas.

Using Maps

Look again at the map on page 179. Find Poland, Hungary, Rumania, Bulgaria, Czechoslovakia, and East Germany. These Eastern European nations are sometimes called "satellites" of the Soviet Union. The word *satellite* may be defined as a body that orbits around a large body. Can you guess why these nations are called satellite nations?

Comparing and Contrasting

To understand one of the differences between communism and capitalism, try this experiment. Study the rules of the game of Monopoly. Is the game a model of communism or capitalism? Do you think the Communists wanted to eliminate the owning of private property from the Communist way of life? Do you agree with what they did? Give reasons for your answers.

Reading on Your Own

If you like adventure stories, read *With Dersu the Hunter: Adventures in the Taiga,* by Vladimir Arsenyev (New York, Braziller). For some interesting pictures, see *Let's Travel in the Soviet Union,* by Darlene Geis (Chicago, Children's Press).

SOUTH ASIA: INDIA

Electricity! Imagine a village that has never had electricity! What a revolution. It hums along the wires, shines in the little bulb that keeps the night away, and brings water to the earth's surface as if by magic!

TAYA ZINKIN

Yesterday and Today

Once there were four blind men. They had never seen an elephant. The first time one came near, the men were puzzled.

As the elephant passed, the blind men put out their hands. The first man felt the trunk and cried, "The elephant is like a huge snake."

The second man felt the leg and cried, "No! The elephant is like a huge tree."

The third man felt the elephant's body and cried, "No, no! The elephant is like a huge granary."

The fourth man grabbed the tail and cried, "No, no, no! You are all wrong! The elephant is like a whip."

But a wise observer remarked, "That is how it is with men who see only part of the truth."

▶ A granary is a storehouse for grain.

UNDERSTANDING INDIA

India is one of the world's oldest and largest nations. It is also one of the most diverse. Understanding India is a problem like that of the blind men—a person must look carefully at all the parts to get a clear picture.

▶ Diverse (də vėrs′) means having great variety.

A look at the parts History and tradition are important to Indians. Many ancient Indian customs are as important today as they were nearly 2,000 years ago. We can learn something about a people by studying their customs.

Geography also gives clues about India. The coming of monsoons or the changing of a river's course affects people's lives.

Other things also help tell a country's story —its people, its religions, and its literature. Even photographs can sometimes help us understand a faraway place.

But none of these things can be studied alone. We need to see all the parts to understand the whole picture. Think about the blind

▶ Tradition is the history, beliefs, and ways of doing things which a group passes on to its children.

▶ Monsoons (mon sunz′) are the winds which come at a certain time of the year and bring the rainy season.

▶ How would these things affect people's lives? How would a flood affect your life?

227

men again. Their picture of an elephant would have been clearer if they had combined their information. And so it is with India. We must combine the clues.

ANCIENT INDIA

Buried cities About 50 years ago, a team of **archaeologists** found traces of two ancient cities in the Indus Valley. No one knows what these cities were originally called. We call them Harappa and Mohenjo-Daro. Evidence shows that they were the centers of early India's culture. They existed about 2500 B.C.

The archaeologists who found the evidence of the Indus Valley civilization were excited. By digging into mounds, they had found buried cities they had not known existed! These scientists learned about the Indus culture by examining the ancient **artifacts** they found.

Looking at the evidence According to the evidence, the Indus civilization was very large. Besides the two cities, archaeologists found evidence of seaports, farms, and trading villages. They even found remains of buildings, streets, and roads. The streets of the buried towns had been laid out in a rectangle.

Archaeologists believe that the city of Mohenjo-Daro was part of a highly developed civilization. Its people were traders, farmers, and craftsmen. The craftsmen made cooking pots from silver, copper, and bronze. They decorated furniture with carved pieces of bone or ivory. They shaped figures of people and animals from clay. The people also developed an advanced technology which helped them build a complicated sewerage system.

◗ Archaeologists (är′ kē ol′ ə-jists) are scientists who study ancient cultures by examining such things as clothes, tools, housing, and art.

◗ hə rap′ ə

◗ mō hen′ jo dür′ ō

◗ B.C. means before Christ was born. A.D. means *anno Domini.* These are Latin words for the time after Christ was born. We use the B.C. and A.D. to talk about dates in history.

◗ Artifacts (ärt′ ə fakts) are objects that were made by humans.

◗ Technology (tek nol′ ə jē) is all the skills and ways of doing things that a people develop. Tools + the knowledge of how to use them = technology.

◗ Sewerage (sü′ ər ij) is a method of getting rid of waste matter.

228

The seals above come from the ancient Indian city of Mohenjo-Daro. They were used to identify the sender of a letter or document, much as signatures are used today. Hot wax or metal was poured onto the letter or document. When the seal was pressed into the hot liquid, it made a copy of its design on the paper. The seals found at Mohenjo-Daro have many different designs on them. Some show scenes of daily life in the city. Others have writing on them that scholars are still trying to understand. Both the seals and art like this statue tell us about the Indus Valley civilization.

▶ Why would the cities have been more crowded after the floods?

▶ Nomads (nō′ madz) are people who wander from place to place to find food or grazing land.

▶ ar′ē ənz

An ancient mystery The Indus Valley civilization vanished. No one really knows why. The archaeologists found evidence that the Indus River changed its course. This meant that there were many floods. Perhaps the people tried to rebuild some of their cities. But these rebuilt cities would have been very crowded. Or perhaps the people moved to another area after the repeated floods. Perhaps the people were killed by invaders.

A new people settle The Indus Valley civilization lasted a thousand years. Then fierce nomads migrated to India from the north. These nomads were warlike people who gradually took over much of India. They may have been the invaders who destroyed the Indus Valley civilization.

These nomads were called Aryans. They did not look like the dark-skinned people who already lived in India. The Aryans had blue eyes and fair skin.

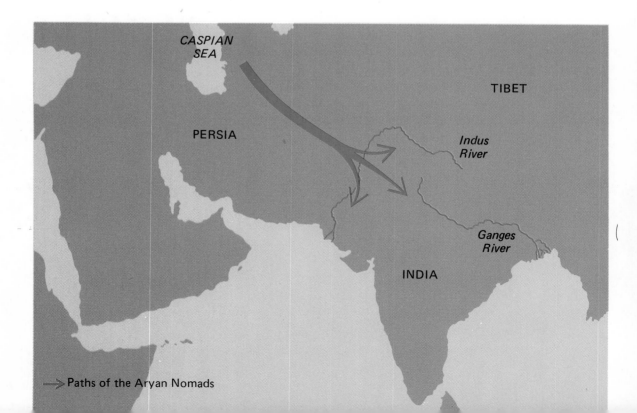

⟶ Paths of the Aryan Nomads

Aryan culture Most of our knowledge of the Aryans comes from their literature. Although little of this literature has survived, there is enough to show that the Aryans were mainly farmers and herders. They measured wealth in terms of cattle. The more cattle a person owned, the richer he was.

The Aryans had learned to tame cows, horses, and sheep. They were the first people to bring horses and chariots to India. We also know that the Aryans used tools of iron, bronze, and copper. And they enjoyed music, dancing, and dice games. What else, besides written evidence, might tell us these facts about Aryan life?

The word *Aryan* can be translated to mean nobleman. The Aryans thought that they were superior people. They treated the darker-skinned Indians like servants. They even set up social classes to keep themselves separate. Many historians believe that the caste system developed from the Aryan system of classes.

◗ Superior means better than someone or something else.

THE CASTE SYSTEM

The caste system forces people into separate social classes. Each person's class, or caste, is hereditary. Each caste has rights and duties.

Originally, there were four major caste groups. From highest to lowest, they were as follows:

Brahman—priests and teachers
Kshatriya—princes and warriors
Vaisya—merchants and farmers
Sudra—laborers, craftsmen, and servants
Later, these major groups were divided into hundreds of subdivisions.

◗ kast

◗ Hereditary (hə red′ə ter′ē) means passed by birth from parent to child.

◗ bräm′ən
◗ kə sha′ tri ya
◗ vīsh′ yə
◗ shü′drə

VEDIC LITERATURE

Early Aryan literature is called Vedic (vād′ ik) literature. It is made up of prayers and myths called Vedas. At first, the Vedas were simply told by one generation to another. Many years later, they were written down. No one knows who first put them in writing. What is the advantage of having these myths written down?

Vedic literature gives clues about early life in India. One of the earliest Vedas is a collection of thousands of prayers. It was composed between 1500 and 1000 B.C.

The lines below are from this Veda. The prayer was to the god who controlled sunshine, rainfall, and the movement of the earth.

Ceaseless are the waters, ceaselessly flowing,
   ceaselessly cleaning, never sleeping.

Ceaselessly flowing in channels. . . .
Rising from the middle of the flood and flowing
   to . . . the sea.
   O god of the great waters,
   protect me.

What were the people praying for? Why?

These ancient people were mainly farmers. Do you think it made sense for them to pray to this particular god? Why?

Sanskrit

Vedic literature is written in Sanskrit (san' skrit), a language that is used only by holy men. Sanskrit forms the basis of many Indian and European languages spoken today. In fact, you frequently use some words that have Sanskrit roots.

English	Latin	Sanskrit
mother	mater	mata
father	pater	pita

Why would language specialists be interested in studying Sanskrit? What could Sanskrit teach them about other languages?

Many familiar western stories, such as "Jack and the Beanstalk," have been traced to Indian sources. How do you think such stories might have traveled from India to the Western world?

The Fire Sacrifice

Sanskrit was used in the mysterious religious services of the ancient Indians. Certain priests would recite the Vedas from memory in front of groups of other priests. While offerings were laid on a fire, the priest reciting the Vedas was supposed to communicate with the gods.

Do you think that the priests would work hard to memorize the Vedas perfectly? Do you think they might have received greater honor for this? Why or why not?

Poetry as Medicine

Besides their use in ancient Indian religious services, the Vedas were also used by priests to cure the sick. Chanting the Vedas to sick people was supposed to relieve pain and make magic spells and drugs work better.

Sometimes the chanting of the Vedas did work to cure sick people. Can you think of any reasons why?

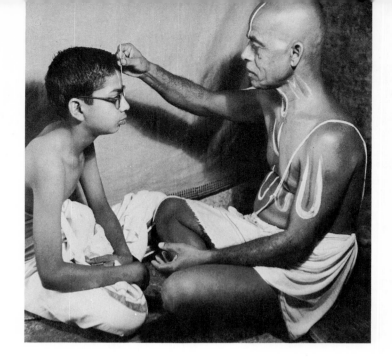

Hindus paint marks on their bodies to show which caste they belong to. Here, a teacher paints a caste mark on the forehead of one of his students.

▶ Inferior means not as good as someone or something else.

▶ Did caste rules make it difficult for people to travel from village to village? Why?

▶ Many Brahman families hired servants. Whom could the family hire as a cook, if it could not eat food prepared by lower caste members?

▶ Does the caste system encourage people to think of new ways of doing things? Why or why not?

Untouchables People outside the four groups were called outcastes. They were considered inferior to everyone else and were called *untouchables*. The untouchables always had the worst jobs in India. They removed dead animals from the streets. They did any job that the other castes would not do. What does the name *untouchables* tell you about them?

Everyday rules Caste determined other things in addition to a person's work. It affected every part of a person's life. Each caste member learned how to do his special work and what foods his caste could eat. No one was allowed to eat food touched by someone of a lower caste. Each caste member learned how to respect older people, higher castes, and others in his family. Each person also learned how to worship the special gods of his caste and his area. All people were forbidden to marry outside their caste.

The caste system was well established by 500 B.C. In Indian civilization, caste became the most lasting reminder of the Aryans.

The high caste of this woman made it easier for her to be accepted as a lawyer. But the caste system also means that the men below must hunt for food among the dogs.

HINDUISM

Hindu gods Hinduism became the major religion of India about the same time that caste started. Hindus believed that there were three major gods—the creator god, the destroyer god, and the preserver god. All Hindus share some of the same beliefs. But people have always been free to practice Hinduism in different ways. Families may feel closer to one god than to another.

Reincarnation Hinduism teaches respect for every living thing. It teaches that the most important part of every living thing is its soul. Hindus believe that this soul, or spirit, never dies. After the body dies, the soul is reborn into some other thing living on earth. This rebirth, called reincarnation, may be in a new

◆ Preserve (pri zėrv′) means to keep or to protect.

◆ Reincarnation (rē′ in kär nā′-shən) means the rebirth of a soul into a new form.

Hindus believe that the Ganges River is holy. They believe that the river washes away their sins. Every Hindu hopes to die along the banks of the Ganges so that he will be made holy before entering his next life.

236

form. So a priest could be reborn a farmer, a cow, or even an ant.

Hinduism teaches that the form of reincarnation depends on how the person has acted in his previous life. Caste existed before Hinduism. But it soon became an important part of the Hindu religion.

Hindus believe that a person who breaks caste rules will be punished by being reborn into a lower caste. But a person who acts as he should will be rewarded with a higher caste in his next life.

If a person is poor or of low caste, Hindus believe he has disobeyed his caste rules in a previous life. A Brahman, they believe, must have obeyed his caste rules to have reached his good life. But a Brahman can always be lowered to another caste in his next life if he disobeys Brahman rules.

▶ According to Hindus, what does it mean "to act as you should"?

▶ A person's actions during his lifetime affect how he will be reborn. Do you think that makes people obey or disobey caste rules? Why or why not?

BUDDHISM

▶ bud′ iz əm

Search by a prince   People became bitter about the unfairness of the caste system. About 500 B.C., a young Hindu prince decided to help. His name was Siddhartha Gautama. Siddhartha saw that the Indian people could not move forward while they were bitter and unhappy. Siddhartha gave up his wealth and high caste. He went to search for the cause of life's unhappiness.

▶ si′där tə gut′ ə mə

After much thought, Siddhartha found an answer. He believed that unhappiness was caused by wanting too many things. If a person could be happy with what he had, he could end his unhappiness. He could do this by following certain rules for living. These rules included self-denial and love for others.

▶ Could denying yourself something make you want it any less?

YOGA

Have you ever tried to hold your breath for a long time and then let it out slowly? This is one of the techniques of an ancient Indian discipline known as Yoga. For thousands of years, people have used Yoga to help search for happiness and contentment.

Students of Yoga often study for as long as 20 years before becoming masters, or Yogi. They learn many different physical exercises. These exercises are designed to put the students in good physical condition. Then they can concentrate on deep religious thoughts without worrying about physical discomforts.

Many Yoga exercises involve putting the body into difficult positions. Some of them are very hard to learn. Have you ever tried to fold your legs over one another? This is one of the basic Yoga positions. It is called the lotus position. Most people find it difficult to stay in that position for even a few minutes. But Yogis train themselves to remain in the lotus position for hours or even days. They are taught to overcome the physical discomfort of holding these positions. Other

exercises and rules teach concentration. Yogis feel this is the key to finding inner peace. This kind of concentration is called meditation.

Yogis and many other people practice meditation. They claim that it makes them feel relaxed and peaceful. Some people say that it makes them feel better—just as good exercise does. But other people claim that it is a way of achieving a strong religious feeling. These people say that meditation helps them feel much closer to God.

The word *Yoga* itself comes from an ancient Sanskrit word meaning "union." What kind of union do you think the word refers to? Why would people want to have this kind of experience?

Many people in the Western world are suspicious of the claims made about the benefits of Yoga. But recently, scientists have proved that Yogis can control their bodies in extraordinary ways. Some Yogis can even control their heartbeats! What do you think Yoga could do for you? Why?

bŭd′ə

▶ To be enlightened is to see the truth.

▶ To which Indians do you think Buddhism was most appealing? Why do you think so?

A new religion Many Hindus were ready to accept new ideas. They listened to the prince. Siddhartha's followers felt that he had found an important truth. They renamed him Buddha, which means "enlightened one." Buddha's followers started a new religion, called Buddhism.

For a time, Buddhism was the main religion in India. It differed from Hinduism mainly over caste. Buddhist missionaries carried the Buddhist religion to other parts of the world. Later, Hinduism became less strict about caste and took over some of the ideas of Buddhism. Today Buddhism is a main religion in Japan, Southeast Asia, and China. But it is seldom found in its own home—India.

TIME LINE

3000 B.C.

      Indus Valley cultures (c. 2500 B.C.)

2000 B.C.

      Aryan invasion (c. 1500 B.C.)

      Vedic literature

1000 B.C.

      Hinduism

      Caste system

      Siddhartha and Buddhism

        (c. 563 B.C.–483 B.C.)

      Alexander the Great invades India

        (326 B.C.)

      Asoka builds pillars (269 B.C.–232 B.C.)

0

      Period of shifting empires

      Golden age of art, literature, science

      Period of invasions

      Islam begins (c. 750)

1000 A.D.

      Arrival of Europeans (c. 1500)

      Great Moslem empire (1526–1707)

      British East India Company

       (c. 1700–1858)

1900 A.D.

      Gandhi (1869–1948)

      Independence (1947)

CENTURIES OF CHANGE

Much of India's early history is guesswork. Written records did not begin until about 600 B.C. We know that India had great empires, but the reasons why they rose and fell are often unclear. Some ages were times of confusion —invaders would arrive, and new groups and classes would arise. But there were golden ages, too, when art, literature, science, and trade were at their peaks.

▶ Do you think there is a connection between the beginning of two great religions and the beginning of recorded history? Who do you think the first writers of history might have been? Why would they have done the writing?

241

The painting below is from a museum in Bombay. It shows an Indian woman fainting. Can you guess from the picture whether the woman is from a high or a low caste? Explain. Indian paintings often show life among the ruling classes. The huge elephant on the right is an example of Indian sculpture.

A search for clues Where have historians found their information? What kind of evidence have they used? Historians have studied the writing on stone pillars built by an early ruler. They have found old coins with dates and inscriptions. And they have studied the writings of observers, such as Buddhist monks who came to India from China.

But India's periods of confusion puzzle historians. Invaders would often destroy architecture when they attacked. Other information sources were also lost in times of unrest. Sometimes more folklore than fact has survived. As a result, historians can only guess about some centuries in ancient India. But these centuries were followed by the rise of a new religion and by the arrival of the Europeans in India. And about these times, historians have a great deal of information.

◗ A pillar is a strong column, often used to support a building.

◗ An inscription (in skrip′shən) is something written or marked on a surface.

◗ Folklore is the traditions and stories passed down through the ages by word of mouth.

◗ Why might folklore be less reliable than fact for some kinds of historical information?

ISLAM

Amid the confusion of the seventh and eighth centuries A.D., a new religion developed. This religion was Islam.

Mohammed Islam's founder was Mohammed, an Arabian camel dealer born in Mecca. Mohammed was troubled about the unfairness of life. One day he had a dream. In the dream, he was a prophet whose duty was to lead his people to Allah, the one true God. Mohammed took the dream as a sign of truth.

Mohammed's message was brotherhood. He preached that all people were equals before Allah. The followers of Islam are called Moslems or Muslims. The word Moslem

Note the contrast between the mosques and the market.

ASOKA'S PILLARS

If you traveled through India today, you could see some of the same evidence that historians have studied. This evidence is a series of stone monuments built over 2,200 years ago by Asoka (ə sō′ kə), an Indian ruler. The monuments are called Asoka's pillars.

Asoka won many wars and ruled a great empire. But then he became a Buddhist. He changed his ways and tried to live a good life. He tried to improve the lives of his people, too.

Asoka wanted the people to know about his change. He ordered pillars, some over 40 feet high, to be built throughout his empire. Each pillar was inscribed with Buddhist teachings and descriptions of Asoka's changes.

Many of these pillars are still standing. The following lines are from some of the pillars.

> Thus speaks Asoka:
> After the battle I regretted the pain I had caused. . . . So I began to follow the message of Buddha and spread his teachings. . . . I have had this inscription engraved so that all my sons . . . will not seek new victories. . . .
>
> I am not satisfied simply with hard work or carrying out the business of the empire, for I consider my work to be the betterment of the whole world. . . .

Why were stone pillars a good way of informing the people of Asoka's time? What ways would a leader choose today?

Asoka's pillars have been found in northern and central India. None have been found in southern India. What clues does this give you about the borders of Asoka's empire?

means "one who submits" (to the will of Allah).

Islamic teachings   Many of Mohammed's teachings were written down and kept. These records later became part of the holy book of the Moslems. This book, which is somewhat like the Bible, is called the Koran.

◗ kô rän'

The Moslems had many enemies, but their religion spread rapidly throughout Asia and Africa. They spread it by conquering nations and forcing their people to convert to Islam. Soon, a great Moslem empire arose.

The Moslems ruled India through most of the sixteenth and seventeenth centuries. But these Moslem invaders were not easily accepted by the Indians. Hinduism and Islam are very different religions. Unlike the Hindus, the Moslems were a united people. Moslems preach the equality of all people; Hindus respect caste divisions. Moslems believe there is only one God; Hindus believe there

The veiled women are a distinct part of Moslem culture.

are many. Islam forbids idol worship; but Hinduism permits images of its gods.

The Moslems' treatment of the Hindus changed from one Moslem ruler to the next. Sometimes Hindus were given important jobs. Other times they were taxed heavily, their temples were destroyed, and they were forbidden to practice their religion. Tension between the Moslems and the Hindus was never eased. It continues to divide the Indian people in the twentieth century.

How do you think the religious differences caused tension between Moslems and Hindus?

The Moslems believed in equality. How do you think they justified this belief with their mistreatment of the Hindus?

ARRIVAL OF THE EUROPEANS

A search for colonies While India struggled against invaders and religious wars within its borders, strong European nations were seeking colonies. Colonies could supply European nations with workers, new markets, new crops, spices, and minerals.

▶ A colony is a territory ruled by another country. The ruling country is often far away from its colony.

Each European king wanted his nation to be the wealthiest and most powerful. One way to do this was to control other nations through colonies. Such a policy is called **imperialism,** or empire building.

▶ im pir′ē əl iz′əm

Trade routes Europeans were also anxious to control trade routes to Asia. They wanted spices, jewels, silks, and tea from Asia and the Middle East. Portuguese, Dutch, English, and French traders fought each other for control of the Asian trade. The British took the lead in India.

▶ Why would the European nations not share these trade routes?

SPICES

Why would Europeans risk their lives searching for spice routes? Why were spices once as valuable as gold?

Spices come from the roots, bark, and seeds of various plants. The climates of the East Indies and the Spice Islands are mild and are therefore ideal for the growth of these plants. Find the places listed here on your classroom globe. Can you see why their climates would be warm?

Some common spices are cinnamon, cloves, pepper, nutmeg, and paprika.

But the Europeans needed spices for an important reason. Spices were used to help preserve food. At that time, there were no refrigerators. People had only crude ways of preserving meat. They could smoke meat in chimneys, soak it in salt, or cover it with pepper and other spices.

Spices were used as seasonings, too. They helped to hide the taste of meat that was not fresh.

Have you ever heard anyone say that something is "the spice of life"? What do you think that means?

▶ A charter is a written grant of permission from the leader of a country to a company or to citizens.

▶ Why would it be easier to gain power in a conflict-torn country than in one with an orderly government?

The British East India Company In 1600, Queen Elizabeth I granted a charter to the East India Company of England. This made it the only British trading company allowed to trade in India. The company set up trading posts along the coast of India.

The British traders sailed to a war-torn India. The Moslem princes were battling each other for control. But these conflicts helped the British. The East India Company took advantage of the situation and became wealthy and very powerful.

How did the British company become powerful? Had it planned to take over India, or did this happen purely by chance?

A new kind of ruler As the Moslem Empire became weaker, the British East India Company feared it would lose its valuable trading posts. The company had to deal with the warring princes. The British offered to help keep peace. In return, the company was given land.

Soon, the British East India Company ruled most of the people of India. The company had to rule and defend its new territory. The British traders became the tax collectors and the "police" in some areas. Sometimes the British fought to increase their power. When angry Indians rebelled against the British, they were beaten back by force.

British rule In 1858, the British government took away control from the East India Company and decided to rule India by itself. Great Britain, a country much smaller than India and located thousands of miles away, claimed India as its colony.

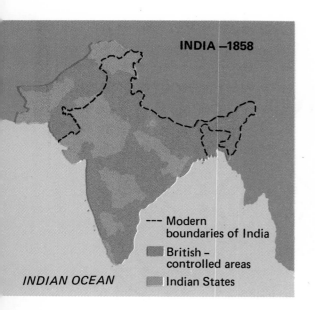

INDIA —1858

--- Modern boundaries of India

British - controlled areas

Indian States

INDIAN OCEAN

There were some parts of India not directly ruled by Britain. These parts were controlled by Indian princes and were called Indian States. Look at the map on page 248. Still, the British ruled a larger area of India than had any rulers of the past.

Under British rule, the Indian princes lost their power. The Indian people feared that the British would not respect India's religions and traditions. They knew that the British were very different in religion, language, and customs. They knew that the British considered the Indians strange. Do you think the Indians were right in fearing the British?

A new way of life The British introduced a system of law and order to India. The British queen appointed a viceroy to rule India and to enforce the law. The viceroy and other British officials replaced the many local rulers. There were no longer costly wars for power when a prince died. When one viceroy ended his term of office, another one was appointed by the British ruler.

▶ What can happen when one country does not respect the religion and traditions of another?

▶ A viceroy (vīs′roi) is an official appointed by a ruler to govern an area.

▶ Do you think it would have been better to have both Indian and British officials?

This picture shows a British officer announcing that Queen Victoria had made herself Empress of India. What traces of British culture can you see in the picture?

▶ Would all Indians have welcomed this change in their tradition? Explain.

▶ Famine (fam'ən) is widespread lack of food and the hunger that results.

▶ Think about the introduction of new machines and inventions to a country like India. Do you think this might cause disadvantages as well as advantages? Explain.

This is a picture of a commuter train in India today. What seems to be the problem with trains in India?

A new court system gave equal treatment to all castes. Under Indian rule, lower castes had received harsher punishments than higher castes.

The British took control of money and business in India. They began to build railroads and put up telegraph lines. They tried to wipe out famine and improve public health. They also encouraged the growth of industries.

Railroads The British completed thousands of miles of railroad in India. For the first time, travel within India was easy. It became possible to move grain quickly into areas with a food shortage. The railroads were able to help relieve famine.

Industry The railroads made it easier to transport goods into India. Machines were brought in to modernize the Indian economy. But many ancient Indian crafts were forgotten as the new ways came to India. And as industry grew, so did Indian cities. The cities quickly developed crowded slum sections where many of the Indian workers lived.

Health The British set up public health programs to attack disease. This helped to lower the death rate among Indians. But even after 70 years of British rule, the average number of years an Indian could expect to live was just over 26.

As health programs brought improvements, the population grew. In the first 300 years after the British arrived, the Indian population almost tripled.

Problems of imperialism A foreign ruler finds it difficult to introduce new ways to an old country — even when the ruler is trying to help. What complaints might the Indian people have had about the British reforms? Do you think colonizing a foreign country is a good idea for a powerful nation? What happened to the British in India?

The British did bring order to the Indian government. With a stronger government, India was able to change and develop. But some historians criticize the British. They say that life improved very little for the Indian people. Some people believe that the British encouraged disagreement between Hindus and Moslems. How would this have helped the British?

Though the government was united under the British, the Indian people had no voice in it. They were not allowed to vote and were not given any important government jobs. But the Indian people did have to pay taxes. These taxes paid for many of the changes which the British made. Indian money was also used to keep up the country's army — the same army that kept angry Indians from rebelling against the British.

▶ Do you think the good points of lengthening people's lives and lowering the death rate were outweighed by the later problems of too many people and too little food? Give arguments for both sides of the question.

▶ Do you think it was fair for the Indians to pay taxes, but not be allowed to vote? Why? Can you think of an example from American history of how another group of people reacted to this?

STEPS TOWARD INDEPENDENCE

Many Indians were dissatisfied with British rule. A few Indians, who had taught themselves English, read about democracy and freedom in books supplied by the British. Indians were beginning to develop a feeling of **nationalism** and a respect for independence. They were ready to unite and demand their rights.

◗ Nationalism is a strong feeling of pride in one's country.

Indian National Congress   In 1885, the Indians began their struggle. A few Indian leaders formed the Indian National Congress. Now Indians could meet and work together on their problems. Delegates from all parts of India — from different castes and different regions — met together for the first time. Delegates had many ideas on what to ask for and how to get it. But all delegates agreed on some basic things — they wanted more jobs, better education, and more self-government. They were not yet asking for the end of British rule, only for reforms in it.

The British responded slowly. They continued to control the money and the key areas of government — taxation, police, foreign trade, and foreign policy. In 1919, the British finally gave the Indians control of education, agriculture, and public health.

◗ What is the difference between these departments and the ones the British controlled? Does this explain the Indians' dissatisfaction?

The Indians were not satisfied. They would no longer ask for reform. They would now demand independence.

A spokesman   Every successful independence movement needs a spokesman — someone to speak for the people and lead them toward their goals. The spokesman for the Indian movement was Mohandas Gandhi.

◗ mō hän′dəs gän′dē

252

GANDHI

Gandhi belonged to a caste of grocers and moneylenders. His family were strict Hindus.

As a young man, Gandhi studied law in London. The Hindu religious leaders had disapproved of his going to London. They had threatened to outcaste him. But Gandhi ignored their threats and went anyhow. Why do you think the Hindu leaders opposed Gandhi's trip?

Gandhi believed in fighting without weapons or force. He called his method nonviolence. He would simply disobey any unfair law or policy. He was willing to be punished for his actions. Gandhi thought that the law would have to be changed if enough people protested in this way. It would show how strongly the people felt about their beliefs.

Gandhi described some of the rules of nonviolence in his autobiography:

A protestor will never try to harm his opponent in thought, word, or deed.

A protestor is never angry. He will put up with the anger of his opponent.

A protestor will never strike back. He will not fear any kind of punishment.

A protestor will let himself be arrested.

If anyone insults an official during a demonstration, the protestor will protect the official even if he must risk his own life.

If a protestor is a prisoner, he will behave courteously and follow prison rules.

To be successful a protestor must carefully follow the rules of nonviolence.

▶ Why didn't Gandhi speak to the people about democracy if that was what he wanted for his people?

▶ Why is nonviolence a good technique for people who follow Hinduism?

▶ Why did the British tax salt? Why didn't they choose another product?

▶ How do you think the British in India reacted to the world news coverage of the march?

Gandhi wanted all Indians to understand the independence movement. He walked barefoot through the villages, speaking to all people — both Brahmans and untouchables. Gandhi explained independence and nonviolence to the people. He did not talk about complicated ideas like democracy. Instead, he quietly explained how Indians could feel free inside for the first time. Many Indians understood Gandhi. His movement grew.

The march to the sea Gandhi urged Indians to protest. He told them not to pay taxes and not to send their children to British schools. But his most famous nonviolent action was his "march to the sea."

The British placed a tax on salt. It became a crime to have salt not bought from the government. Since all Indians needed salt, there was little they could do but obey the law. But Gandhi had a plan. He led thousands of people to the seashore. There he showed them how to boil sea water to remove the salt. If the people could make salt, they could avoid the tax.

The government was furious. The government said it was illegal for people to make their own salt. The British arrested Gandhi and thousands of his followers. Newspapers around the world reported the protest and arrests.

INDEPENDENCE AND PARTITION

After World War II, the British realized they could no longer keep India as a colony. The Indians had shown their determination by their protests. The British flag came down in 1947. But the Indian victory was spoiled by two events: a Hindu-Moslem war and the assassination of Gandhi.

The Indian people honored Gandhi with the title Mahatma, *which means "Great Soul." Gandhi was an unusual kind of leader. He vowed never to make money for himself. He always wore simple clothes and sandals. At his death, he owned little more than a few clothes, his eyeglasses, a book, and his rice bowl.*

Hindus and Moslems Ill feeling between Hindus and Moslems was not new in India. Tensions caused by religious, cultural, and political differences had existed for hundreds of years. Moslems invaded around 1600. During harsh Moslem control of India, Hindus had often been denied their rights.

The Indian National Congress tried to unite the two groups, but failed. The Moslems wanted a separate Moslem state. They made up only 10 percent of the Indian population and feared being a minority among the Hindus.

Partition Under the British plan for independence, India was divided into a Moslem state and a Hindu state. The new Moslem state was called Pakistan. The Hindu state kept the name of India.

Partition was made according to religion. Where there was a majority of Hindus, the area

▶ Why would the Moslems have feared a minority role? How might the past have added to their fears? Do you think the Hindu-Moslem split hurt the Indian independence movement? Why or why not?

▶ Partition (pär tish′ ən) means division.

▶ How do you think the people felt about leaving their homes and moving? Do you think they felt their real "home" was with their own people?

◆ Tolerance (tol'ər əns) means patience toward different ideas and opinions.

▶ Do you think different languages divide people? If so, in what way?

◆ bäng' la desh

was usually made India. Where there was a majority of Moslems, the land was usually made Pakistan. How do you think Moslems living in Hindu areas felt? Hindus in Moslem areas?

Over 11 million people fled across the new borders after independence. Both Moslems and Hindus wanted to be with their own people. It was a sad time. Thousands of people died as they fled—some from disease, famine, and floods. But many were also killed—by their neighbors of a different religion.

Assassination Gandhi and the National Congress had opposed partition. They had sought peace between the Hindus and Moslems. But many people could not understand Gandhi's tolerance. One of these people shot and killed Gandhi in 1948.

TROUBLE IN PAKISTAN

East and West Pakistan Partition did not solve all problems for the Moslems. Pakistan was split into two parts. Industry and political power were centered in West Pakistan. East Pakistan was settled mostly by poor farmers. People in West Pakistan looked down on people from East Pakistan. The people of each area spoke different languages.

Bangladesh In 1971, East Pakistan made a desperate move. With the help of the Indian army, it fought a bitter war. Finally, East Pakistan declared itself the independent nation of Bangladesh.

Study the chart and record of events. Can you see reasons for the breakup of Pakistan?

	WEST PAKISTAN	EAST PAKISTAN
Area (square miles)	310,403	55,126
Population	55,000,000	75,000,000
GNP	$12,000,000,000	$6,000,000,000
Per capita yearly income	$130	$77
Moslems	99%	89%
Government jobs	80%	20%
Foreign trade	35%	65%
Government aid	70%	30%

◗ GNP (Gross National Product) is the total amount of goods and services bought and sold in a country. GNP measures a country's wealth and growth.

◗ Per capita means for each person.

Record of Events

NOVEMBER, 1970
A cyclone strikes East Pakistan. Damage is enormous, but the West Pakistani government sends little aid.

DECEMBER, 1970
National elections are held. The East Pakistani party wins a majority and asks for greater self-rule.

MARCH, 1971
The West Pakistani government delays the opening of Parliament and jails the East Pakistanis' leader. Troops from West Pakistan invade East Pakistan. Ten million easterners flee to India.

DECEMBER, 1971
The Indian army and East Pakistanis defeat West Pakistan's troops.

JANUARY, 1972
Bangladesh becomes an independent nation.

1. Which section of Pakistan had more people?
2. Which section had greater foreign trade income?
3. Which section received more government aid?
4. Why do you think India helped East Pakistan?

AFTER THE WAR

A shattered land When the fighting stopped, millions of people who had fled Bangladesh came back. They returned to a land that was shattered. Even before the war, Bangladesh had been one of the poorest areas on earth. It had one of the highest population densities of any country—1,200 people per square mile. And it had all of the other problems of a developing nation—few resources, little industry, and a shortage of food.

The people of Bangladesh also must live with the problems created by the war. Millions of people lost their homes and everything they owned. Many now live in filthy, overcrowded tent camps. They live without food or hope.

The people who still have homes and businesses suffer, too. No one has any money. Businesses can hardly survive. Many of the dikes that held back the rivers and the sea were destroyed by the war. So floods threaten farmers.

Foreign aid Some countries have been sending small amounts of aid to Bangladesh. Most observers agree that this aid must continue for many years if the country is to survive.

▶ Why would businesses suffer when no one has money?

▶ Dikes are banks of earth used to hold back water.

1. Name some artifacts that were found in the Indus Valley. What can artifacts tell us about the daily life of a people?
2. What does the word *Aryan* mean? Explain how the Aryans began the caste system in India.
3. Look at the list of jobs which the different Aryan castes were allowed to have. What does the order of the list tell us about the values of Aryan culture?
4. Name three religions once practiced in India.

The Land and the People

"Educated boys—well, they are of no use to me in the field," says an Indian father, referring to his own sons. "But when I go into a government office no one will even look at me or pay any attention to what I have to say. If I take my sons with me, however, the work gets done in time. They are useful there."

Ten boys from this village are studying "Englis," as they put it. Not one of them has gone back to work on the land.

THE GEOGRAPHY OF THE NATION

As much as any country in the world, India is influenced by its land. The lives of its people are tied to the soil, to the rains, and to the weather. Yet India is an old land. In many places, the soil is worn. There are too many people for the land. The rain itself brings life and death. How? What kind of land is India?

Look at the landform map on page 262. The land itself is like a funny-shaped triangle that juts out into the ocean. In the north, the Himalayan Mountains separate India from China. To the west and the east, mountains called the Ghats separate the mainland from the sea.

The Indo-Ganges Plain South of the Himalayan Mountains, there are fertile plains. Three rivers provide these lands with water. Find the three rivers on the map and name them.

The Deccan Plateau South of this area of fertile plains is the Deccan Plateau. Find the Deccan Plateau on the map. A plateau is a flat area of land high above sea level. Like most plateaus, the land of the Deccan Plateau is dry

▶ him′ ə lā′ ən

▶ The word *ghats* (gäts) means steps.

▶ dek′ən pla tō′

▶ Sea level is the surface of the sea. Mountains and landforms are measured as so many feet above sea level.

260

and infertile. Food crops cannot grow there without irrigation; yet there are few rivers and little rain.

Look again at the landform map. Now compare it with the population map. Where do you think most of the Indian people live? Why do you think so many people live there?

Latitude and longitude Climate may be one of the most important elements in the life of a people. Climate means the weather of an area over a very long time. The climate of an area often depends on how far north or south it lies from the equator. We measure this distance north or south in degrees and minutes of latitude. We measure how far east or west a place is in degrees and minutes of longitude. The symbol for a degree is °. The symbol for a minute is '. The equator is labeled 0° by geographers. The North Tropic Line is 23° 27' north latitude—that is, it lies in a latitude 23° 27' north of the equator.

Many Indians irrigate their land the same way it was done thousands of years ago. These men are flipping the baskets from side to side to water the rice seeds. Why do Indians not use more modern ways of irrigation?

◗ Parallels of latitude (lat' ə-tüd) are imaginary lines that circle the globe at set distances north and south of the equator.

◗ Meridians (mə rid' ē ənz) of longitude (lon' je tüd) are those lines on the globe east and west of a set line drawn from the North to the South Pole.

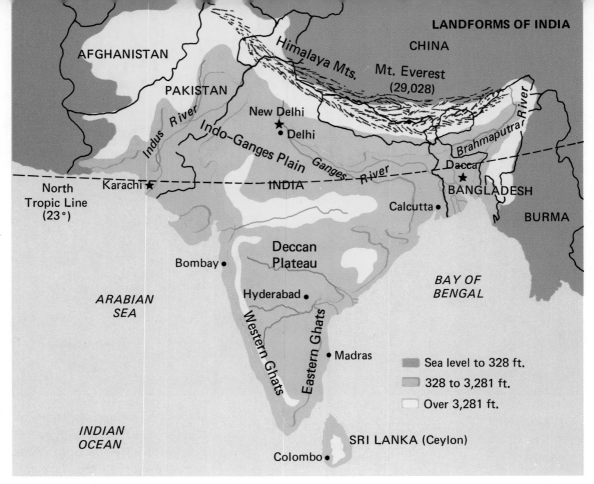

LANDFORMS OF INDIA

AFGHANISTAN

CHINA

PAKISTAN

Himalaya Mts.

Mt. Everest
(29,028)

Indus River

New Delhi ★
• Delhi

Indo-Ganges Plain

Ganges River

Brahmaputra River

North
Tropic Line
(23°)

Karachi ★

INDIA

Dacca ★
BANGLADESH

BURMA

Calcutta •

ARABIAN
SEA

Bombay •

Deccan
Plateau

Hyderabad •

BAY OF
BENGAL

Western Ghats

Eastern Ghats

• Madras

	Sea level to 328 ft.
	328 to 3,281 ft.
	Over 3,281 ft.

INDIAN
OCEAN

SRI LANKA (Ceylon)

Colombo •

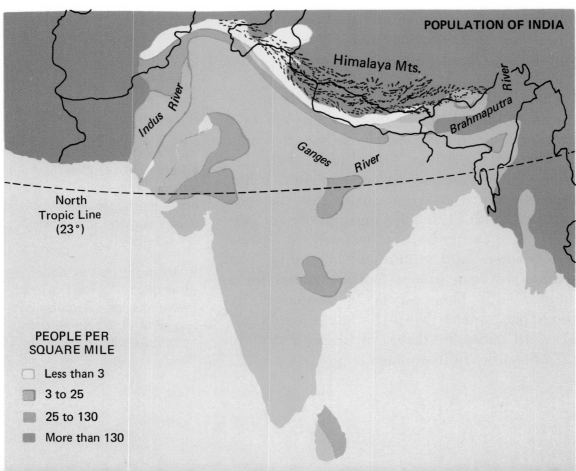

POPULATION OF INDIA

Himalaya Mts.

Indus River

Brahmaputra River

Ganges River

North
Tropic Line
(23°)

PEOPLE PER
SQUARE MILE

	Less than 3
	3 to 25
	25 to 130
	More than 130

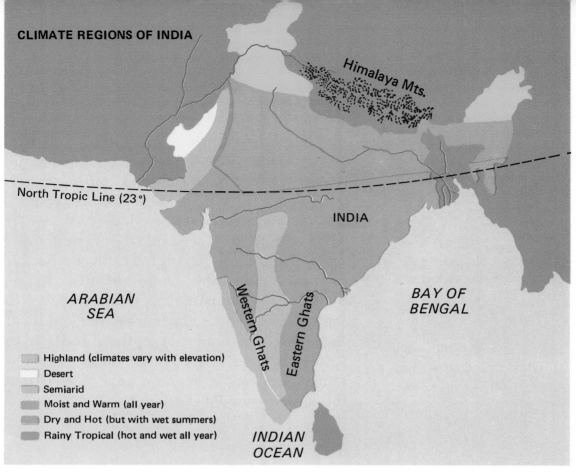

CLIMATE REGIONS OF INDIA

Himalaya Mts.

North Tropic Line (23°)

INDIA

ARABIAN SEA

Western Ghats

Eastern Ghats

BAY OF BENGAL

- Highland (climates vary with elevation)
- Desert
- Semiarid
- Moist and Warm (all year)
- Dry and Hot (but with wet summers)
- Rainy Tropical (hot and wet all year)

INDIAN OCEAN

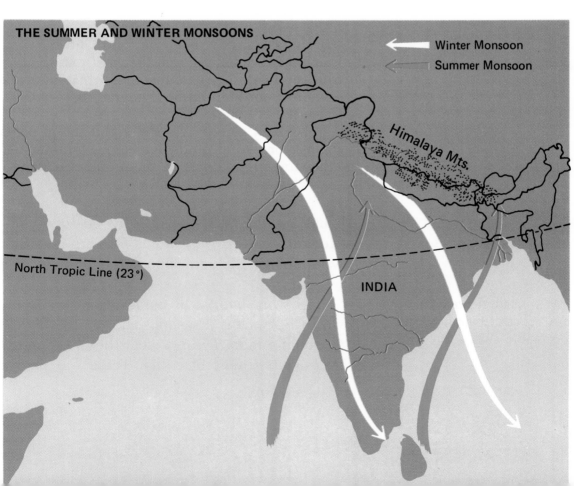

THE SUMMER AND WINTER MONSOONS

→ Winter Monsoon
→ Summer Monsoon

Himalaya Mts.

North Tropic Line (23°)

INDIA

▶ A tropical (trop′ ə kl) area is a place where the climate is usually very hot.

▶ Look at the climate regions map on page 263. How many major climate regions does India have?

India's climate The northern half of India lies north of the North Tropic Line. What do you think the climate is like there?

The southern half of India extends to just 8° north of the equator into the hot, wet tropics. There are places in northern India so cold that people must stay indoors day after day. Yet there are also places in the mountains of tropical India where nothing can grow because of the endless cold. There are many reasons for this. Most important is that the higher the land, the colder the climate. So, while it is cold in the high mountains of southern India, in the valleys below it is always hot. Trace the mountain ranges on the map on page 263. Do you think many people can live here?

THE MONSOONS

It rained so hard and so long that the thought of no rain caused a mild wonder. It was as if nothing had ever been but rain, and the water found every hole in that thatched roof to fall in through and drip onto the already damp floor. If we had not built on high ground the very walls would have melted. . . .

As night came . . .—the eighth night of the monsoons—the winds increased, whining and howling around outside the hut as if seeking to pluck it from the earth. . . .

What are the monsoons? Why do they cause life and death? Why don't farmers and their wives leave the monsoon lands and go elsewhere?

The word *monsoon* comes from an Arabic word; it means season. The monsoons are seasonal winds. Twice a year they blow across the subcontinent of India. Trace the path of

▶ What does this tell you about contact between Indian and Arabic cultures?

264

the monsoons on the map on page 263. Which monsoon carries more rain to the lands? Which monsoon do you think is more important?

How are the monsoons important? Listen to the words of one expert:

Because in 1965 the monsoons failed to arrive, India has been suffering from the effects of a long drought. Agriculture in the whole of India has always been ruled by her monsoons. The life of the Indian farmer so depends on the monsoon that a delay of only a few days in the arrival of the rains can make the difference between plentiful food or none. Two-thirds of the rice crop is rain-fed rice.

It takes approximately 125 days for rice fields to be tilled and for the rice to be planted and picked.

Each day of the monsoon is vital for the rice. If the rains last too long or are too heavy, the rivers flood. If the rains are too short, there is drought. Nothing grows, people starve.

▶ A drought (drout) is a long period without rain.

▶ Rain-fed rice is grown in land that is not irrigated.

▶ Do you think the monsoons provide a secure way of life?

The rice crop depends on the coming of the monsoons. What things in the picture tell you that a monsoon storm can begin at any moment?

In Indian villages, people depend almost completely on what they can do with their hands. What activities are these villagers doing? What things in the pictures are handmade? Is there anything shown that is machine-made?

266

Most Indians do not live in large cities, but in villages like the one shown above. Though radios and better roads are breaking down the isolation of these villages, daily life has changed very little.

HOW PEOPLE LIVE

Maps and charts help show some of India's problems. But they do not always give the entire story. Do you think that maps show how people really live? Explain your answer.

Village life An American writer has described Indian village life. Read her description and look at the photographs. Does her article add to the information on the maps? If so, how?

Flying over the Indian countryside after dusk, one can sense the poverty of the villagers. Few lights can be seen for miles. Most villages do not have electricity. Millions of villagers spend their evenings in darkness. Some people own kerosene lanterns. But they do not use them often. They cannot afford much kerosene.

The layout of villages and the building materials for houses change from village to village. In southern India, houses are usually separated by fruit trees. Vegetable fibers are used to make the walls and roofs of the houses. In the north, villagers fear invaders. They build their houses close together in small groups. Most of the houses are mud huts. Rain can easily wash them away.

Most village homes have only one or two rooms. These homes are dark even in the daytime. They have no windows because the people fear robbers. Most people can afford only one lock—for the front door. Families often bring the cattle indoors at night to protect them from robbers.

Many Indians are undernourished, but economists believe the people spend 66 percent of their income on food. They use only about 20 percent for housing, kerosene, and debts. Most villagers own few things. They have copper and earthenware pots for cooking and storing grain; a few cotton quilts for warmth; some religious articles; and cots made from woven string.

▶ Kerosene (ker′ə sēn) is an oil for burning.

▶ Do the Indians make good use of the land in building their homes and planning their villages? Explain.

▶ Undernourished (un′ dər-ner′ isht) means not having enough food.

▶ Why do you think the people are undernourished if they spend such a large part of their income on food?

A few rich people may have private wells. But village life usually centers around one or two common wells. Women come here to get water for cooking and drinking. Close to the village is a pond of stale water. The cattle drink from it and women do the washing here.

Most villages have no shops. A village money-lender may keep some cloth, salt, kerosene, and soap for sale. Villagers buy and sell at nearby market towns or along the road.

Although homes are generally very clean, the villages as a whole are not. Garbage is still dumped in the narrow lanes near the houses. And the lanes turn to mud in the rainy season.

Most of India's people have lived in small villages for hundreds of years. They are used to the old ways. They have preserved their rural culture.

City life Most Indians live in rural villages. But some people live in cities. The percent may seem small, but it represents almost 97 million city dwellers.

How did it begin? Where did these cities come from? In India, cities can be traced as far back as 2500 B.C. Most of India's largest cities, however, were founded in the seventeenth century by the British East India Company. Many are transportation and trade centers.

Urban growth Cities in India are growing almost three times as fast as rural areas. Why is the urban growth rate so high? In the United States, people often move to cities in search of jobs and a better way of life. But thousands of Indian villagers are moving to cities where they have no friends and can find no jobs. Why?

Look at the statistics for rural population density on page 273. Perhaps the villages are

▶ Rural means in the countryside. Urban means in or near cities.

▶ Some major Indian cities are Calcutta (kal kut'ə), Bombay (bom bā'), Madras (mə dras'), Delhi-New Delhi (del' ē), and Hyderabad (hid'ə rə-bad). Find these cities on the map on page 262. How might geography explain the growth of some of these cities?

▶ What evidence of cities in 2500 B.C. do you know about?

▶ Many new arrivals in the cities can find no better "home" than the sidewalk. How do you think people feel when they arrive in a strange place with no home and no job?

Cities have brought opportunity to many Indians. Some people have started successful businesses like the selling of flower petals shown at right. But millions have fled their native villages only to find slums and misery in the overcrowded city streets.

becoming so crowded that people are moving to the cities to find more room. But in the cities of India, their luck is not much better. Here is what a newcomer to Delhi would see.

Delhi is a typical Indian city—a confusion of tenements, shacks, and stalls. All of these are scrambled together on narrow streets. There are few sidewalks. Cars, buses, and ox-drawn carts share the streets with pedestrians and rows and rows of bicycles.

Life in the city is depressing. People often sleep six or eight to a room. There are no playgrounds and the city streets are dirty.

Bagichi Ramchand is a typical Delhi slum. It was built up about two centuries ago, in what was then open country. It was a place where people stopped on their journey to a nearby temple.

Today 300 families crowd into the slum's two and one-half acres. Some people live in two-story tenements; others live in one-room mud hovels. The slum has only a few outside toilets and water faucets. Pedestrians, bicycles, wandering animals, and children at play all use the muddy lanes surrounding the slum.

The people of Bagichi Ramchand do not really care about their surroundings. They consider their real homes to be the villages of their ancestors. They do not feel close to their neighbors who come from different castes and regions. There is no feeling of living in a neighborhood for these people.

▶ A tenement (ten'ə mənt) is a building divided into small cheap rooms and apartments in which many people live.

▶ bä gē' chē räm' shund

▶ A slum is an area with many people, run-down buildings, and few things like running water and toilets.

▶ A hovel (huv' l) is a very small, unpleasant place to live.

▶ How would the caste system affect neighborhood unity?

1. Describe what India's climate is like in the valleys south of the North Tropic Line. What is it like above the North Tropic Line? In which region do most Indians live?

2. Read the villager's quote at the beginning of the chapter. Why will his sons not help him in his field? Do you think there will be a place for them to live and work in the city?

Case Study: Economic and Social Change

A STATISTICAL VIEW

Sometimes numbers can tell us as much about a nation as maps and other written materials. Numerical facts are called **statistics.**

◗ stə tis′ tiks

The following statistical charts compare India and the United States in the late 1960s. Use the statistics to discover some of India's problems. Compare the figures for India and the United States.

Population Distribution

	INDIA	UNITED STATES
Land area (square miles)	1,262,000	3,618,000
Population	536,984,000	203,213,000
Rural population	82%	25%
Urban population	18%	75%
Density (per square mile)		
Total	426	57
Rural	297	26
Urban—sample cities	Delhi	Chicago
	43,000	16,138
	(population 3,500,000)	(population 3,555,000)

◗ Density means people per square mile.

1. Which country is more crowded? How would this affect the amount of space available for housing?
2. Which country is more urbanized?
3. How does density affect the amount of land available for farming?
4. Does India have a population problem? Why or why not?
5. Which city is more crowded: Delhi or Chicago? How would crowding affect the way people in cities live?

Agriculture

	INDIA	UNITED STATES
Rice production	64,042,000 tons	3,655,000 tons
Wheat production	20,560,000 tons	43,766,000 tons
Milk production	23,451,000 tons	58,099,000 tons
Egg production	2,200,000 tons	68,692,000 tons
Cotton production	1,195,000 tons	2,403,000 tons
People in agriculture	70%	5%
Grams of proteins eaten per day	47.9	96.8

1. According to this chart, which country is producing more food?

2. Review the population figures on page 273. How many times greater is the Indian population than the United States population? Notice that except for rice, India produces much less food than the United States. In fact, the total Indian food production is about half as much as the amount the United States produces.

3. In which country is a larger part of the population engaged in agriculture? Notice that even with this percentage of farmers, India can produce only about half as much food as the United States.

4. Food-growing in India is difficult. Indians cannot always get the food they need. Proteins are an important part of a person's diet, since they help body cells grow. Proteins are gotten from food. Scientists recommend that people get 58–70 grams of protein a day. From the chart, tell which people have a better diet. Explain.

5. Wheat can be grown well by using machinery instead of labor. But rice requires much labor. Why would India grow almost three times as much rice as wheat?

Wages and Prices

	INDIA	UNITED STATES
GNP	$46,000,000,000	$931,000,000,000
Income per person	$73 year	$3,167 year
Salary		
unskilled worker	$15 month	$507 month
skilled worker	$86 month	$732 month
Rent	$5 month	$89 month
Food		
milk	$.11 quart	$ .30 quart
lamb	$.30 pound	$2.04 pound
rice	$.16 pound	$ .23 pound
flour	$.10 pound	$ .13 pound
Clothing		
jeans	$4	$8
sari or dress	$4	$15

▶ A sari (sä′rē) is a dress of wrapped cloth worn by Indian women.

1. Which country is wealthier? How do you know?
2. How much do average skilled and unskilled workers in India and the United States have to spend on food and clothing each month?
3. What do you think Indian families will spend the most money on? Why?

PEOPLE AND FOOD

A "compulsory fast" All the people—city dwellers and villagers—need food. But India has too little food and too many people. The death rate has been lowered, but the birth rate has not. This means that the population of India continues to increase. There will never be enough food unless the population growth is lowered. Until then, many Indians must

◆ Compulsory (kəm pul′sə rē) means forced or without any choice.
◆ A fast is a period of going without food. Gandhi sometimes fasted as a way to protest.

▶ Even if farmers could afford the newest farm equipment, would it be practical to use large machines on such small farms? Explain your answer.

▶ India has problems in many areas—agriculture, health, industry, and education. But the government dealt with agriculture first. Would you have made the same decision? Why or why not?

▶ Do you think "miracle rice" is the answer to India's food shortage? Explain.

endure what Gandhi called a "compulsory fast."

The Indian government has to buy food from other nations to keep its people from starving. Why can't India produce enough food on its own? The average Indian farm is only about 5 acres. It grows only enough food for one family. The average United States farm is about 375 acres. It provides food for more than 25 people. Does this explain part of India's problem?

It is difficult for small farmers to care for their land or to get good equipment. Many farmers have only an ox or water buffalo to help them prepare their fields.

Rescue for farmers The farmers need help, and the Indian government knows it. Changes are being made. The government has set up a special farm program. Teams of experts are teaching the villagers new and better ways of farming. They also give advice on how to plan smaller families. Why would this help solve the hunger problem?

"Miracle rice" Scientists also help the farmers. In the 1960s, a new type of rice was developed. Some people called it "miracle rice" because it grew so well. Community advisers taught farmers how to grow the new rice. The rice grows so fast that farmers have had more than one harvest a year. This means more rice and bigger profits.

How do you think the farmers felt at first about the new rice? Remember that sometimes it is hard for people to change the ways they have used for generations. Read the following story to better understand this problem.

These pictures show an old and a new way in which Indians control the land they live on. A driver signals an elephant by moving his feet behind the animal's ear. Would elephants be useful on large farms? Could machines be used in thick forests?

Ram is a farmer who is now living in a small village near Bombay. One of the government advisers came to discuss the new method of rice growing.

Ram was excited about the idea of a better rice. But he was unsure about trying a new way. "I have only three acres of land from which to feed my family," he thought. Suppose he failed? It was a big risk.

The adviser reassured Ram. Farmers nearby were using the new way and increasing their crops.

But Ram's friends warned him against the experiment. Even his own father warned him against changing his ways. "Take whatever God gives you," he said. "Don't ask for too much."

Ram was confused. He knew that his land was producing fewer crops each year. At last he agreed to the new plan.

Many years later, Ram looked back on the changes he had made.

He had learned to use fertilizer. He was now borrowing tools from the village's new cooperative. He was buying good seed. He was using a new plow and sickle that were better than the ones his father and grandfather used.

And all the advice was free. The advisers were there to help him when he needed it.

All of this puzzled Ram's father. He remarked, "You are getting everything—good seed, fine fertilizer, and good tools—as if a spirit is bringing all these to you."

BETWEEN TWO WORLDS

A job in the city Things may be better for farmers, but villagers are still being pushed out to live in the cities. Many cannot find jobs. Vasuedo is nineteen years old and a member of a low farming caste. But he left home and moved to New Delhi. Luckily, he found a job.

▶ A cooperative is an organization owned and operated by its members. The members share the benefits and losses.

▶ Why are villagers being pushed toward the cities?

▶ vä swā′dō

278

I was born in a small village that used to be far from the city. But the city has spread out so far that now the village is part of New Delhi.

My father is a farmer. When the city grew, he had to buy new land farther away from the city. That's how fast things are going today.

My father grows wheat and other grain on his new farm. He's tried some of the new seeds and they're better than the old ones. He's producing a lot more. But the new farm will probably be swallowed up by the city, too.

I am one of nine children. My father's farm could not be divided into parts. So I left home three years ago to become an apprentice. I worked one year without pay. I do auto repairs. I still don't get much pay, but I like my work.

I haven't seen my father's new farm. I can't go back there. That's my father's life — not mine.

Decision Vasuedo is one of seven brothers. His father's farm is only five acres. What do you think would happen if all the brothers decided to remain at home and farm? Would there be enough land for all to make a living? What would they do? What would you do in the same situation?

INDUSTRIALIZATION

A revolution Once, long ago, most Americans were farmers. But about a hundred years ago, something important changed our way of life. It was called the Industrial Revolution. Any major change in a way of life is a revolution.

For a long time, people made things by hand or used tools and animals to help them. Animals pulled simple machines. Then someone invented a machine that ran by steam. The change from muscle power to machine power—

▶ Why does Vasuedo think the city will get even bigger?

▶ An apprentice (ə pren′tis) is a person who is learning a trade.

▶ Steam is one kind of power. What other kinds of power for machines can you name?

279

MARRIAGES OF THE *TIMES*

When Arvind, a 28-year-old Delhi architect, recently married Renu, a young college graduate, they followed the pattern of traditional Indian marriage. The girl's family judged the boy's job future. And the boy's family investigated the girl's background and character. The couple's financial future was discussed. Then Arvind's parents gave Renu the traditional pre-wedding gifts of clothes and jewelry.

After the wedding, Renu moved into the home of her husband's parents. There she assumed the traditional role of daughter-in-law. All this was exactly according to ancient Indian custom.

Yet, despite appearances of Indian tradition, the modern world had crept in— Renu and Arvind met through a newspaper advertisement! Renu's father placed the ad in *The Hindustan Times,* a well-respected national newspaper:

WANTED: A handsome, well-educated young man for a beautiful, well-educated girl. . . .

Arvind's father is an executive with the Ford Motor Company of India. He explained why he looked in the newspapers to find a bride for his son:

One has to depend on modern resources—there's no shame attached to it.

You want a good match for your child—someone who is well-educated and from a good family. The newspaper ads widen your circle of choices.

His son and new daughter-in-law agree. They share the feelings of many young Indians who accept newspaper ads, placed by their parents, as the ideal way to find a mate: "We trusted our parents completely," said Arvind.

How do these attitudes about marriage compare to those of your culture? Do you know anyone whose parents arranged their marriage? Would you like the Indian system of marriage? Why or why not?

Social scientists explain that marriage through newspaper ads is becoming more common in India. They say that it is one sign of social change.

Previously, Indian parents would arrange marriages with the sons or daughters of their friends and neighbors. Now Indian society is not as stable as it was in the past. People move all the time and do not get to know the people in their community well. "Newspaper marriage ads have definitely increased in the past five years as more and more people migrate to jobs all over India," said one social scientist. The ads show another change, too: "A girl is still expected to be attractive and a good housekeeper. But families are also looking for girls and men with an education. Caste and status are becoming less important." Do you think that the newspaper marriage ads are an important social change in India? Explain.

Indian textiles have found markets all over the world. They are colorful, interesting, and inexpensive.

▶ Why can't all Indians who want to, be farmers?

the Industrial Revolution—affected the lives of all people.

Think about automobile manufacturing. What do automobile factories provide for Americans? Cars, of course. American streets are crowded with cars. But what else? Jobs. American workers can afford to buy cars because they have jobs. They buy their cars from car salesmen. Can you see how one industry can affect many lives?

A revolution is happening in India now. It, too, is an industrial revolution. Since all Indians cannot be farmers, many are learning to be factory workmen. The Indian people are buying manufactured goods at the same time that they continue making home-woven cloth.

Agriculture and industry The government is the chief developer of agriculture. It is also the major planner of India's industry. Better farming requires modern tractors, plows, and fertilizer. Only modern factories can produce these. And factories need electricity, steel, and workers. Farmers need more water for crops and better transportation to bring food to market. But irrigation and roadways need many workers and modern equipment, too. India certainly has enough people. But India needs money to build factories and train workers.

Government help The government has taken over industry left by the British and helped develop new industries. The government controls many areas—electrical plants, water and atomic power plants, steel production, irrigation systems, and railroads. India's industrial growth depends on these.

The government helps out privately owned industries, too. It provides them with cheap electricity, low factory rents, and money to train workers.

▶ How does government aid help industry grow?

Made in India India is the world's second-largest cotton producer. For centuries, Indians have woven cotton into cloth. Cloth can be made on simple looms as well as on complicated machines. It made sense to expand the textile business. More Indians work in textiles than in any other industry.

▶ Textiles are cloth or the weaving of fibers into cloth.

Many people in India still work in small home industries. They make jewelry, brassware, and embroidery. But Indian factories also produce locomotives, paper, bicycles, and electronic equipment.

▶ Do you think the textile industry depends on good agriculture? Why?

In some areas, India has become a leader. In Asia, India has the most miles of railroad track. It has the largest fertilizer plant. It is also Asia's third-largest steel producer. And India still has valuable supplies of iron ore, coal, tin, and copper which have not yet been developed.

▶ Do you own anything made in India?

Old and new skills are combined in the cities of modern India. The potter still turns his wheel. But the growth of the cotton industry has given new jobs to people on farms, in marketplaces, and in factories.

Education and change Education is a problem for both farmers and factory workers — in villages and in cities. New government factories need skilled workers to run the machines. Farmers must learn to work their new equipment. Many teachers are needed to show the people these new ways. They are also needed to teach people to read and write.

Sometimes just building more schools does not help. Imagine you are a farmer. You have a wife and three children. You cannot afford to hire anyone to help on the farm. The entire family must help you raise food. If they do not, there will be no food. There is a school a few miles away from your farm. Your children can learn to read and write there. Will you send them to school? Why or why not?

Better education sometimes brings its own problems. Many people do not want to work on farms after they learn to read and write. So they leave their villages. But in the cities, there are not enough jobs for even the educated people.

▶ Think about the future. Imagine that one of the farmer's children grows up and decides to move to the city to work. Do you think it would be difficult for a person who cannot read and write to move from a small village to a large city?

INDIA TODAY AND TOMORROW

The people of India have followed the same ways for generations. But with new ways and more education, traditions are changing.

Caste today The caste system may have helped to strengthen Indian society. Each person knows what is expected of him. But caste has also weakened India. Most people accept low caste and its burdens. The system has made people unwilling to change. Businessmen like to give jobs to people of their own caste. People still feel most at home with members of their own caste.

For thousands of years, Indian leather workers were outcastes, or untouchables, because they worked with the skins of dead animals. But now the leather workers are slowly gaining status.

▶ Can laws always change traditions? Can the government law against untouchability work? Why or why not?

▶ har'ə jänz

▶ Why did Gandhi think it important to change the name of untouchables?

▶ Why do you think caste rules have broken down in the city faster than in the country?

The government has tried to help improve the system. It has outlawed the rules of untouchability. Mistreatment of untouchables is a crime. Gandhi decided to rename the untouchables. He called them *Harijans,* which means, "the children of God."

The growth of cities and factories helped change caste, too. Here is one change a reporter saw.

The bus has broken down caste barriers. The Harijans and the Brahmans ride the bus for the same fare. Hens, market goods, and people from all castes squeeze together on crowded Indian buses.

The Brahmans may protest about riding with people of lower castes, but the bus driver pays no attention. He knows that throwing out the Harijans would be bad business. And it might cause him trouble if someone reported it to the government.

People and change How do the people feel about changes in their lives? They know that changes can improve things. But they are cautious.

A villager once told two missionaries how he felt about his people and change.

We may seem unfriendly, backward, and stubborn. Those things are always said of people who resist change. At times you become very impatient with our caution. But consider some of our feelings.

If untouchables want to rise to something better, who will keep our villages clean? Each of us has been born to his appointed task. Each of us has this task because of his former life. Everything is in the hands of the gods. This we do know—the old ways have served us well for centuries. What if untouchables try to be farmers, and farmers try to be carpenters, and carpenters try to be teachers? There would be confusion and work would be badly done. Once change begins, how far will it go?

▶ What does the villager mean when he says "former life"?

▶ Do you think the villager's fears are reasonable? How would you reply to the man's remarks?

1. How did improving health conditions in India make the food problem worse? What did Gandhi mean by a "compulsory fast"?
2. How has modern science helped Ram? How has the growth of modern cities affected Vasuedo's family?
3. Why does the Indian government aid privately owned industries?

INVESTIGATING THE UNIT

Doing Research

Without the work of archaeologists, the early history of South Asia would not be known. From books or encyclopedias, find out how an archaeologist does his job. What kinds of tools does an archaeologist use? Why must he take special care during diggings? How does an archaeologist know the age of the evidence he digs up? How does an archaeologist decide where to start digging for evidence? Are there any land features that give clues about where evidence might be buried?

Looking at the Evidence

One of the most interesting parts of an archaeologist's job is evaluating the evidence. Reread the section on the Indus Valley civilization. What pieces of evidence might have shown that people had lived on farms, in seaports, or in villages? Play archaeologist yourself. Judging by the evidence, what skills and technologies would you guess the people of Harrapa and Mohenjo-Daro had?

Using Maps

There are several different kinds of maps in this unit. Pretend that you had to send all the information on one of these maps to a friend in another coun-try. You do not have enough money to send the map itself, so you must write out, as exactly as possible, all the information the map gives. After everyone has completed the map descriptions, make a class decision. Which are more accurate means of giving information—maps or written descriptions? Which helps a person gather information faster—map language or written language?

Comparing and Contrasting

India and the United States were both colonies of Great Britain. Both won their independence from Britain. Compare the ways in which each fought for independence. Did both nations use the same methods of protest? Did both fight wars? Can you think of any reasons why different methods were used in the two nations?

Reading on Your Own

For an interesting book on the mixing of old and new in modern India, read *My Heart Has Seventeen Rooms,* by Jean Bothwell (New York, Macmillan). *Story of India,* by Seymour Fersh (New York, McCormick-Mathers) is a good introduction to Indian life and history. And for some interesting pictures, see the book *Indian Pictures* (New York, Visual Geography Series, Sterling).

EAST ASIA: CHINA AND JAPAN

Somehow the old keeps pace with the new in East Asia. Somehow part of
what happened before remains to remind us of a living past. The camel
and the cart keep their place beside the truck and the automobile.
The new is added to the old like another color in a painting.

WALTER FAIRSERVIS, JR.

Yesterday and Today

One of every four people in the world lives in East Asia. Since the beginning of man's culture, people there have farmed, raised their families, and worshiped their gods.

Find East Asia on the map on page 324. What major nations make up these lands? Who are the people who live here? What are their cultures like?

China's culture is very old. Much of the Chinese way of life began in times long past. These ways of life influenced those of Japan and Korea, China's neighbors. As you read, look for the ideas and the values that are important to the people of China and its neighbors. How did these ideas and values develop? And how are they changing? How are East Asian values like yours? How are they different?

THE SHANG DYNASTY

According to Chinese legend, the universe was first ruled by the Twelve Emperors of Heaven. Each emperor ruled for 18,000 years. Next, the universe was ruled by the Eleven Emperors of Earth. Each of these emperors also ruled for 18,000 years. Then the Nine Emperors of Mankind ruled for 45,000 more years. Still other rulers came after them.

These rulers and emperors, said the Chinese, gave mankind all the things it needed to live. One god invented agriculture, another fire, and still others, hunting, fishing, writing, and medicine. The early Chinese thought that all of civilization had begun in their part of the world.

Modern historians do not believe in these legendary Chinese emperors. They base their knowledge of ancient Chinese history on evidence found by archaeologists. Even according

▶ A dynasty (dī′nə stē) is a series of rulers who all belong to the same family.

▶ According to Chinese legend, is China an old or a new culture?

▶ An archaeologist (är kē ol′ə-jist) is a scientist who tries to learn how ancient people lived by studying the remains of their cultures—things like ruins of buildings, art, and written records.

291

▶ shäng

▶ What evidence do you think archaeologists found that shows the Shang raised pigs and dogs?

▶ Can you think of any reason why a people might choose bones with which to "speak" to their dead ancestors, rather than some other material?

to this evidence, though, people have been living in China for more than a million years.

Many historians believe that the first important dynasty in China was that of the Shang. The Shang people lived about 4,000 years ago, in the area north of the Yellow River. Look at the map on page 294. Find the center of Shang culture.

Historians consider the Shang an advanced culture. We know, for instance, that the Shang people lived in villages. We know that the farmers raised wheat and millet. Millet is a kind of grain. Archaeologists have found evidence that the Shang raised pigs and dogs. We know, also, that the Shang worked with bronze, a hard metal. We have found bronze bowls.

But the most important evidence we have of the level of Shang culture is writing.

Picture writing A hundred years ago, Chinese farmers began to find old bones in some of their fields. The bones were cracked and had pictures drawn on them. For a time, they were ground up and used for medicine.

About 50 years ago, archaeologists and other scholars figured out that the pictures on the bones were writing.

The Shang believed that the cracks were the voices of their ancestors. Since they could not speak directly to their ancestors, they drew pictures to ask questions. They scratched the pictures on special bones and threw the bones into a fire. The bones cracked from the heat. A special group of people then looked at the cracks and explained what they meant.

People would ask their ancestors for advice about everyday matters. They believed that they could learn from their ancestors whether

WRITING
AND CHINESE CULTURE

This is a Shang character: 𗈬 . The upper half represents a closed-in place. The lower half is a man crouching. The meaning of the entire character is a closed-in place where people live—a city.

This is another Shang character: ✗ . It is a tree, showing branches and roots. This character shows two trees: ✗✗ It means grove or forest. The modern form for this word is 林 . You can see how the character has changed. But it is still related to the Shang character.

The Shang characters expressed ideas as well as objects. They did this by combining or changing characters. This is their character for "sun": ⊖ . Their idea of east was the sun rising behind a tree: 東 . The modern character is 東 . The Shang character for west was a tiger, because tigers came down from the western mountains.

Shang writing is the basis for all Chinese, Korean, and Japanese writing. It differs from Western writing because each of its characters stands for an object or idea. Western writing uses letters. Only combinations of letters form words. The words, not each letter, represent objects or ideas. Today, too, every Chinese character stands for a word. Words cannot be broken down into letters since there are no letters.

Because there are no letters, it is impossible to sound out a Chinese word. People all over China can read: 東 They all know what it means, but they may pronounce it in completely different ways. People from different areas of China will not understand one another unless they write the character. Unfortunately, there are so many characters that many people cannot read.

The Japanese adopted Chinese writing in the sixth century. But they made an important change in it. They made characters stand for syllables, not whole words. Written Japanese looks like written Chinese to a Westerner, but the languages are very different.

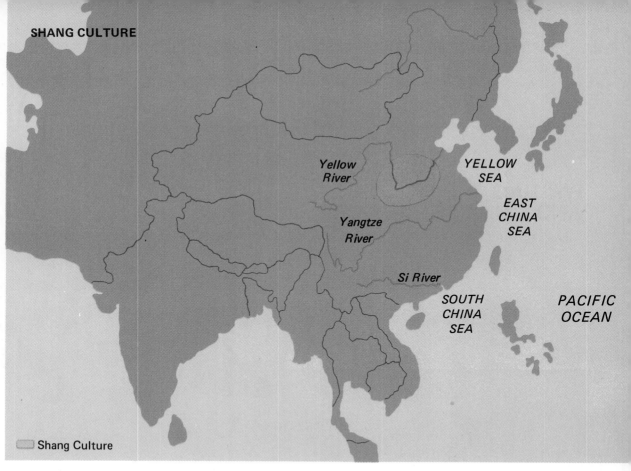

SHANG CULTURE

Yellow
River

Yangtze
River

Si River

YELLOW
SEA

EAST
CHINA
SEA

SOUTH
CHINA
SEA

PACIFIC
OCEAN

Shang Culture

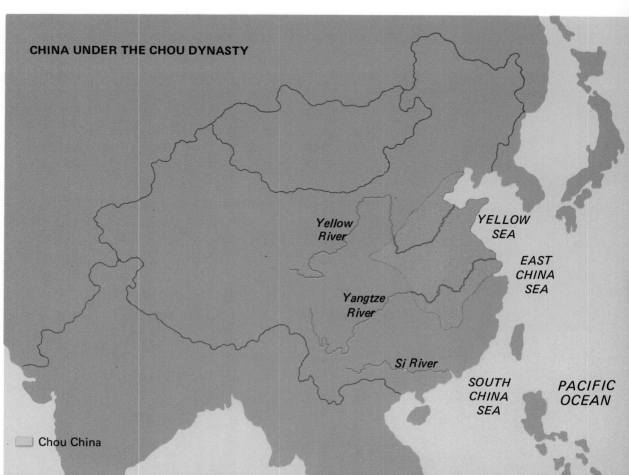

CHINA UNDER THE CHOU DYNASTY

Yellow
River

Yangtze
River

Si River

YELLOW
SEA

EAST
CHINA
SEA

SOUTH
CHINA
SEA

PACIFIC
OCEAN

Chou China

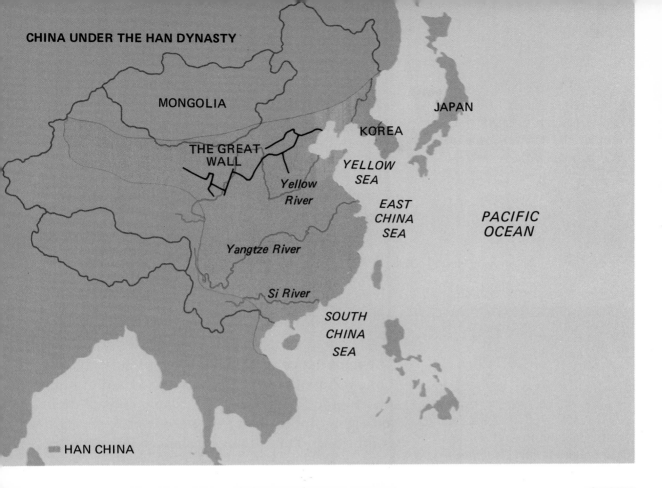

CHINA UNDER THE HAN DYNASTY

MONGOLIA

JAPAN

KOREA

THE GREAT WALL

YELLOW SEA

Yellow River

EAST CHINA SEA

PACIFIC OCEAN

Yangtze River

Si River

SOUTH CHINA SEA

▨ HAN CHINA

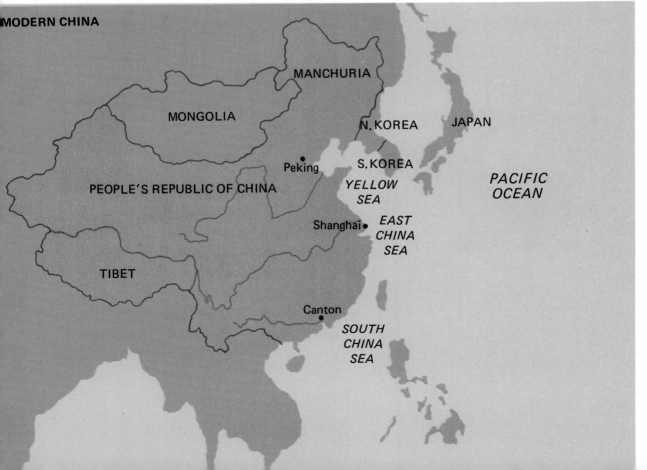

MODERN CHINA

MANCHURIA

MONGOLIA

N. KOREA

JAPAN

Peking •

S. KOREA

PEOPLE'S REPUBLIC OF CHINA

YELLOW SEA

PACIFIC OCEAN

Shanghai •

EAST CHINA SEA

TIBET

Canton •

SOUTH CHINA SEA

▶ A drought (draut) is a long period of time when no rain falls. Would farmers be afraid of droughts? Why or why not?

▶ Look at the map on page 294. What river were the Shang near? In this area of China, there are sometimes heavy rains. Can you see why the people would fear floods? Why would they fear droughts?

▶ yin

▶ yäng

a flood or a drought was coming. Do you think that Shang farmers would be anxious to learn what their ancestors could "tell" them?

The power of ancestors The Shang believed ancestors controlled all events of the future. The Shang people believed that ancestors brought the spring rains and controlled success at planting and hunting. People thought that kings and princes had the most powerful ancestors.

The importance of balance The pictures on the bones show that the Shang were afraid of both floods and droughts. The Shang asked their ancestors for a balance between these two conditions. This idea of balance became very important. The Shang people came to believe that balance and harmony were necessary in every area of life.

The Shang believed that two kinds of energies kept life going. One was called Yin, and the other was called Yang. Yin and Yang were opposite ideas. One was male, one female; one was light, one dark. The Shang prayed to their ancestors to keep a perfect balance between Yin and Yang forces.

When Yin and Yang combined perfectly, the Shang believed, life would continue peacefully. They saw this combination at work in nature. For example, as daylight became stronger, it was a sign that night was getting nearer.

Caring for the ancestors The Chinese people believed their ancestors controlled the Yin and Yang energies. Therefore, the Shang developed ways to care for their ancestors.

Ancient Chinese art often
showed the idea of
harmony and balance. Do
you see balanced lines
and colors in these two
objects?

The Shang believed it was the duty of all males to keep the ancestors happy.

All Shang boys were taught their duties. They learned to care for their ancestors' graves. They were taught to have many children to keep the family name alive. If the ancestors were not cared for, the Shang believed, they would become unhappy "wandering ghosts." This could cause bad things—like a poor harvest or flooded fields—to happen to the ancestor's family.

All people were afraid of one day becoming wandering ghosts. Therefore, they taught their children that the most important duty was respect for parents and grandparents, living or dead. Why do you think that parents and grandparents taught this?

The family Shang family life was organized around this idea of respect. Loyalty to one's family was the most important thing children could learn.

Parents were more anxious to have boys than girls. Only men were allowed to care for the ancestors. And men were expected to take care of their old parents. Boys were also thought to be more helpful in the fields.

Women There is a Chinese saying about the role of a woman: "At her parents' home, she obeys her father; after marriage, her husband; when he dies, her son."

A woman could not carry on the family name. When she married, she had to take the name of her husband. A woman's family had to pay her husband money or goods before the husband would marry her. This payment is called a dowry.

▶ Do you think people would want to care for their ancestors? Why or why not?

▶ What does this tell you about a woman's rights in ancient China? Do you think that all women could be that obedient? Do you think that mothers would always obey their sons?

▶ In very poor families, parents sometimes murdered their infant girls. Why do you think they did that?

▶ dou′ rē

For thousands of years, Chinese peasants have used this method of carrying heavy burdens.

The Shang dynasty lasted until about 1000 B.C. Then a strong people invaded the Shang lands. The culture of China went through many changes under these new people. But the role of women which the Shang developed changed little. A woman's place in Chinese society stayed the same for thousands of years.

THE CHOU DYNASTY

The people who invaded the Shang lands are called the Chou. The Chou lived to the west of the Yellow River Valley of the Shang. No one knows exactly why the Chou people were such good warriors. But for hundreds of years, they had defended their lands against nomads to the north and west. They conquered more and more areas around them. Finally, the Chou conquered the Shang. A new era had begun.

▶ jō

299

▶ Would it be easy to rule a large kingdom if transportation and communication were poor? Have you read about the Roman Empire? Do you know what the Romans had that helped them govern their large empire?

▶ Have you read about the Middle Ages in Western Europe? If so, do you remember what feudalism means? Which came first, the feudal period in China or the feudal period in Western Europe?

▶ Do you think this was a sensible way of organizing the Chou states? Would you rather have your enemies far away where they could do little harm or up close where you could watch them?

▶ Oppressive (ə pres′ iv) means harsh and unjust.

▶ A proverb (prov′ erb) is a short, wise saying.

Kings and nobles   The Chou added many new territories to the Shang kingdom. Look at the map on page 294. What areas of China did the Chou conquer? Was the Chou kingdom much bigger than the Shang kingdom? Did the new territories include mountains and deserts?

The Chou lands were too big for one group to rule. Roads and methods of communication were not very advanced. So the Chou split up their kingdom into small states. Each state was ruled by a chief. These chiefs became the nobles of China. The people who worked their lands were peasants. This period is sometimes called the feudal period of China.

The Chou states were organized like a series of circles. At the center of the circle was the capital. Here the king governed. The circle of states surrounding the capital was governed by the king's advisers. These were usually his close relatives.

More distant relatives governed the third circle, while lords who had helped topple the Shang governed the fourth circle. But most Chou people were not advisers and nobles. Most were peasants.

Life of the Chou peasants   What kinds of lives did the peasants lead? A clue comes from an ancient Chinese proverb. "An oppressive government is more terrible than tigers," goes the proverb. The government's oppression fell on the heads of the Chou peasants. A typical peasant family lived in a one-room house with a dirt floor. The house had no furniture. A peasant had to raise food for the noble who ruled his circle. Since so much of the food he raised went to his lord, a peasant had to fish and hunt to get the food for his family.

This suit is made of jade threaded with gold. It held the body of a princess. The ancient Chinese thought that these beautiful materials would help preserve her dead body.

Peasant families lived together in groups. The land they lived on was divided into sections. There was one section for each peasant family to farm. In addition, all of the group had to farm an extra section for the lord. They planted his crops and harvested his fields before they could tend to their own.

In almost every way, the Chou peasants were servants of their lords. Besides caring for his fields, they made farm tools, wove cloth, and sewed clothing for his household. They also built roads and dikes and dams to protect the land they lived in. And, when a noble needed to defend his land, it was the peasants who were called from the field to do the fighting.

The peasants were the least powerful people in the Chou kingdom. But without their work, the Chou system of government could not have existed.

▶ A dike is a wall. In China, the dikes were often made of mud. Do you think mud walls last well against a raging river? Why or why not?

▶ lē′

▶ Do you think the attitude of the nobles toward the peasants was honorable? Explain your answer.

Here is a Chinese artist's portrait of Confucius.

▶ kən fyü′ shəs

The honorable nobles The Chou nobles lived a different kind of life. They ruled the states and commanded the army. They learned music, arithmetic, archery, and poetry. They behaved according to a special code of manners, called *li*. *Li* meant doing the right thing, or being honorable.

The nobles looked down on the peasants, who farmed and did not have learning or manners. Peasants had no power. They had to obey laws made by the nobles. They could not rise to important positions. They were not taught to read and write. They were not even given last names. And last names were needed to worship ancestors.

The decline of *li* In time, nobles began to fight among themselves. The more they fought, the less they followed *li*. This era in Chinese history was called the Period of the Warring States.

During this period, a group of nobles became worried about the decline of *li*. They thought the ancestors must not be happy. They thought that if Chou nobles followed the proper rules of behavior, heaven and earth would be in harmony again. Life would then be more prosperous and happy. The leader of this school of thought was named Confucius.

A NEW PHILOSOPHY

Confucius lived from about 551 to 479 B.C. He was a high official of the government, but he resigned because he said his prince was not honorable enough. So he wandered through all the other Chinese states, looking for an honorable noble to serve.

On his travels, Confucius taught that the nobles must obey the rules of *li*. He said a noble should be an example of honor. He said the noble should serve the people, so the people would obey the noble.

Confucius insisted on the honor and goodness of past ages. He said that men should be like the heroes of Chinese legend. He argued for moderation, self-control, and devotion to duty. Confucius called these qualities the Great Way.

Confucius and the Great Way Here is a story about Confucius. By reading it, can you tell what Confucius valued?

> Once Confucius was taking part in a ceremony. After the ceremony was over, he went for a stroll along the top of the city gate and sighed in a sad way.
> A follower of his asked, "Why does the gentleman sigh?"
> Confucius replied, "When the Great Way was practiced, the world was shared by all alike. The deserving and the able were promoted to office. Men practiced truth and lived in affection.
> "The aged found a fitting end to their lives. The young were well educated. Widows, orphans, and the sick were cared for.
> "Men had their tasks and women had their homes. They did not waste, but they did not hoard. They worked hard, but not just for themselves. All evil plotting was prevented in this way, and thieves and rebels did not arise. People could leave their outer gates unlocked.
> "Now the Great Way has become hidden and the world is the possession of private families. There is little affection among people. Goods and labor are used for selfish purposes. Walls and moats must be built for safety. Therefore secret plans and plotting come about and men take up arms."

▶ Moderation (mäd′ə rā′shən) means neither too much nor too little.

▶ In Confucius' time, was China ruled according to these qualities? Was China stable? Did Confucius value moderation?

▶ Respect for elders and people in high positions was a value Confucius praised. What sign of respect can you see in the question of his follower?

▶ Hoard (hôrd) means to keep stored or hidden away.

▶ A moat (mōt) is a deep, wide ditch, usually filled with water, that is dug around a castle or town for protection against enemies.

▶ A virtue (ver′chü) is a quality that shows the goodness of a person or thing.

Confucius believed that there were five virtues: (1) people should do good to each other; (2) people should *be* good as well as do good; (3) people should honor and respect each other; (4) people should be wise; and (5) people should be sincere.

Confucianism was not the only important philosophy of ancient China. Many other notable philosophies competed for attention. But the ideas of Confucianism have lasted for more than 2,000 years.

But Confucianism and other philosophies could not save the Chou dynasty. For many years, there was civil war. Noble fought noble. A new dynasty took power and quickly lost it.

Then one family again became more powerful, and a new dynasty was founded. This new dynasty added another new idea to the development of China. The dynasty is called the Han dynasty, and it ruled China for more than 400 years. But most importantly, it ruled its people with a new system of laws.

While hunting, Confucius spied a bird at rest. But he did not think it was fair to shoot a resting bird, so he waited until the bird flew off before taking his shot.

THE HAN DYNASTY: A NEW TYPE OF GOVERNMENT

One of the most important things any government does for its people is to protect them from outside enemies. For centuries, China had been threatened by neighboring people living near its borders. Many of these neighboring people were much poorer than the Chinese. They often raided Chinese villages and farms. Look at the map on page 295. Would China need a large army to defend its borders? Why or why not?

The Han government, like governments today, protected its people against criminals.

Just before the Han dynasty came to power, a cruel emperor used force to unite China. He burned books and killed scholars. He also began building a wall to keep outsiders away. The emperor sent thousands of people to build a wall 1,500 miles long. To this day in China, people say that every stone in the Great Wall cost a human life.

The emperors drew up laws for the whole empire.

Governments today try to increase industry and trade in their countries. The Han government also tried this by building roads and canals so that goods could be moved easily all over the country. But China is a very large country. So building roads and canals everywhere required a great deal of money. The Han emperors, like all other rulers, had to get that money from their people. They collected taxes.

Han officials All the activities of the Han government—protecting the empire, enforcing laws, building roads and canals, taxing people—required many trained and educated people. Government officials needed to know how to read and write and do arithmetic.

People who wanted to become government officials had to study for many years and take

▶ Why would government officials need to know how to read, write, and do arithmetic? Look back at the Chinese writing on page 293. Would it take a long time to learn the Chinese system of writing?

DISSATISFACTION CHANGES THE WORLD

Ts'ai Lun (tsī' lun') lived when the Han dynasty ruled China. He was one of the emperor's most trusted ministers. Ts'ai Lun was in charge of building roads and canals over the whole empire. Every day messengers delivered his orders to engineers and workmen all over China.

In those days, messages were written on silk or bamboo. Silk was very expensive. Bamboo was cheaper, but it was too bulky to be used very much. Can you imagine a whole book written on bamboo strips? Would you be strong enough to carry your textbook home if it were written on bamboo?

Ts'ai Lun was dissatisfied. He decided that a new material was needed to write on. He experimented for years with many different materials. Finally he found that if you soaked the inner bark of the mulberry tree in chemicals, then pressed it dry, you could write on it. He tried this method on other materials. Mulberry bark was cheapest. But the best paper came from two other things: old rags or old fishing nets!

The art of making paper spread quickly to all parts of China. But the Chinese managed to keep the method a secret for hundreds of years after Ts'ai Lun's death. Finally, two European monks smuggled the secret to the West.

a number of tests. It was very hard to become an official. But the road was open to anyone who would work for it. Even a poor peasant boy could study hard and become an official. Passing the tests was a way to move up to a higher position in life.

Under the Han dynasty, government officials became very important people in China. They were respected in the same way that Chou nobles were respected. One of the early Han emperors announced, "Officials are the rulers of the people. It is right that they should have better clothes and carriages. These things show how important officials are."

Scholars and the government In periods of civil war, emperors had killed scholars and burned their books. They were afraid that learning might create rebellion against the rulers. But the Han government talked to the scholars. The emperor convinced the scholars that Confucius had taught perfect obedience to the emperor. Soon the scholars were teaching this way of life to the people.

Another way the Han emperor kept his power was by reminding his people of an old Chinese idea—that the emperor was divine. This meant that his power came from heaven. He called himself the "Son of Heaven." The Han officials believed that it was their duty to rule for the people's good. This was what Confucius had taught. And it helped China stay stable and united for many hundreds of years.

The end of the Han dynasty In spite of the Han system of government, invaders managed to conquer a large part of China. Many historians

▶ Do you think this system is better than the Chou system of government by nobles? In what ways did government officials help the Han rulers control China?

▶ Do you agree that officials should be the rulers of the people? Explain your answer.

▶ Under the Han system, was it possible for a poor person to become wealthy and respected? How?

▶ Do you think Confucius really taught this? Would people be likely to revolt if they believed this?

blame the Han emperors. They say that the last Han emperors were busier making sure of their power than fighting the invaders.

But there are other reasons why China was conquered. All of the roads, canals, and palaces built by the Han government were very expensive. The emperor had to get more and more money by taxing his people. People started making their own coins. There were many coins, but most were not made of gold or silver and were not worth very much. So taxes got even higher.

It was mostly the peasants who had to pay the higher taxes. Eventually, large numbers of peasants refused to pay any more taxes. The Chinese empire began to break up. Outside invaders seized control of some parts of China. Other parts were taken over by army generals. The Han slowly lost their whole empire.

The collapse of the Han dynasty brought about an important change in Chinese culture. It marked the beginning of a new religion for the Chinese people. The religion was Buddhism.

BUDDHISM COMES TO CHINA

◗ bü′diz əm

Buddhism was not a new religion. It had been practiced in India for centuries. In fact, it was brought to China by two Indian monks.

◗ nir vän′ə

Buddhism claimed to offer everlasting happiness to its followers. This everlasting happiness was called Nirvana. Nirvana was the Buddhist idea of paradise. Buddhists said that the perfect man had been an Indian of the sixth century. The man's name was Siddhartha Gautama, or Buddha. Buddha means the "enlightened one."

◗ si′där tə gaut′ə mə
◗ bud′ə

Buddhism taught that there are four Noble Truths: (1) people are doomed to suffer; (2) suffering is caused by selfishness and jealousy; (3) the only way to end suffering is to overcome one's selfishness; (4) the only way to overcome selfishness is to be gentle and kind to others.

Buddhists said that Buddha had reached Nirvana, and that anyone could join him. To join him, people must not look for wealth. People must learn to control their feelings and desires.

Buddha had never intended to become a god. He had only set out to better the lives of his people. So Buddhism, unlike most Western religions, has no prayers or special ceremonies. Yet many Buddhists do have certain prayers that they use.

The Chinese changed Buddhism to fit their beliefs. They said that there were many

▶ Buddhism came during years of war and change. Do you think other religions also become popular in times of confusion? Explain your answer.

Japanese Buddhists honor these shoes as the sacred sandals of Buddha.

THE MONGOLS AND MARCO POLO

In 1279, new invaders came to China. These were the Mongols. Find the land of the Mongols on the map on page 295.

The Mongols were a barbaric people. Their law did not let them farm or trade. They were allowed only to hunt and make war. Mongol law even forbade bathing.

The Mongol leader was Genghis Kahn (jen' gəs kän'). He conquered Persia, Arabia, Turkestan (tər kə stän'), Russia, Hungary, Germany, and Korea. His law said that if a city resisted attack, it would be destroyed and all its people killed.

The Mongols first defeated northern China, destroying cities and murdering millions of people. Then they defeated the people in southern China.

The Mongols ruled China for almost a hundred years. Their rulers became interested in Chinese affairs. They supported learning, religion, and the arts. They built a beautiful capital and encouraged trade and business. They hired many foreigners to work in the government. One of them was an Italian traveler named Marco Polo (mär' kō pō' lō).

Marco Polo studied Chinese and Mongolian customs for 17 years. Then he returned to Italy and recorded his impressions. For centuries, his impressions were practically the only knowledge Europe had about China.

Marco Polo was impressed by the Mongol court. He did not see the weaknesses in its rule. The Mongols had murdered many Chinese and were hated by the Chinese people. They had to hire foreigners to work in the government because they could not trust the Chinese. The foreigners did not care about the local people, so the Chinese were cheated and treated harshly.

What do you think happens when historians have only one source of information? Do you think Europe's idea of China was completely accurate?

Buddhas, not just one. They said the Buddhas had become gods with great power. They also said the gods were interested in prayers and ceremonies.

In later years, different Buddhist theories of reaching Nirvana became popular. One emphasized deep thought. Another stressed doing good things for others. Still another stressed saying special words. But all different routes led to the same goal—Nirvana.

THE MIDDLE KINGDOM AND THE OUTER WORLD

About 200 years ago, the king of England wrote to the emperor of China. He asked that English merchants be allowed to trade manufactured goods for China's beautiful silks and painted pottery. The Chinese emperor wrote back: "We have no need for your country's manufactures. We have everything we need in our kingdom."

Hundreds of years ago, life at the emperor's court reached a high level. Complicated ceremonies made the emperor seem like one of the gods. Can you think of a reason why this way of life made the emperors feel that they had little to learn from other nations?

How does such an idea grow? Look at the map on page 295. What are China's western and northern borders? Find the mountain ranges to the south and west of China. Now look at the great desert that separates China from the north. What countries lie across China's eastern borders?

Do you think these natural boundaries would be hard or easy to cross? Do you think China had much contact with the outside world throughout most of its history?

▶ What are the borders of the United States? Do you think Americans have ever feared close neighbors?

▶ Do you think a nation can be a good neighbor if it fears outsiders? Why or why not?

A target Despite natural protection, China has often been attacked by its neighbors. For thousands of years it has feared its neighbors. China has attacked some of these neighbors. In recent decades, China and India have fought along India's northern borders.

You have read about times when China was peaceful and its people prosperous. Often, nomadic tribes looked at the prosperous Chinese with envy. They saw good farms. They saw wealthy city people and fine silks and beautiful pottery. So they came down from the north and west. They attacked the people and destroyed homes and crops.

The Chinese worked to keep out attackers. They built the Great Wall. Emperors kept large armies. But still the attackers came.

The Chinese also saw that their culture was farther advanced than those of the other peoples they met. Their meetings with others influenced the Chinese to believe that their way of life was the most advanced in the world. For a time, they welcomed traders from other lands, since they felt they had nothing to fear. Arab traders and merchants from southeast Asia sailed ships to China's lands.

Tea was picked and sent to Canton, where it was traded to Western merchants. From there, fast clipper ships transported the bales of tea thousands of miles to Europe and America.

East meets West Then in 1516, the first European ships arrived in China. At first, the Chinese welcomed European seamen as they welcomed other foreign merchants. But the Europeans destroyed their own welcome. The Europeans believed that they, not the Chinese, had the most advanced way of life. They robbed and murdered and did not feel guilty. Often they tried to convert the Chinese to Christianity — by force. The Chinese answered by driving the Europeans out by force. They called them Ocean Devils and treated them like pirates.

For the next 200 years, China was ruled by a powerful dynasty. It could welcome European traders or not — as it wished. The Chinese wanted the money that Europeans paid for Chinese goods. There was no way to get this without trade.

So the Chinese reached a compromise. They opened one city — Canton — to the Europeans. Europeans were not allowed into any other ports.

But about 200 years ago, things began to change. China underwent a period of civil war. Its government was weakened. It could no longer throw out the hated Europeans.

China and modern nations Why was China so weakened? One reason was technology. China had not modernized; its enemies had. The soldiers of the emperors fought with spears and rocks. The soldiers of England and Japan fought with modern rifles.

By 1900, China had grown so weak that European nations and Japan were able to take control of much of China. For the first time, China was in the hands of its enemies.

▶ kan′tän

314

In 1911, the Chinese government fell apart. The last emperor resigned, and government by dynasty was over. A republic was founded. But the republic was weak, and China's problems were not yet over. Civil war raged in China. Some people followed the leaders of the republic. Some people followed the leaders of a new group—the Communists. The leaders of the republic believed that China should be modernized. They believed that property should be privately owned. They believed that change was needed, but not too fast.

The Communists, however, believed that China was too old-fashioned to change slowly. They believed that all things, including land and big factories, should be owned by all the Chinese people together. They believed that real change could never come until the majority of people—poor peasants—owned all the land.

For a time, the followers of the republic and the Communists fought together against a frightening enemy: the Japanese. In 1931, Japan conquered Manchuria. Find Manchuria on the map on page 295. In 1937, Japan conquered eastern China. Although both republicans and Communists fought against the Japanese, they could not cooperate with each other.

▶ man chur' ē ə

You have probably read about the great war that took place from 1939 to 1945. Historians called it World War II. When the war was over, Japan had been defeated. But the fight between republicans and Communists continued. The leader of the republicans was Chiang Kai-shek. The leader of the Communists was Mao Tse-tung. In 1949, the republicans retreated to Formosa. Find Formosa on the map on page 295. The Communists took over the mainland.

▶ jē äng' kī' shek'
▶ mau' dzə' dung'

▶ Mainland is the continuing body of land that makes up the main part of a nation.

315

THE CASE OF THE MISSING CASES

It was 1941. A small group of American soldiers stationed in China were being sent home. The Japanese were on the attack. All through northern China the fighting was severe. Japanese dive bombers made travel by train and truck difficult. Slowly the American group made their way towards the coast.

The Americans had with them about two dozen large wooden packing cases. The cases were sealed and none of the soldiers knew what was in them. The boxes were supposed to go with them. But the cases never arrived. The Americans were attacked before they reached the ship. In the confusion, the boxes disappeared and were never again found.

The soldiers might have been surprised to learn that the cases contained nothing but some old bones. But these were not ordinary old bones. They were the remains of about 30 early men who had lived hundreds of thousands of years ago in China. Scientists decided to call people from that time Peking (pē' king') man.

The bones had originally been dug up in the 1920s near Peking. Scientists who examined the bones while they were still in China concluded that Peking man had lived over 375,000 years ago. The scientists thought that Peking man was over five feet tall, almost the size of modern people. Peking man's brain was also almost as large as that of modern man. Scientists believe that these early men lived in small hunting groups and used simple tools.

Scientists had hoped to make a much more careful study of the bones in the United States. But the bones never got here. Most people believe they are still in China. Scientists only hope that the bones will not be buried for another 375,000 years.

COMMUNIST CHINA

The leader of the new government was Mao Tse-tung. He had led the Communist party for many years. They had fought against the Japanese and against the republicans.

Mao Tse-tung is chairman of the Communist party. In both the Soviet Union and China, this is the most important position in the government.

Mao Tse-tung and the Communists completely changed Chinese culture. In a little red book, available all over the world, Mao has printed his thoughts. Here are some of them:

> Every Communist should be a friend of the masses and not a boss over them.
>
> The masses are the real heroes.
>
> Our policy . . . . should rest on our own strength . . . through our own efforts.
>
> There is no construction without destruction.
>
> Destruction . . . means revolution.

Political power grows out of the barrel of a gun.

Read these sayings again. What do the sayings mean? Do you agree that political power grows out of the barrel of a gun? Do you think destruction is always good? Do you think it can be good at times? Do you think Confucius would agree with these statements?

New values   Mao did not believe that China could change if its values remained the same. Mao introduced new values into China. Wealthy people were no longer permitted to keep their wealth. They were no longer permitted to work in the government.

The government was organized around the

Chinese women work in industrial jobs and are an important part of the Chinese army. The poster below calls for national unity. Would you expect to see such a poster in the United States?

全世界无产者同被压迫人民、被压迫民族联合起来，反对

peasants. Peasants met together and decided who would do certain jobs and how much they would be paid for them. The government took away all private property. It brought the peasants together on large farms called communes. It set up schools to teach all the people to read. The government also tried to modernize industry and to teach new ways of working to the people.

The government reorganized the army. It had the army build roads and dams with the help of the people. In addition, it trained its men for fighting.

The government worked hard to replace the ancient Chinese values with Communist values. The Chinese people do not have a choice of candidates at elections. Chinese newspapers cannot print complaints against the government. They cannot quit their jobs or leave the country when they want to.

▶ Do you think Confucian ideas would help or hurt the Communist leaders? Why do you think so?

Yet most of China's huge population has enough to eat. Chinese cities are clean; there are no slums. The most important question about China is, "What has happened to the old values?" Children no longer worship their ancestors. They no longer study Confucius. They are interested in good housing and new clothes, rather than in Buddhism. Are the old values dead, or will they reappear? The thoughts of Confucius lasted 25 centuries. Have the thoughts of Mao replaced them forever?

▶ Can you name any other countries with millions of people? Do they have trouble feeding their citizens? Do they have communist governments?

This is a mystery for the future. Perhaps in your time, you will be able to tell if Mao's government has completely changed China's culture. And maybe you will be able to predict how long Mao's culture will remain unchanged.

This old Japanese picture includes a poem. Both the picture and the poem have the title "Praying for Rain."

JAPAN LOOKS TO CHINA

The power of the clans About the time that Buddhism came to China, Japan was still ruled by many groups of families, called clans. There was an emperor, who was said to be descended from the gods. But the emperor did not have much power. Each of the clans controlled the area close to its home.

The emperors take charge Gradually, the emperors became more powerful. But they had to work hard to gain their power. They sent people loyal to them to China. There they studied the secrets of Chinese greatness. They brought Chinese culture to Japan.

The Japanese emperors welcomed Buddhist monks to settle in Japan. The monks brought with them Chinese methods and inventions. And they brought their religion. Since that time, Buddhism has found a home in Japan.

The shogun takes command The borrowing from China started a flowering of Japanese culture. And it contributed to the glory and power of the Japanese emperors. But some people soon became jealous of the emperors. About 800 years ago, an army general, or shogun, seized power. He allowed the emperor to stay on the throne. But the shoguns ruled for over 700 years after that.

Japan progresses The shoguns always defended their power against the lesser nobles who ruled in local areas. When the shogun was weak, each of the local lords was stronger in his own area. When the shogun was strong, he ruled over the other nobles.

Throughout this long struggle, Japan continued to develop as a nation. Trade grew. Towns became larger and more beautiful. The Japanese developed their own traditions in literature, music, dance, and the theater. By the time European explorers first came to Japan about 500 years ago, they found a culture that was as rich as that of Europe.

Japan keeps out the world European traders and missionaries were allowed into Japan for a short period. But as they became more eager to build their religion and trade, the Japanese rulers grew suspicious. Foreigners were soon excluded from Japan. Foreign ships were chased away from Japanese shores. Even though many Japanese merchants wanted contact and trade, Japan was isolated for hundreds of years.

Another Japanese emperor Isolation caused Japan to fall behind the developing nations of Europe. Many Japanese realized that they had much to learn from the rest of the world. About 100 years ago, the shogun was overthrown and the emperor restored. The Japanese began to modernize their society, government, and industry. They succeeded so fast that they astonished the rest of the world.

1. How has the family been important in traditional China?
2. Explain the importance of Confucianism in traditional China.
3. Why was it possible for the Chinese Communists to gain control of China's government in 1949?

The Land and the People

From break of day
Till sunset glow
I toil.
I dig my well,
I plough my field,
And earn my food
And drink.
What care I
Who rules the land,
If I
Am left in peace?

What do you think these lines mean? Do you think people care who rules them as long as they are left alone?

These lines were written in China thousands of years ago. Yet much of what they say is probably true even today. Most of the Chinese people are farmers. And even in crowded, industrialized Japan, the land is carefully cultivated.

LAND AND THE WAY PEOPLE LIVE

To a great degree, the standard of living of a people depends on their nation's natural resources. Yet there are many nations with limited natural resources and high standards of living. You may already know, for instance, about places like Denmark, Norway, Switzerland, and England.

There are many kinds of land in East Asia. There are mountains and deserts. There are lands that are rolling and fertile. But in much of East Asia, the land has been farmed for thousands of years. The soil is worn, and there is difficulty growing enough food to eat. Look at the maps on pages 324–325. How many people live in China today? How many people live in Japan?

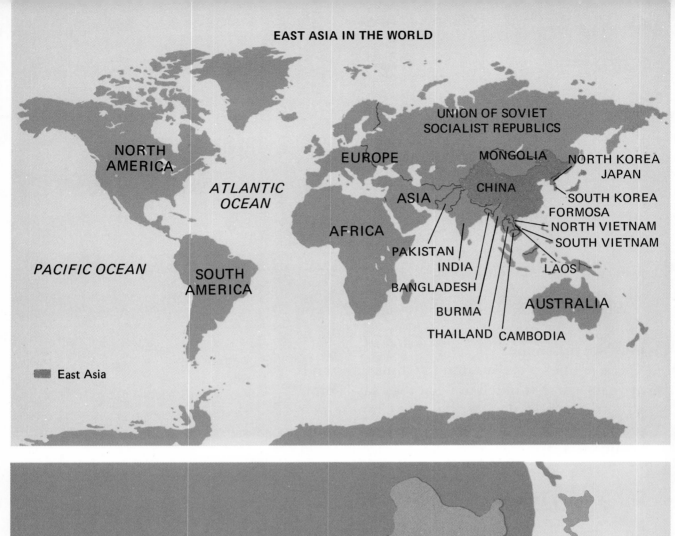

EAST ASIA IN THE WORLD

NORTH AMERICA

ATLANTIC OCEAN

EUROPE

UNION OF SOVIET SOCIALIST REPUBLICS

MONGOLIA

NORTH KOREA
JAPAN
SOUTH KOREA
FORMOSA

CHINA

ASIA

AFRICA

PACIFIC OCEAN

SOUTH AMERICA

PAKISTAN

INDIA

BANGLADESH

BURMA

THAILAND   CAMBODIA

NORTH VIETNAM
SOUTH VIETNAM

LAOS

AUSTRALIA

■ East Asia

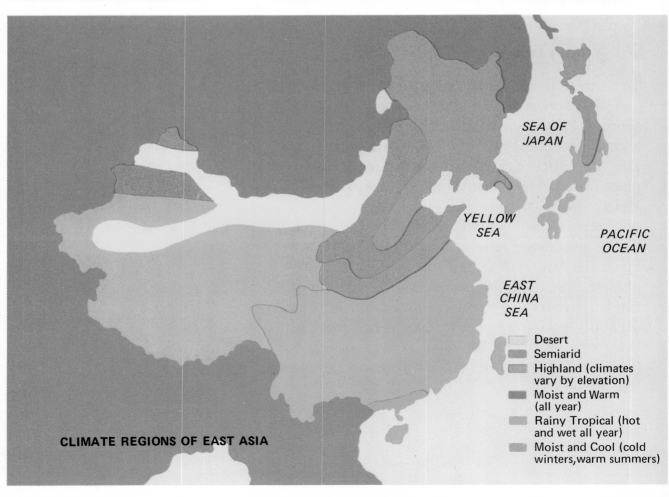

CLIMATE REGIONS OF EAST ASIA

SEA OF JAPAN

YELLOW SEA

PACIFIC OCEAN

EAST CHINA SEA

Desert
Semiarid
Highland (climates vary by elevation)
Moist and Warm (all year)
Rainy Tropical (hot and wet all year)
Moist and Cool (cold winters, warm summers)

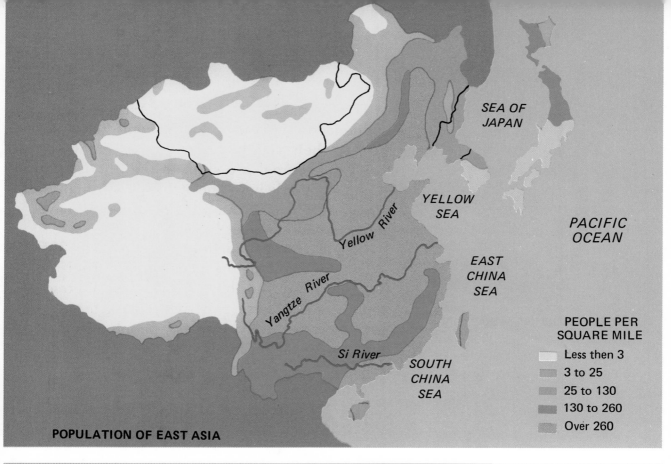

POPULATION OF EAST ASIA

SEA OF JAPAN

YELLOW SEA

PACIFIC OCEAN

Yellow River

Yangtze River

EAST CHINA SEA

Si River

SOUTH CHINA SEA

PEOPLE PER SQUARE MILE
- Less then 3
- 3 to 25
- 25 to 130
- 130 to 260
- Over 260

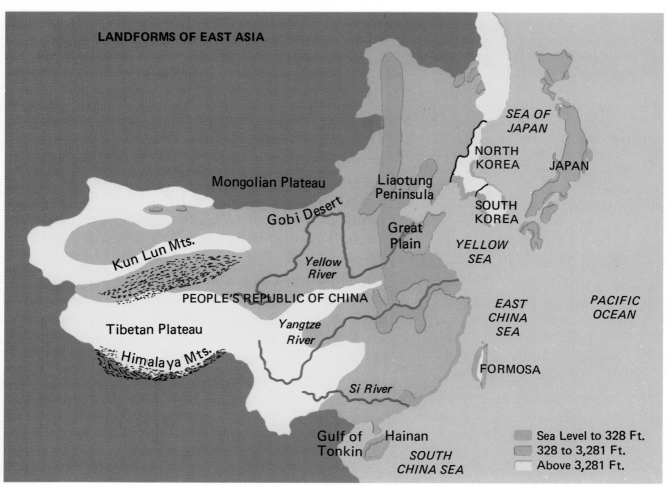

LANDFORMS OF EAST ASIA

SEA OF JAPAN

NORTH KOREA

JAPAN

SOUTH KOREA

Mongolian Plateau

Liaotung Peninsula

Gobi Desert

Great Plain

YELLOW SEA

Kun Lun Mts.

Yellow River

PEOPLE'S REPUBLIC OF CHINA

EAST CHINA SEA

PACIFIC OCEAN

Tibetan Plateau

Yangtze River

Himalaya Mts.

Si River

FORMOSA

Gulf of Tonkin

Hainan

SOUTH CHINA SEA

- Sea Level to 328 Ft.
- 328 to 3,281 Ft.
- Above 3,281 Ft.

The standard of living in East Asia is strongly influenced by the land. Yet people there are raising their standard of living, even where natural resources are slim. In the tiny islands of Japan, people have one of the world's highest standards of living. And in China, people have more to eat than ever before.

Look at the population map on page 325. Where do most of the people live? Find the Yangtze River and the Yellow River and trace their routes. These two rivers mark the area in which the early Chinese people lived. It was here that Chinese history developed. And it is here that most of the Chinese people live today.

THE LANDS OF NORTHERN CHINA

Mud and geography   In the north of China, both the land and the water are muddy yellow. Once yellow was the national color of China, and the emperor was called Lord of the Yellow Land. He even wore yellow robes.

The land and the waters of the Yellow River are yellow because the earth there is yellow. The yellow earth is called loess. Loess is a fertile, dusty soil. In the summer, when there is rain, good crops grow in the loess. But in the winter, when there is little rain, the loess forms a hard crust. In the wind, the crust crumples into yellow dust.

A river changes its route   The Yellow River has changed its route many times. Loess is the reason. Sometimes almost half the river is made up of this yellow mud. As the river moves along, the loess settles on the bottom of the riverbed. What happens when you pile sheets and blankets on a real bed? The bed grows

For thousands of years, the Chinese people have depended on the Yellow River. They have used it as a highway for their boats. And they have built terraces into the hills above the river. The terraces create level patches of land for farming. The terraces also keep the soil from washing into the river.

higher and higher. As loess settles in the Yellow River, the riverbed also grows higher.

Since they began to settle along the banks of the Yellow River, the Chinese people have built dikes to control its waters. In some years, heavy rains have fallen. In these times, the river sometimes rises 40 feet higher than the land surrounding the high walls of the dikes.

Sometimes the dikes break, and the high waters rush out over the land. When this occurs, the land is flooded, sometimes for hundreds of miles.

How does all this change the route of the river? When loess piles up to a high level, it acts like a dam and stops the water from flowing through. The mouth of the river has changed position many times in this way.

Breaks in the dikes have also changed the course of the Yellow River. The water that rushes out of the dike cuts a path through the earth. The river then permanently follows this path.

A river floods Pearl S. Buck has written about the lives of the Chinese along the Yellow River. Mrs. Buck was an American writer who lived almost half of her life in China. This writing is taken from one of her books — *The Good Earth*.

Much of what you will read tells how life *was* in China. In the last 20 years, the government has worked hard to control the Yellow River. Today the river is not as frightening.

The rains, which should have come in early summer withheld themselves. . . . The fields, although Wang Lung cultivated them desperately, were dried and cracked. . . .

▶ Suppose a farmer's land was near the path of a river changing its course. Might the flooding waters cover his land?

▶ What would happen to lands if the river turned far away? Would farmers still have good land?

▶ wäng lung

Month passed into month and still no rain fell. As autumn approached the clouds gathered . . . and in the village street one could see men standing about, . . . their faces upturned to the sky. . . .

From his fields Wang Lung reaped scanty harvest of . . . beans. . . . He set . . . two little boys to sifting the dust of the threshing floor between their fingers after he and the woman had flailed the bean vines, and he shelled the corn upon the floor in the middle room, watching sharply every grain that flew wide. When he would have put the cobs away for fuel, his wife spoke out,

"No — do not waste them in burning. I remember when I was a child in Shantung when years like this came, even the cobs we ground and ate. It is better than grass. . . ."

Wang Lung stood there in his dooryard where year after year he had threshed his good harvest, and which had lain now for many months idle and useless. There was nothing left in the house to feed his [family]. . . .

The years passed, and Wang Lung grew richer. He was able to buy land. In good times, the land along the Yellow River is very fertile because of the loess.

Then it all came to pass as Wang Lung had foreseen. The river to the north burst its dikes. . . . and the river swelled and rolled like a sea over all the good farming land, and the wheat and the young rice were at the bottom of the sea.

One by one the villages were made into islands and men watched the water rising and when it came within two feet of their doorways they bound their tables and beds together and put the doors of their houses upon them for rafts. . . .

There were no harvests of any kind that year and everywhere people starved and were hungry and were angry at what had befallen them yet again. Some went south, and some who were bold and angry . . . joined the robber bands that flourished . . . in the countryside. . . .

▶ What were the little boys doing? Why were they doing it?

▶ shan′ təng′

▶ What do you think the river to the north is?

The pictures here and on the following pages were taken by an American couple who lived on a Chinese commune. They arrived when the people were clearing a new field.

Do you think drought and flooding are a new problem to the Chinese farms? Why would people live in a region that has brought them disaster many times? Do you think the Chinese people would have moved to a better region if they could have?

The Yangtze River is more regular than the Yellow River. It seldom floods. Look at the population map. Do you think more farmers could settle along the Yangtze?

THE LANDS OF SOUTHERN CHINA

The lands of southern China are very different. The climate is warm and damp. There are many

What methods are the commune members using to clear stones from their fields? Do you think that American farmers would use the same methods?

lakes and ponds—and thousands of miles of canals have been built there.

North and south Even in the United States, where trucks and trains speed different kinds of food from one section of the country to another, people often eat the foods that are common in their region. Do you think more people eat lobster in Maine or Missouri? Do you think more people eat grits in Alabama or Alaska? Well, in China, more people eat rice in the south than in the north.

Rice grows well in the wet lands of southern China. The lands are green with growing plants, and the lakes and ponds are full of fish.

▶ If there is a Chinese restaurant near where you live, go in one day and ask the chef about northern and southern China. Find out what people in the north eat. Then find out what people in the south eat. Is your restaurant a northern or a southern restaurant?

▶ In which region—north or south—do you think farming is a safer way of making a living? Check the map on page 325 again? Where do most Chinese people live?

331

The commune has changed stony ground into productive fields. The commune members store the crops they raise and give each family an equal share.

▶ Do you know of any other countries where workers live together on land that they all share equally?

THE LAND AND ITS OWNERS

For thousands of years, China's land was worked by peasant farmers and owned by wealthy landlords. The peasants had enough to eat—when harvests were good. Sometimes, hard-working peasants could save up enough to buy their own land. But this did not happen often.

You have read about the revolution that took place in China more than 20 years ago. This revolution brought about more than a change in government. It brought about a whole new way of life. Land was taken from the landlords. Millions of people were organized into groups to work together on farms. Such farming villages, where the people work together and share their goods, are called communes. Other people were joined into groups working in factories or building dikes.

332

A model commune Sometimes the best way to learn about something is to look closely at a small part of it. We are going to take a close look at one farming commune in China today. It is a model commune. That means that life is better on this commune than in most others in China. Therefore, the government uses it as an example to show outsiders—and as an example to the Chinese themselves. As you read, ask yourself if life is good there. Can you see any things you would not like? Think back to what you have read about Wang Lung. How is life different for the people who live in this commune? How is life the same? Do you think Wang Lung would be happy in this commune?

While the women of the commune work in the fields, their children play in the village.

The model commune is in the province of Shansi. Look at the map on page 334. Find the province of Shansi. What great river is it near? What do you already know about that river?

333

History of the commune In 1945, a small village in Shansi had one landlord, four rich peasant families, and about 70 poor peasant families living in it. The poor families were almost always in debt, since they had to borrow money from their richer neighbors to buy seeds and tools.

Today, that poor village is the model commune we are studying. All the families living there share all the land. They work in a group, called a brigade. The land is owned by the government.

About 420 people or 83 families live in the village and make up the brigade. They have 100 horses and mules, 150 pigs, 400 sheep, and 53 acres of farmland. They also have thousands of fruit and nut trees.

▶ A brigade (bri gād') is a group of persons organized for a certain purpose.

▶ Can you figure out about how large an average family is in the village? Do you think this is large for a country with a population as large as China's?

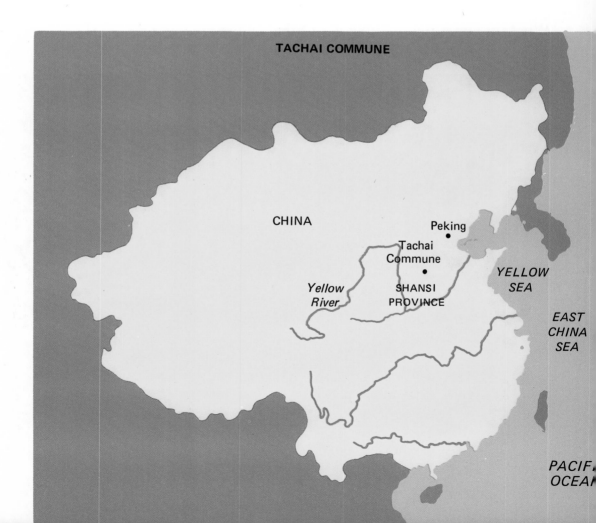

TACHAI COMMUNE

CHINA

Peking

Tachai Commune

Yellow River

SHANSI PROVINCE

YELLOW SEA

EAST CHINA SEA

PACIFIC OCEAN

Floods In 1963, the village suffered seven days of heavy summer rain. The storm destroyed all the terraces and many of the people's homes. But the brigade rebuilt all the homes and terraces without outside help. It is considered a model brigade because of its self-reliance.

Every year the farmers build more stone terraces to prevent another disaster. They now have stone buildings that will not wash away. The farmers build small dams and reservoirs in the terraces. They dig ditches for irrigation in case of drought.

The farmers of the village have a few machines—water pumps, small tractors, and bulldozers. Once mules carried stones and fertilizer to the top of the village's slopes. Now machines that work like ski lifts do this.

Each family in the commune is allowed a small piece of land for itself. They buy things they do not get from the land or from the commune at the commune store.

The commune also has small workshops, like this of the blacksmith.

Families live in small houses. Most of the houses are new, though they have few rooms. Some houses have electricity, but there are few appliances. Most families own a few chickens for themselves, but the rest of the livestock belongs to the brigade. The people farm wheat, corn, vegetables, and fruit and nut trees for the brigade. They share everything but the chickens. They grow almost everything they eat. They even have grain stored for emergencies.

The brigade has three shops—a bookstore, a general store, and a clothing and shoe store. What used to be the landlord's home is now a hospital.

Life is not this regular on all communes. But the commune system has worked in many parts of China. Think of the problems of China: many people, not enough good land, and often droughts and floods. Do you think a group of individuals could work well together to overcome these problems? Do you think it is more important to have freedom to own private land or to be united to improve the land?

Geography influences agriculture, industry, and trade. We have talked about farmers in China because China is primarily agricultural. There is also, of course, industry and trade in China.

In Japan, on the other hand, industry and trade are more important than agriculture. Try to discover the geographic reasons for this.

JAPAN

The Japanese live in a mountainous land surrounded by ocean. Only about 20 percent of Japan can be farmed. Because of this, the

Life on the commune is hard. Women work in the fields and workshops and still have housework to do. There are always new projects like this greenhouse. After their work was done, the members of the commune put on their best clothes for a party honoring their American guests.

A GEOGRAPHIC PUZZLE

In one brigade farmers working together have reclaimed land once covered by large stones. The area where the brigade was working was famous for the tea grown there. But on this land, the brigade departed from a 4,600-year-old tradition—it grew rice instead of tea.

A visitor asked the brigade leader, "For generations your people have planted and harvested tea; there is nothing you don't know about it, and the climate here is ideal. Why not stay with the thing you know, and buy your rice from places where it is more easily grown?"

"If we did that, the nation would have to provide us with rice" answered the brigade leader. "We do not want to be a burden to the rest of our people."

"Not at all, since you would be delivering tea, which is more valuable . . . because it can be sold abroad. . . ."

"You don't understand," the brigade leader argued. "We are following the words of Chairman Mao. He says that everyone must store away food reserves for use in case of war."

With whom do you agree? Why? What would a general decide? an economist?

Japanese farm intensively—that is, they grow as much as possible on as little land as possible. How would that help solve the problem? Name methods by which the Japanese have learned to farm their mountainous lands.

It is natural, though, that the Japanese have turned to the sea to add to their livelihood. Japan leads the world in shipbuilding, fishing, and whaling. It builds more ships and catches more whales and fish than any other country, including the United States and the Soviet Union. Its 104 million people eat such foods as raw fish and seaweed—unusual foods to most people, but proof that the Japanese people depend on the sea.

Do some research. Find out how many of Japan's people live by the sea. Is the sea really necessary to Japan?

Japanese industry When you go home, ask your parents how many things that you own are Japanese. Look at the chart on page 341. Do you own a Japanese camera, a Japanese car, or a Japanese television? How could a country with very few resources become one of the most industrialized nations on the earth? There are many reasons. Japan has little room for farming, but it has many streams and rivers to provide hydroelectric power. It also has plenty of coal for energy. Hydroelectric power and coal are basic ingredients for industry. Why?

Japanese industry today Industry and trade have been extremely successful. Japan is now the world's second-largest automobile manufacturer (after the United States). It is third in steel production (after the United States and the Soviet Union). This means that there are a

Japan was a poor nation one hundred years ago. But it has become one of the most modern nations in the world. Farming, industry, and exports have helped Japan move ahead.

lot of factories in Japan. Though Japan is a very small country, its capital, Tokyo, is the largest city on the earth.

Look at the chart below. What is Japan's biggest import? What reason can you suggest for this? What are other major Japanese imports? What do you think such imports are used for? What are Japan's biggest exports? Which of these are manufactured products?

Imports (billions of $)		Exports (billions of $)	
Textile material	1.0	Cars and trucks	1.3
Oil	2.2	Ships	1.4
Machinery	2.3	Televisions and radios	1.5
Food	2.6	Textiles	2.4
Ore and scrap metal	3.0	Finished metals	3.8

Since 1945, both China and Japan have gone through many changes. In less than 25 years, the people of these two ancient nations have completely turned around their ways of life. China and Japan show how the worst problems of history and geography can be overcome by a people open to change.

1. In which region of China do the most people live? Explain why most Chinese people live in this region.

2. Explain the commune system in China.

3. Discuss how Japan has become an industrialized nation.

Case Study:
The Modernization of Japan

A MODERN FAMILY

Let's look at a modern Japanese family, the Ono family. Grandfather, father and mother, and Michi, their son, live together in a four-room apartment in Tokyo. The walls between the rooms are not much thicker than paper. The family can easily hear the people in the next apartment. There are modern appliances in the kitchen. A small color television set is in the living room. The living room is also used as Michi's bedroom.

Grandfather Ono fought in China during World War II. He was an old soldier who volunteered to serve the emperor. He never questioned an order. He fought for the honor and glory of Japan and the emperor.

Mr. Ono works in a large chemical plant. He is an office manager. The plant was small when he first started working there after the war. It grew tremendously because of the great demand for chemicals. Now it is a huge company. Its owners travel to New York and Europe and Africa to do business.

Mr. Ono is willing to work hard, but he does not have much work to do at the plant. The company never fires anyone, so there are many people to do the work. Loyalty is an important idea in Japan. Workers are thought of as children of the company; a company would never fire its children.

Mrs. Ono is from the country, where her father was a messenger for the government. Her marriage to Mr. Ono was arranged by their families before the war, when she was very young. She was taught to obey and respect her husband.

Mrs. Ono is troubled. Her son, Michi, shows

▶ Is this how employees are treated in American companies?

343

▶ What values is the grandfather talking about? What
does he mean by the "ancient
soil"?

no respect for his elders. He stays out late and belongs to the Communist party at his university. Father says Michi will get tired of it, but the family is not in harmony. Mother prays every morning.

Michi himself is not content. He feels cramped in their little apartment. He is bored with his father, who admires money so much. He does not bother to listen to his grandfather. His grandfather is always complaining about "lack of values" and "lack of purpose." He says Japan has not been the same since the war. "Once we knew who we were. We were the twigs of a mighty tree, rooted in ancient soil. Now the tree has fallen."

This bores Michi. He pulls on his cowboy boots and leaves the house.

What are the main problems of the Ono family? What is the difference between Michi and his grandfather? How are times changing in Japan?

THE BEGINNINGS OF MODERNIZATION

The modernization of Japan began in the early twentieth century. Japan's rulers were interested in learning from foreign countries. They modernized the Japanese army and government methods along Western lines. They encouraged trade and industry. They knew what they wanted. They wanted to catch up with the West. They wanted to have wealth and power, just like the United States and Europe. They were very successful. Increased trade made the nation richer. Small businesses grew into large industries, with jobs for everyone. The rulers felt, "We are a small island in a big world; we have been isolated a long time. We

Japanese families are often stricter than American families. Parents still arrange marriages for their children. But some Japanese young people have rejected the ideas of their parents and their government.

▶ Are you taught these things? Why were these things taught to Japanese children? What was the purpose of their education? In what ways would this kind of education help to modernize Japan?

must study and pull hard together to be strong."

The rulers built many schools. By 1905 about 95 percent of the children your age were in school. That is a greater percentage than in many countries today.

Besides regular subjects, Japanese children were taught discipline, loyalty to their emperor and their country, and respect for authority.

JAPAN'S ECONOMY TODAY

Japan's economy has changed a great deal in the last 25 years. You can see how much the economy has changed by studying statistics. Statistics are numbers that state facts. Statistics can tell you the value of all the goods and services produced in a country in a year. If you spend $15 for a pair of shoes, you are spending $15 for goods. If you pay the doctor $20, you spend $20 for services.

Gross national product If you add up all the goods and all the services produced in a country in a year, you have the GNP. The GNP is the gross national product. The GNP shows how big the economy is.

	GNP (in billions of dollars)	
	JAPAN	USA
1955	$ 25.0	$398.0
1960	45.0	503.7
1965	91.0	684.9
1970	198.0	976.4

1. Which country had a larger GNP in 1970?
2. Which country doubled its GNP between 1960 and 1965?

3. Which country's economy seems to be growing faster?

Agriculture The next chart tells what percentage of the working population in Japan are farmers.

FARMING POPULATION	
1962	24.7%
1969	18.0
1971	11.0

1. Were there more or fewer farmers in 1971 than in 1962?
2. Do you think this is a sign that more people are working in industries?
3. Does it mean Japan is growing less food?

Read these statistics before you make up your mind.

RICE PRODUCTION	
1947	9,800,000 tons
1965	12,409,000
1970	12,700,000

Growing rice requires skilled and patient labor. Workers must pull weeds by hand. They also must thin the plants.

Japan used to import 15 to 20 percent of its rice. Today it exports rice. How do you explain the fact that fewer farmers are producing more rice?

Japan produces more rice per square mile than almost any other country. That is important to Japan because it has to feed 536 people per square mile. The United States has only 57 people per square mile. Do American farmers have to be as efficient as Japanese farmers? What are some other effects of having so many people per square mile?

Japan has a low birth rate. The population grows only about 1.1 percent a year. Is a low birth rate good for a crowded country? Why or why not?

Economic achievements Today Japan is the world's leading shipbuilding nation. It catches more fish and whales than any other country. It is the world's third-largest steel producer and second-largest automobile producer. It conducts a great amount of trade with China — one of the world's largest nations. About three-fourths of Japanese families have washing machines. About 92 percent have televisions.

Reasons for growth Japan had some special advantages that explain these economic achievements.

In the 1950s, the cost of labor in Japan was very low. Many people were unemployed. Do people without jobs demand a lot of money for their work? How do you think Japanese businesses profited from unemployment?

Today, the Japanese government spends very little money on defense. Less than 2 percent of its income goes toward defense. The United States spends about 30 percent of its

▶ The birth rate is a statistic that tells you how many babies are born for every 1,000 people in the population.

▶ Why is China a good country to trade with?

income on defense. What can Japan do with the money that might have been spent on defense?

The people of Japan are eager to work and are loyal to their employers. Many Japanese workers, like Mr. Ono, can depend upon lifetime employment. At some factories, workers have a company song or a pep cheer.

CHANGES AND PROBLEMS

Today, however, Japan is changing. Some of the country's economic advantages no longer exist.

Labor costs As you remember, Mr. Ono's company never fired anyone. Japan today has more workers than are necessary. This means that companies have to pay wages to workers they do not need. Weaving a silk scarf, for example, costs a company two or three times as much in Japan as in Italy — because of the extra workers.

Trade Japan sells most of its goods to the United States, Western Europe, and China. But up until now, Japan has not let these countries sell many goods in Japan. These countries are beginning to pressure the Japanese. Soon Japan will have to let in more foreign goods. Then Japanese industries will have more competition. What will they have to do to meet this competition? What do you think will happen to the price of goods in Japan?

A crowded, polluted country Many things are wrong with Japan today. The Ono family lives in a cramped apartment. Outside their window, the city is noisy and smelly. Factories and cars spread pollution.

▶ How do you think lifetime employment affects the loyalty of Japanese workers to their companies?

▶ Why do you think these countries want to sell goods in Japan?

Pollution is a tremendous problem in Japan today. The government of Japan and the Japanese people are trying to find ways to deal with the pollution problem. The following newspaper article reveals how a 15-year-old Japanese boy would solve the problem of pollution. The newspaper article is an interview between the boy and Eisaku Sato, who was premier of Japan until 1972.

UTSUNOMIYA, Japan, September 21 — Premier Eisaku Sato pledged to a 15-year-old high school boy today that he would not permit industrial growth at the cost of polluting the environment and spoiling the lives of the people.

Mr. Sato came to this city 60 miles north of Tokyo to conduct a one-day hearing on environmental problems.

The schoolboy was one of seven questioners selected from 71 citizens in the region who had expressed their desire to air their views at the hearing.

A calm figure in a neat black school uniform, the youth ticked off the evils of pollution point after point, as well as the failure of the government to do anything. He asked, "Isn't the government treating the people more or less as livestock?" The audience of 1,000 residents and 200 newsmen burst into laughter and applause.

If he were premier, he said, he would set up a government department of environmental problems. "But since we trust the government, we are asking you to do these things, and to protect nature, to protect our lives and our families from environmental problems."

Hardly a day passes in these narrow islands without a newspaper or television story on pollution of some kind, whether it be smog from automobile exhaust or lead poisoning from factory wastes, or dead or deformed fish dredged up from polluted rivers, lakes, or seas.

Every political party has seized on pollution as a way in which to criticize the government.

"This is my public pledge," Sato said, looking directly at the high school student. "You can say, this is what Sato said, and you can hold me responsible for it. Industry exists for us, not we for industry."

In his opening speech, Mr. Sato reviewed Japan's astonishing economic growth during the last 10 years.

This fast growth was accompanied by an increasing number of people crowding into urban areas, by mountains of industrial and other waste, and by pollution.

The Premier's speech was his strongest statement on pollution to date. As for the high school student, he told reporters after the hearing that he had enjoyed the opportunity to come into direct contact with politicians, but that he had hoped for more specific answers.

Visitors to Japan today can hardly believe it is the same country they saw pictures of in 1945. In less than 25 years, Japan has rebuilt itself into a modern and respected nation. A land without great resources has shown the world how a country can peacefully grow into an industrial power. But, along with the high school student, the world must ask itself what price we are willing to pay for this kind of industrial growth.

1. How is the Ono family like your family? How is the Ono family different from your family?

2. Name some problems that have been brought about by Japan's rapid industrial growth.

INVESTIGATING THE UNIT

Doing Research

Imagine that you have an assignment from a major national magazine to report on Chinese schools and students. Before you go to China, you want to gather background information for your story. What kind of information would you need? Where might you find it? Go and consult some of these sources. How does this background contribute to an understanding of your subject?

Looking at the Evidence

Find out what life was like for Chinese peasants before the Communist revolution. Is life better or worse for the peasants now? What advantages do Chinese peasants have now that they did not have before? What do they lack that Americans take for granted?

Compare and Contrast

Imagine you are an official from the People's Republic of China on a study visit to the United States. You are taken to a car factory in Detroit, to Wall Street in New York City, and to the Capitol in Washington, D.C. What might you see in these places? What contrasts and comparisons might you make with China?

Using Maps

You are an official of an American company that has just sold a large amount of wheat to China. Only people in the northern part of China use wheat in their diet. Can you find three or four large seaports in that part of China where you can unload your grain? Check a population map to see if these ports will get your grain to a large part of the Chinese population. Look at a climate map and temperature chart. Will the ports be free of ice all year?

Reading on Your Own

Here are two books that will tell you more about the land and the people of modern China: Hal Buell, *The World of Red China* (New York, Dodd, Mead); and Cornelia Spencer, *The Land of the Chinese People* (Philadelphia, J. B. Lippincott).

AFRICA

God bless Africa, / Bless its leaders.
Let Wisdom, Unity, and Peace be the shield of Africa and its people.
Bless Africa, / Bless Africa,
Bless the children of Africa.

FROM THE NATIONAL ANTHEM OF TANZANIA

Yesterday and Today

For hundreds of years, many people believed that Africa had no culture. They believed that the way of life in Africa was less developed than the way of life in Europe and America.

Yet Africa has hundreds of cultures, some of them very old. Why did people outside the continent not know about African cultures? If you look at the map of Africa on page 356, you will see that Africa is almost entirely surrounded by water. Most Europeans did not have ships large enough to travel to Africa. So the only way for most people to reach Africa was across land.

▶ Why would ships have had to be very large to travel from Europe to Africa?

Scholars know quite a lot about the cultures north of the Sahara Desert. This area is quite close to Europe and Asia. Find Egypt on the map. Can you think of one reason why scholars know about the history of Egypt? People have lived south of the Sahara Desert for just as long as they have lived in Egypt. Yet much less is known about these southern people.

▶ sə här′ ə

In many places in the world, scholars can learn much about past cultures by examining things that have been buried in the ground. Often broken tools and household goods can show how a people lived and what they used.

▶ How would the Sahara Desert affect people who wanted to travel in Africa?

But in most of the lands south of the Sahara Desert, insects destroyed much that was buried. Few buried artifacts have survived. How does this affect what we know about these cultures?

▶ An artifact (är′ tə fakt) is any material object that people use as a part of their culture.

The African cultures that scholars know most about are the ones that used writing. Most of these cultures used Arabic, the language of the Arabs of North Africa. Many Africans who came in contact with the Arabs learned to use the Arabic language and system of writing. Wherever this writing was used, there are records

▶ ar′ ə bik

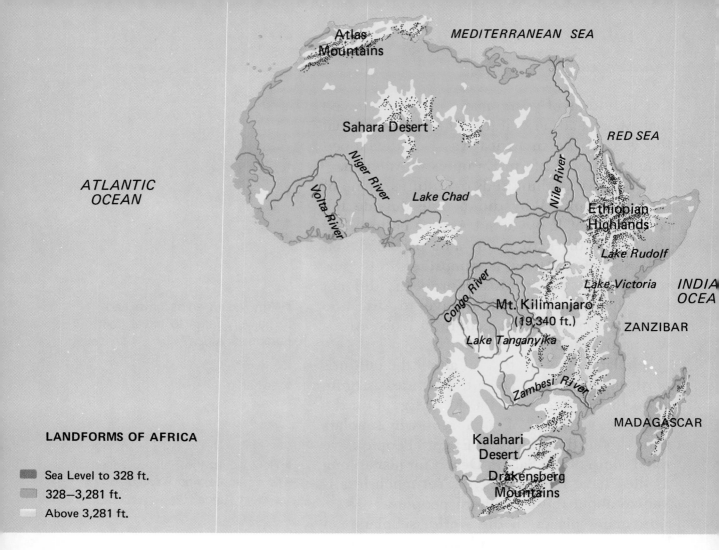

ATLANTIC
OCEAN

MEDITERRANEAN SEA

Atlas
Mountains

Sahara Desert

RED SEA

Niger River

Volta River

Lake Chad

Nile River

Ethiopian
Highlands

Lake Rudolf

Congo River

Lake Victoria

INDIAN
OCEA

Mt. Kilimanjaro
(19,340 ft.)

ZANZIBAR

Lake Tanganyika

Zambesi River

MADAGASCAR

Kalahari
Desert

Drakensberg
Mountains

LANDFORMS OF AFRICA

Sea Level to 328 ft.

328–3,281 ft.

Above 3,281 ft.

that can tell modern scholars about the past cultures of Africa.

CULTURES IN CONTACT

Scholars have found out enough about different African cultures to learn that many of them had a great deal of contact with one another. How do cultures come into contact? Three ways in which cultures come into contact are through warfare, trade, and religion.

Patterns of warfare The map on page 358 shows the main centers of African culture from ancient times to the nineteenth century. The arrows on the map show the main patterns of warfare in Africa. Look at the patterns of warfare in North Africa. What directions do they go in? It is hard for armies to cross mountains and deserts. Soldiers cannot find the food or water they need there. How do the geographical features of North Africa explain the main patterns of warfare in this region?

South of Egypt, the arrows follow the Nile River. The Nile has large stretches of rough water and rapids called cataracts. Look again at the map on page 358. Name two cultures in this area of northeastern Africa. These cultures were not easy to conquer or control. What geographical features can you find in the area that would explain this?

◗ kat′ ə rakts

Hundreds of years ago, Arab traders sailed from the east coast of Africa to India in boats like these.

357

▶ mäl'ē

▶ sông' hī

▶ Why do you think rain forests are called by that name? What do you think a rain forest looks like?

The cultures along the north coast of Africa were conquered over and over again. Armies marched along the same routes that other armies had followed hundreds of years before. They set up kingdoms in the same places.

Just below the Sahara, in the western part of Africa, were a group of large African kingdoms. Some of these kingdoms, like Mali and Songhai, were as large as the whole continent of Europe.

The great kingdoms of West Africa never conquered the lands of rain forests to the south of them. The rain forests were too strange and dangerous.

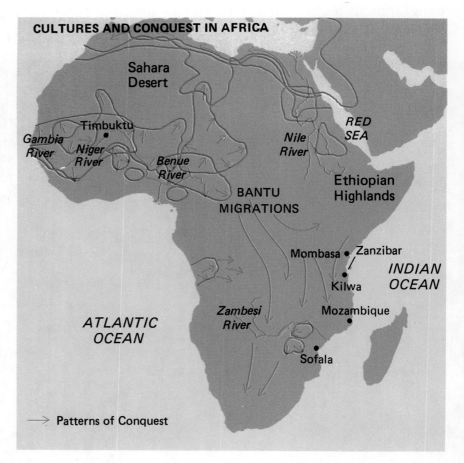

CULTURES AND CONQUEST IN AFRICA

But there were many cultures in these lands. And some of these cultures were very old and had developed greatly. The people of Benin, for example, were skilled workers who built large and beautiful cities.

◆ be nin'

Patterns of trade The kingdoms of western Africa were rich. Their wealth came partly from the huge caravans that they sent north through the desert. But they also traded within their own area. Look at the trade map on this page. What products were traded in western Africa? Where did these products go?

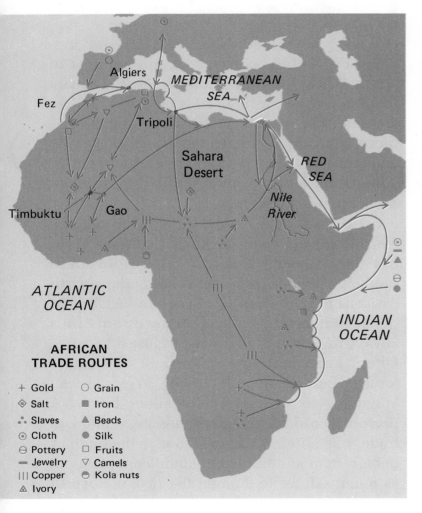

AFRICAN TRADE ROUTES

- + Gold
- ◈ Salt
- ∴ Slaves
- ⊙ Cloth
- ⊖ Pottery
- — Jewelry
- ||| Copper
- △ Ivory
- ○ Grain
- ■ Iron
- ▲ Beads
- ● Silk
- □ Fruits
- ▽ Camels
- ◓ Kola nuts

Many activities go on in African marketplaces. What do you think is the most important activity? Can you think of any others?

▶ Why do you think people travel together when crossing the desert? Does it remind you of how people crossed the western frontier of the United States?

▶ An oasis (ō ā' sis) is a patch of trees and shrubs in the desert. It is usually watered by underground wells or streams.

▶ Can you think of one reason why West Africans and people of the rain forests did not talk to each other?

▶ A tribe is a group of people who speak the same language and follow the same rules and customs.

Trade also helped these West African kingdoms come into contact with the cultures of North Africa. The trade routes across the Sahara had been used for thousands of years. Traders crossed the desert in caravans. Sometimes these caravans included thousands of people and camels. They might travel for months, going from oasis to oasis, until they reached their final destination.

Look again at the trade map. What did the North Africans bring south with them? What did they take back north? Where did these products finally go? What did the North Africans get in return for these products?

The rain forest people of southwestern Africa always traded with the people closest to them. Often, trade between the people of the rain forests and the people of the West African kingdoms took the form of silent barter. A person would leave something he wanted to trade, like an elephant tusk, out in the open. A person from another **tribe** would come and put as much salt as he thought the tusk was worth beside it. If the owner of the tusk thought the deal was fair, he would take the salt. If he did not think the deal was fair, he would wait until more salt was offered.

Most of Africa did not trade directly with Europe. The people of North Africa acted as go-betweens or **middlemen** in this trade. Naturally, they made a profit from it. For centuries, they believed that it would be better for them if no one else could trade across the desert. So they acted as a barrier between Europe and Asia and the rest of Africa.

Patterns of religion About 1,400 years ago, a new religion began in Arabia and swept across northern Africa. It was called Islam. The followers of Islam, called Moslems, believed in one god, whom they called Allah. They believed that one of Allah's commands was to convince other people to become Moslems. Therefore, wherever the Moslems traveled or traded, they brought their religion with them.

Look at the religion map on page 362. What areas of North Africa did Islam spread to?

▶ Middlemen are the people who buy goods and then sell them to other people. A store-owner is a kind of middleman. Can you think of any other types of middlemen?

▶ Islam (is läm′) means "the way of Allah (al′ ə)."
▶ moz′ ləmz

▶ How does the spread of Islam compare to the patterns of conquest and trade in Africa? How are trade, conquest, and religion related in North Africa?

Today, Islam is the fastest-growing religion in Africa. About one out of every four Africans is Moslem.

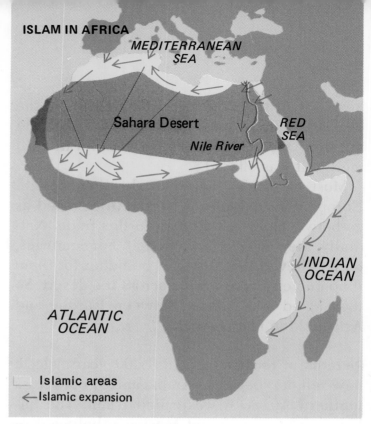

ISLAM IN AFRICA

MEDITERRANEAN SEA

Sahara Desert

Nile River

RED SEA

INDIAN OCEAN

ATLANTIC OCEAN

Islamic areas
←Islamic expansion

AN AFRICAN KINGDOM

The West African kingdom of Mali is one African kingdom that scholars know a great deal about. Mali became a kingdom about 800 years ago.

For much of its history, Mali was ruled by Moslem kings. So Moslem traders and travelers from North Africa, the Middle East, and even India found that they could travel and trade there safely.

A famous traveler One of the most famous Moslem travelers to Mali was a man named Ibn Battuta, who lived 600 years ago. Ibn Battuta was a world traveler. On the backs of camels, donkeys, and horses, on foot, and in ships, he traveled thousands of miles in Africa, the Middle East, and India. On one of his journeys, he set out across the Sahara Desert. After more than two months of travel, he reached the court of the king of Mali. Here is what he saw:

▶ ibn ba tü′ tä

362

On certain days the king gathers some of his people in the palace yard. There is a platform for him there, covered with silk. Over it is a silk umbrella with a large bird made entirely of gold on it.

The king comes out of a door in a corner of the palace. On his head is a golden skullcap. He usually wears a red tunic of an expensive foreign cloth. In front of the king march his musicians with their instruments of gold and silver. Behind the king are 300 armed slaves.

The king walks slowly. When he takes his seat, the drums, trumpets, and bugles are sounded. A slave runs to get the commanders of the army. The rest of the people stand in the street under the trees.

Modern Americans might not be impressed by the display of the Mali king. But Ibn Battuta was. He had traveled far and seen dozens of kingdoms. But he had never seen a kingdom quite like Mali.

A kingdom based on trade For hundreds of years, Mali had supplied much of the world with gold. Huge caravans brought the precious metal across the Sahara. The caravans might be gone for months at a time. When they came

▶ A tunic (tü′nik) is a long slip-on robe or gown.

▶ What expensive metal is mentioned in Ibn Battuta's report? Where do you think the people of Mali got it from?

▶ What do you think Ibn Battuta found in Mali that impressed him so much?

Almost 500 years ago, Europeans thought Africa was a very rich continent. This map, drawn around 1500, reflects this attitude.

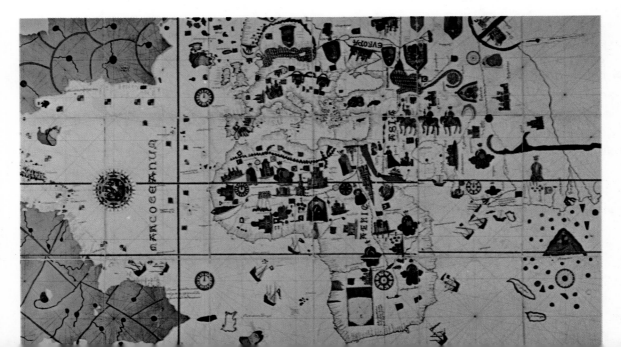

SALT—AS GOOD AS GOLD

Salt, that ordinary stuff you sprinkle on eggs and meat, is a mysterious substance. Scientists know that salt is really a combination of two things—a gray metal called sodium and a poisonous green gas called chlorine. But the real mystery of salt goes even deeper. This combination of metal and gas is not only a good food-flavorer, it is also something that people cannot live without. People who do not get enough salt will become sick.

Luckily, salt is plentiful and cheap in most parts of the world. There are some places, though, where salt is hard to find. One of these places is West Africa. In the days before airplanes could bring food to all parts of the world, salt was a very precious item in West Africa. Traders were as anxious to get salt as they were to get gold! Are people often willing to pay a great deal of money for something that is necessary, but hard to get? Can you think of some examples?

Even today, in our language, we can find evidence of the value of salt. For example, if you're worth your salt, you'll be able to figure out where that expression comes from.

back, they carried expensive cloth, pottery, jewelry, and salt from faraway places.

Wherever Ibn Battuta traveled in Mali, he found the people friendly and helpful. In every Mali village, he bought the local food—grain pounded up and mixed with honey or milk. Ibn Battuta did not like this dish very much. He preferred the fish he could buy when he was near a river. In the market towns, he could buy fruits and grains from all over the kingdom. He could even get dates and figs that came from his own country over a thousand miles away.

To pay for his food, Ibn Battuta carried a bag of salt with him. Salt was so valuable in Mali that it was used as money. Salt was even more valuable than gold!

Trading for gold Ibn Battuta found that gold was all over the kingdom. Women in many Mali

▶ Do you think water is very valuable? Would it be more valuable in a desert community? Can you guess why salt is so valuable in Mali?

In what ways do you think these modern African women use streams and rivers?

villages found it in streams of water. They put some of the sand from the stream in a shallow basin and swirled it around. Gold was usually heavier than anything else in the basin. So it settled to the bottom of the basin. If the women found any large chunks of gold, or nuggets, they had to give these to the king. But the tiny grains of gold they could keep for themselves.

It was Mali's gold that the traders from the other side of the desert wanted more than anything else. To get it, they would bring to Mali all kinds of beautiful things from far away — cloth, beads, and jewelry. The important people in the cities of Mali used these foreign goods. When Ibn Battuta ate with the wealthy merchants or scholars of Mali, he found that they had beautiful cups and bowls of brass. The men of Mali wore rich, brocaded clothes. The women, too, had rich clothes and jewelry.

In the hot afternoons, the ladies sat with their friends in large, cool houses. There, they might sit on thick rugs listening to musicians. In the evenings, people visited with their friends.

The people of Mali   Ibn Battuta had noticed that there was a difference between the people of Mali and other peoples. In his travels, he had come to expect to be robbed and cheated everywhere. But in Mali, things were different. Ibn Battuta found:

1. There are very few mean or unfair acts done here. That is because the people of Mali hate anything that is not good and honest. Their king will pardon no one who does a bad act.
2. The land is safe for any traveler. A traveler is as safe in the streets here as he would be at home. He never has to worry that he will

▶ Brocaded clothes have raised designs on them in silver and gold.

▶ If Ibn Battuta had written about this rich African kingdom over 600 years ago, why didn't Europeans know about it?

366

be robbed or that someone will harm his wife or daughters.

3. If a man from another land dies in this country, they do not take his money or possessions. They order one person to take care of them until the dead man's family or friends can come and get them.

The end of Mali A little over a hundred years after Ibn Battuta visited it, Mali was conquered by a neighboring kingdom. Some of Mali's cities were destroyed during this invasion. But others managed to survive and hold onto much of their old wealth. For more than a century, these cities kept up their age-old trade routes.

THE COMING OF THE EUROPEANS

Europeans had known little of Africa for over a thousand years. The Arabs who lived in North Africa had carefully guarded their trade routes through the Sahara. It was not until the Europeans learned more about navigation and sailing that they were able to sail down the coast of Africa.

The remaining cities of Mali were eventually conquered, too. An invading army came from the kingdom of Morocco, a thousand miles across the desert.

▶ Can you think of a reason why the Arabs may have done this?

▶ Look at the map on page 358. Does sailing down Africa's west coast help Europeans avoid North Africa?

▶ Look at the map again. Why do you think the Portuguese were the first Europeans to sail to Africa?

About 500 years ago, the Europeans invented a new type of steering oar and new types of sails With these they could sail against the wind more easily Would that help them go down the coast of Africa?

The winds on the coast of West Africa blow from south to north. Look at the map of Africa. Would the winds help the Europeans coming down the coast?

The first European traders The first country whose ships sailed far down the African coast was Portugal. These first sailors were looking for a new eastward route to India. And within a few years, they had found it. But they also found things of value on the coast of Africa. Gold and ivory were certainly things worth returning for. There was a demand for gold

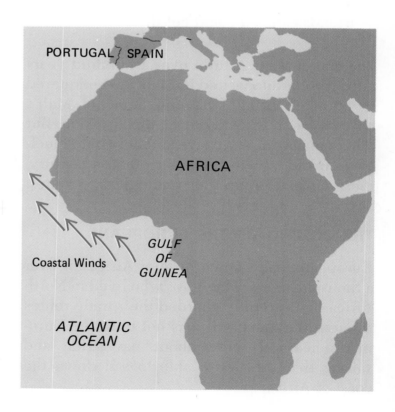

When Europeans first came to Africa, they treated their hosts with great respect. This picture shows Dutch traders kneeling before the king of the Congo.

throughout Europe. And ivory could be carved into beautiful things. But, in a matter of years after the Portuguese first sailed to Africa, they found an even more profitable object to trade.

THE SLAVE TRADE

Slavery had existed throughout Africa long before the coming of Europeans. Some slaves, usually those taken as prisoners in wars, were treated harshly and sold like pieces of property. This kind of slavery is called **chattel slavery**.

But most slaves within Africa were not treated this way. Many of them were trusted servants. Sometimes slaves even became trusted government officials. Many of them got the chance to buy their freedom. Slavery of this kind is called **domestic slavery**.

◗ Chattel (chat′ l) means movable possessions.

The European slave trade was much crueler. To the Europeans or Americans, an African slave was just a piece of property. When an African was captured, he could be treated as cruelly as his owner cared to treat him.

Capturing slaves The Europeans did not like the tropical heat and dangerous swamps of the African coast. So, very early in the slave trade, they began to depend on the African people along the coast to get their slaves for them. In return for the slaves, the Europeans would trade beads, cloth, iron bars, and guns.

The slaves traded to the Europeans usually did not come from the coast. Instead, coastal people captured or bought these slaves from inland people. Sometimes the slaves had to march for many days. During this march the slaves were chained together.

▶ Why do you think the slaves were chained together?

Here is one account of the slave trade. It was written by a slave.

My father had many slaves and a large family. I was the youngest son and my mother's favorite. From the time that I was very young I was trained to be a warrior. I learned how to shoot with a bow and arrow and throw the javelin.

▶ A javelin (jav′ ə lin) is a light spear.

When the adults of our village went away to work in the fields, we children used to play together in the houses. One of us used to stay up in a tree watching for men of other tribes who might want to kidnap us and take us into slavery. One time it was my turn to watch. I saw some stranger prowling around the village and ran to tell the biggest boys. They held the man until our parents came from the fields.

But when I was about 11 years old, I was not so lucky. A man crept up behind me and put his hand over my mouth so that I could not cry out. Then he carried me off and sold me in a far-off town. I was sold to many different people and

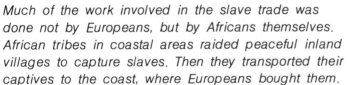

Much of the work involved in the slave trade was done not by Europeans, but by Africans themselves. African tribes in coastal areas raided peaceful inland villages to capture slaves. Then they transported their captives to the coast, where Europeans bought them.

371

carried to many strange lands far from home. About six months after I had been kidnapped, I was taken to the sea coast. There I first saw the sea and a sailing ship. I was terrified when I was thrown on the ship and tossed around by the sailors. I found out later that they were just testing to see if I was healthy enough to make the trip. But at the time, I was convinced they were going to cook me in the big iron pot they had boiling on the deck. I was sure they were going to eat me right then.

At last they put us down below the deck of the ship. The ship started to sail. I had no room to move. It smelled so bad and I was so afraid that I soon became sick. I wished I were dead. Some of the other slaves tried to jump overboard and drown themselves. But they were usually caught and beaten. The sailors tried to make me eat. But when I refused, they beat me badly, too. After months of beatings and sickness, we finally came to a new land. There I met some old slaves who told me that I would not be beaten. I would just have to work. I decided to work hard enough to buy my freedom.

Slaves in the New World Once the slaves arrived in the New World, there was almost no hope for freedom. Usually, they were slaves all their lives. And their children were slaves, too. Many were so cruelly treated that they died within a few years. Of the slaves who managed to win their freedom in the New World, very few found their way back to Africa. Instead, they spent their lives in a strange new land.

The effect of the slave trade on Africa After more than 300 years, the countries of Europe decided to stop the slave trade. The Europeans realized what this trade had done to slaves. But they did not always understand what the slave trade had done to Africa.

▶ North America, South America, and the islands of the Caribbean Sea were known as the New World. Some African slaves also went to Europe and Asia.

Does this picture show one effect the Europeans had on Africa? Explain.

One of the effects of the slave trade was that Africa lost many of its young people. Often, the slave traders captured the strongest and healthiest men and women.

▶ How would this affect the African societies these people came from?

Another effect of the slave trade was to destroy any other form of trade in Africa. The profits of the slave trade were so great that many African merchants also took part in it. Instead of making tools and other goods for trade, these merchants simply traded human beings.

▶ How would this affect Africa's manufacturing?

One of the worst effects of the slave trade was to increase warfare between the kingdoms and tribes of Africa. Many African tribes traded slaves captured in war to the Europeans.

▶ How did the slave trade lead to war between tribes?

Africa after the slave trade The slave trade injured Africa in many ways. But the ending of the slave trade harmed Africa even more. The

African kingdoms that had taken part in the trade tried to develop new products to sell to the rest of the world. But these products were not as profitable as slaves. The Africans who had been made rich by the slave trade were now poor. Why?

EUROPEANS TAKE COLONIES

The Europeans who came to Africa about a hundred years ago found a poor and war-torn continent. Most Europeans did not understand the reasons for the bad conditions in Africa. They believed that the Africans could not manage their own continent. Many Europeans thought that the Africans needed to be educated. Some Europeans wanted to convert Africans to Christianity. And almost all wanted to control Africa's natural resources.

▶ What are some of the reasons why Africa was poor and war-torn? What part did the Europeans play in causing this?

▶ What do you think Africans thought of the Europeans' attitude? Give reasons for your answer.

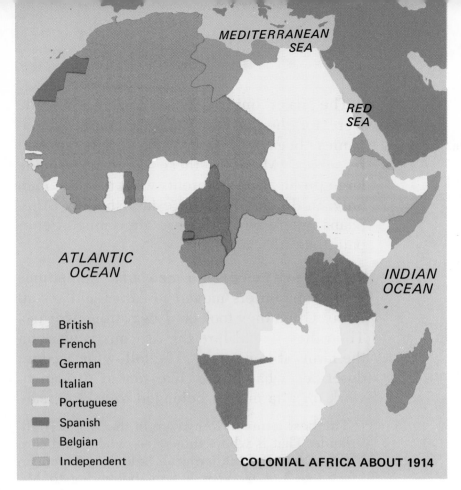

British

French

German

Italian

Portuguese

Spanish

Belgian

Independent

COLONIAL AFRICA ABOUT 1914

Carving up a continent For the same reasons, about a hundred years ago, Europeans began to carve up Africa into colonies. Each European nation competed with the others to grab as much land in Africa as it could. By the beginning of this century, nearly every part of Africa was controlled by Europeans.

Many European nations wanted to control Africa. But once they had their colonies, they often did not know what to do with them. The governments of many European nations were not willing to pay for the cost of governing their colonies. They tried to make the people of their colonies pay the cost themselves. For a long time, almost nothing was done to develop industry for Africa or to raise the standards of living of the African people. Education and medical services were left to missionaries.

▶ A colony is a country that is ruled by another country.

375

▶ Do you think that this was fair to Africians? How do you think Africans felt about what the Europeans were doing to their countries?

▶ kēn′yə

▶ Why do you think Mr. Brown "fences in" his workers?

The major improvements Europeans made were for themselves. European mining companies began to tap Africa's rich mineral resources. Many of these companies made large profits. But the profits went to white men only. In the few factories established by Europeans, white workers were often much better paid than Africans.

Working on a European-owned farm Sometimes European settlers moved to Africa and set up farms. Often they took land away from Africans. Then they would hire the Africans to work on the farms at low wages. The following account describes what it was like for an African to work on a farm that belonged to a European.

The best farms in Kenya are in the White Highlands. That is where the coffee, wheat, and corn are grown. But the farms all belong to European settlers. Let us visit a farm belonging to Mr. Brown.

If you are an African, you must change your clothes before you go. Put on dirty old clothes, the more ragged the better. Mr. Brown knows educated Africans by the way they dress. He does not allow these people to visit his farm. He says that they are lazy and that they have strange ideas that his workers do not need to know. Perhaps he is afraid the outsiders will notice some things.

When you look around his big farm, you wonder where his workers live. All you see are some mud huts you might think are for animals. A barbed wire fence and a big ditch surround these huts. Mr. Brown has told his workers that the fence and ditch are necessary to keep thieves away. But Mr. Brown's house, which is nearby, has no fence or ditch. You might think that Mr. Brown just wanted to fence in his workers.

The farm is very large and rich. It has many good fat sheep cows, and pigs. But the workers are thin and hungry-looking. They all have dirty, ragged clothes. Yet they are very friendly and will take you to their homes. You might not have dreamed that people can live so miserably. The hut is their kitchen, dining room, bedroom, and bathroom. Everyone in the family sleeps there. The children all sleep on the floor with the fleas and sheep.

The family wakes up at 4:30 A.M. The mothers cook for their children. Then everyone except the youngest children go to the fields. The youngest children are left alone all day. As soon as the people get to the field, they meet Mr. Brown and his men. All the people work at very hard jobs. The women clear the bush. The men follow and dig up the hard earth. Then the boys come and break up the large lumps of earth.

As soon as a boy is over five years old, he begins to work in the field for Mr. Brown. Mr. Brown says that education makes a person lazy. He will not allow his workers to build a school. He says that sending young boys into his fields is the best way of training them for their future jobs — digging his fields.

What profit, if any, do you think workers like these might have gotten from their labor?

All of the workers do their jobs without any rest. If they stop for a minute, they might make Mr. Brown so angry that he will not pay them for the day. Go near where the people work. The earth shakes under the men's heavy hoes. They do this job from 6 A.M. to 8 P.M. with only 15 minutes for lunch. Lunch is only porridge and one or two sweet potatoes. You wonder if this is enough food when you think of the amount of work they have to do. But Mr. Brown will tell you that a person who eats more will grow fat and lazy. That is why he only pays his workers a few dollars a month.

After lunch, all the workers continue working in the blazing sun. The men and boys take off their shirts. Streams of sweat run off their bodies. Often they use their torn handkerchiefs to dry themselves. But they do not take a minute to do this. Mr. Brown is quick to notice any "lazy people," as he calls them.

At eight o'clock the workers start for home. The mothers begin cooking for their families. First they feed the small children, who have not had food all day. Then they give food to their tired husbands and older children. After supper everyone is so exhausted they quickly go to bed.

▶ What is the writer's attitude toward white farmers in Africa?

MOVING TOWARD INDEPENDENCE

About 50 years ago some of the European nations began to realize their mistakes in Africa. Some of these countries, like Great Britain, started to think of their colonies differently. They realized that Africans wanted independence for their countries. Some of the European nations now believed that they had to help these countries gain independence. They started training Africans to run their own countries. They built more schools and hospitals. They tried to encourage industry to grow.

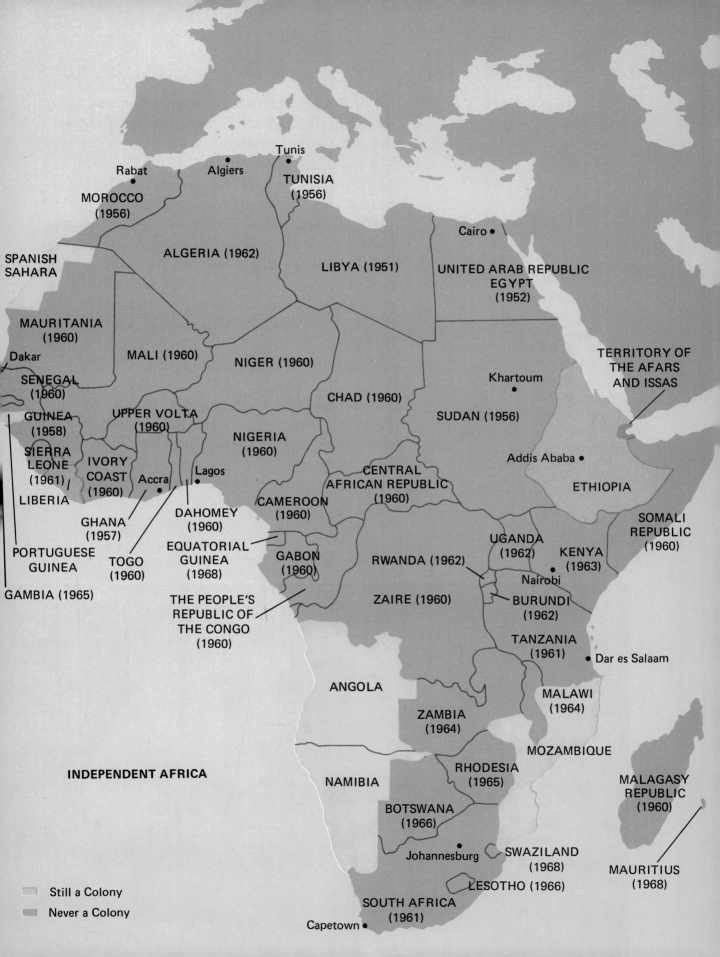

Rabat •   Algiers •   Tunis •

MOROCCO
(1956)

TUNISIA
(1956)

SPANISH
SAHARA

ALGERIA (1962)

LIBYA (1951)

Cairo •

UNITED ARAB REPUBLIC
EGYPT
(1952)

MAURITANIA
(1960)

Dakar •

MALI (1960)

NIGER (1960)

TERRITORY OF
THE AFARS
AND ISSAS

SENEGAL
(1960)

Khartoum •

CHAD (1960)

SUDAN (1956)

GUINEA
(1958)

UPPER VOLTA
(1960)

NIGERIA
(1960)

Addis Ababa •

SIERRA
LEONE
(1961)

IVORY
COAST
(1960)

Accra •

Lagos •

CENTRAL
AFRICAN REPUBLIC
(1960)

ETHIOPIA

LIBERIA

CAMEROON
(1960)

SOMALI
REPUBLIC
(1960)

PORTUGUESE
GUINEA

GHANA
(1957)

DAHOMEY
(1960)

UGANDA
(1962)

KENYA
(1963)

GAMBIA (1965)

TOGO
(1960)

EQUATORIAL
GUINEA
(1968)

GABON
(1960)

RWANDA (1962)

Nairobi •

THE PEOPLE'S
REPUBLIC OF
THE CONGO
(1960)

ZAIRE (1960)

BURUNDI
(1962)

TANZANIA
(1961)

Dar es Salaam •

ANGOLA

MALAWI
(1964)

INDEPENDENT AFRICA

ZAMBIA
(1964)

MOZAMBIQUE

NAMIBIA

RHODESIA
(1965)

MALAGASY
REPUBLIC
(1960)

BOTSWANA
(1966)

Johannesburg •

SWAZILAND
(1968)

MAURITIUS
(1968)

LESOTHO (1966)

SOUTH AFRICA
(1961)

Capetown •

☐ Still a Colony

■ Never a Colony

▶ bel′ jəm

▶ Look at the map on page 379. When did the first African country win its independence? How long did it take before all the other countries were independent? What African countries are still not independent? Which European country rules them?

But other European nations did not have this attitude. Some, like Belgium and Portugal, did not train any Africans to run governments. They did not build many schools or hospitals. At the same time, these countries made millions of dollars from African resources.

Other European countries, like France, tried to help their colonies but did not help in the right way. They insisted that Africa be a part of France. So Africans were given the same education as French people. Africans learned the names of French kings. They read French literature. But they were not taught about African kings or African literature.

Africa becomes independent Some of the European countries were helping their colonies learn to rule themselves. But none of the Europeans realized just how badly Africans wanted to be free. There were riots and even

The man in this picture is working on a modern locomotive. Why do you think modern forms of transportation are important to Africa today?

This African wood will be made into beautiful furniture in another part of the world.

warfare before Europeans granted Africans their freedom.

Some African countries won their independence before they were really ready. Often they faced difficult problems. Usually the nations that were least prepared by their European rulers had the worst problems when they became independent.

Problems of independence One example of this is the Republic of Zaire. It had been governed by Belgium. When Zaire became independent in 1960, there was not a single African university graduate in the whole country. There were almost no trained people to run the government. The richest part of the country wanted to break away. The army revolted. Years of civil war was the result.

Other African nations were better prepared by their colonial rulers. But even these nations had problems after independence.

▶ Before 1971, Zaire was known as the Congo.

▶ Do you think Belgium prepared Zaire for independence? What could the Belgians have done that they did not do?

381

In most countries, there was not nearly enough money to develop industry Without industry, many people did not have jobs. They could not earn enough money to support their families So large numbers of Africans were poor.

Many of the African countries depended on crops like peanuts, palm oil, kola nuts, or cocoa. These are useful crops. Palm oil is used to make soap; cocoa is used to make chocolate. But palm oil and cocoa are not nearly as valuable to other countries as manufactured goods—products turned out by industries. The African countries cannot make enough money without building up their industries.

Other African countries have rich natural resources. But they do not have the railroads or roads to transport these resources. They do not have the money or the skilled workers to build transportation systems. And they do not have the money to pay others to build for them.

The countries of Africa have not been independent for very long. And some of the difficulties of running governments still exist. But Africans are sure that, in time, they will be able to solve their problems. They have a great history behind them. They are sure that the future will be just as bright.

♦ Kola nuts are used to make a popular drink. What do you think the drink is?

♦ What manufactured goods can you name? What countries are they made in? Are industrial countries usually wealthy countries?

1. How did warfare, trade, and religion in Africa bring African cultures into contact with one another?
2. What effect did the coming of the Europeans have on Africa?
3. What are some of the problems independent African nations face today? Explain the roots of these problems.

The Land and the People

Africa is a giant land, three times larger than the United States. It is a land of almost every type of climate and geographical feature. It has scorching deserts. And it has thick rain forests where trees and shrubs grow so closely together that sunlight never shines through. It has mountains that have rain forests at the bottom, grasslands further up, and snow at the top.

African people have managed to adapt to every type of climate on their enormous continent. There are three main types of climate and vegetation areas in Africa — savanna, desert, and rain forest.

THE AFRICAN RAIN FORESTS

Many people think of Africa as a continent completely covered by rain forests. Africa does have rain forests. But look at the vegetation map on page 386. Are the rain forests spread out all over Africa? What line crosses the middle of Africa from east to west? How close are the rain forests to this line?

The middle part of Africa is hot all year round. In most of this area, heavy rains fall throughout the year. This hot, wet region is the home of Africa's rain forests.

Look again at the vegetation map on page 386. What is the largest rain forest area in Africa? What river is it near? Notice how the rain forest surrounds this river and the other rivers that flow into it. Why do you think this area is called the Congo basin?

The people of the rain forests There are two groups of people who live in the rain forests — Bantu villagers and Pygmies. The two groups

▶ A savanna (sə van′ə) is a mostly flat region, usually covered with grass and a few trees.

▶ ban′tü
▶ pig′mēz

384

There are not many roads like this through the African rain forest. The heavy rains make the roads almost impossible to use through a part of the year.

have very different ways of life. But they have learned to survive in the rain forest by depending on each other.

Pygmy hunters The Pygmies are different from any other group of African people. They are very small. Adult Pygmies are usually only 4 to 4½ feet tall. They live as hunters in the rain forest. They live in groups of three or four families. The men of the families hunt together, and the women and children sometimes help them.

Some Pygmies live in larger groups and hunt with nets. The men go to an area where they know there are animals. They hold up nets, which are sometimes as long as 300 feet. Then the women and children spread out and chase the animals into the nets. This kind of hunting requires great cooperation from everyone in the group—men, women, and children.

▶ How tall are you? About how tall are most adults in the United States? Would being small be an advantage or a disadvantage in the jungle? Explain your answer.

▶ Are children needed to get food for families in the United States? How would you feel about working the way Pygmy children work?

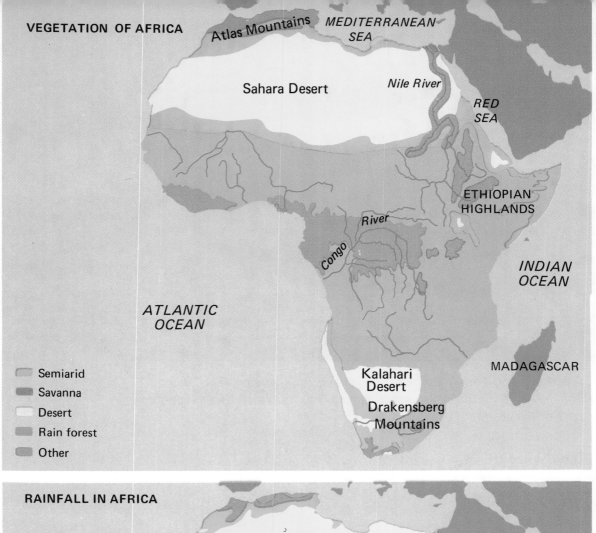

VEGETATION OF AFRICA

Atlas Mountains

MEDITERRANEAN SEA

Sahara Desert

Nile River

RED SEA

ETHIOPIAN HIGHLANDS

River

Congo

INDIAN OCEAN

ATLANTIC OCEAN

MADAGASCAR

Kalahari Desert

Drakensberg Mountains

Semiarid
Savanna
Desert
Rain forest
Other

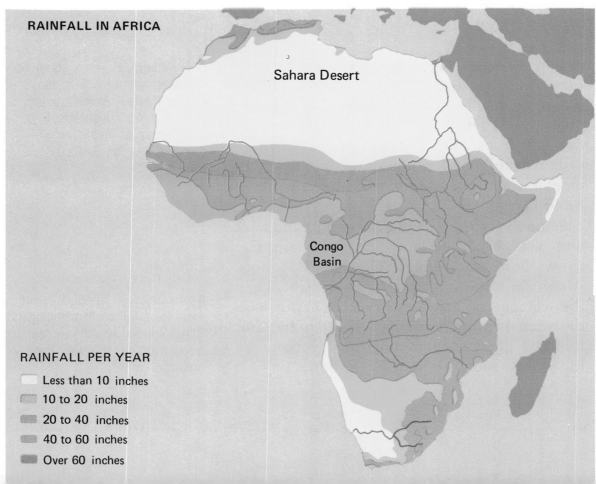

RAINFALL IN AFRICA

Sahara Desert

Congo Basin

RAINFALL PER YEAR
Less than 10 inches
10 to 20 inches
20 to 40 inches
40 to 60 inches
Over 60 inches

DROUGHT!

The fierce, hot winds and violent dust storms that sizzle across the desert sands do not stop at the desert's edge. They move as far as the areas which border the desert. But normally, rain will come to these border areas. Little rain falls in the desert.

There are some years when rain does not fall anywhere—the years of drought (drout). Recently, south of the Sahara Desert, there was no rain for five years. Grass and shrubs dried up first. Then the water holes dried up. Cattle died. Crops failed.

The desert grew larger and larger as more of the Sahara became too dry to support life. New crops would not grow. Soon grain supplies were exhausted, and millions of people began to starve. Emergency supplies of food trickled in from the United States and other nations. But poor transportation prevented the supplies from reaching many of the starving. What effects would cities and farms south of the desert feel as millions of people fled their northern homes in search of food and water?

People suffered for five years before the rains finally came to these dry lands. But not before the lesson was clear: Drought is still among the worst disasters people can live through.

Hunting is a full-time job for the Pygmies. It means that they cannot live in permanent villages. They must follow the animals all over the forest. Women and children are not left behind in villages. They are needed for hunting, too.

But over the years, the Pygmies have learned to enjoy some of the luxuries of village life. Their forest foods of meat, fruit, nuts, and berries are enough for them. But the Pygmies also enjoy some village foods—like rice, beans, peanuts, and vegetables. They also need some metal tools, like knives, axes, and machetes, that are made in the villages.

The Pygmies could build their own villages. But they prefer not to settle down that long. Instead, they have made friends with other peoples who have built villages in rain forest clearings. The Pygmies live with these villagers for a few weeks every year.

▶ A luxury is something that is not needed for survival. An ice cream cone or a movie is a luxury.

▶ Machetes (mə shet′ ēz) are very long knives that are used to hack away at grass, vines, or shrubs.

Pygmy children perform important tasks. Do children in our society have similar responsibilities?

388

Unlike the Pygmies, the Bantu villagers do not hunt in the rain forest. The women and children usually stay close to the village and do tasks like those in the picture above.

Hunters and villagers   The villagers are Bantu. Both they and the Pygmies like the arrangement they have made. The Pygmies get the things they need from the villagers. And they do things for the villagers in return. The Bantu cannot keep cattle in the rain forest. There is not enough room for the cattle to feed. And an insect called the tsetse fly infects the cattle with terrible diseases. So the Bantu are given meat by the Pygmies.

The Pygmies also do other work for the Bantu. The villagers are afraid of the rain forest. To them it is a dangerous, evil place. But to the Pygmies it is familiar. So the Pygmies do things for the villagers that involve going into the rain forest. They fetch firewood and guard the village fields from wild animals.

▶ Have you ever seen cows grazing in a field? Can you see why they could not graze in a leaf-tangled rain forest?

▶ tset′sē

▶ Do you think that the Bantu want to stay friendly with the Pygmies? Why or why not?

389

Village farming The villagers must work very hard to clear their fields. Once they are cleared, the villagers must fight continually to keep the rain forest from taking over again. The soil of the rain forest is so poor that the farm crops soon wear it out. So the land can only be farmed for a few years. Then the villagers must give the land back to the forest and clear more.

The villagers do not understand why the soil wears out. They think that the land belongs to the forest god. They believe that the god curses the soil and makes it infertile.

The lives of both the Pygmies and the Bantu are hard. But they survive in better harmony with the rain forest than other people who have tried to live there. For example, one farming company tried to clear away a rain forest. The company wanted to start a peanut plantation there. But the soil quickly wore out and became as hard as concrete. Hundreds of thousands of acres of land were made useless.

AFRICAN DESERTS

There is another type of climate and vegetation area that is just as hard to live in as the rain forest—the desert. Study the vegetation map on page 386. What areas of Africa are desert? What is the largest desert in Africa? This desert is also the largest in the world. It is as large as the United States, and it covers more than a quarter of Africa.

The Sahara When you think of a desert, do you think of oceans of sand under a blazing sun? The sun certainly blazes in the Sahara. Temperatures in the daytime can go as high

▶ Would this idea of the forest god make the villagers even more afraid of the jungle? Why or why not?

▶ Which do you think is better for the jungle—the Pygmies and the Bantu, or the farming company? Explain your answer.

Bushmen use their knowledge to survive in a harsh environment. Do people in our culture need this kind of knowledge to survive?

as 180° Fahrenheit. Then, at night, they can fall to near freezing.

The Sahara does have oceans of sands. But it also has large areas of infertile, stony gound. In addition, there are infertile mountains.

The Bushmen of the Kalahari   At the other end of Africa is a desert that is just as harsh and infertile as the Sahara. Yet people who live here have managed to make a home and live in harmony with the land. The people are the Bushmen. And their home is the Kalahari Desert of South Africa.

The Bushmen look a little like the Pygmies of the rain forest. They are a few inches taller than the Pygmies. And, like the Pygmies, they make their living through their knowledge of a difficult and dangerous home.

◗ Fahrenheit is the temperature scale used most frequently in the United States.

◗ kä′ lä hä′ rē

391

SHIPS OF THE DESERT

What has long, graceful eyelashes, tiny ears, and a long, curving neck? What can carry heavy loads through the hot and waterless sands of the desert? It's the desert dweller's best friend—the camel.

If you should ever meet a camel, do not be fooled by its eyelashes and friendly smile. The camel is a mean and lazy animal. It bites and spits at anyone— even the person who feeds it. If a desert caravan should stop, the camel will kneel down and roll over so that its heavy load falls off its back. It may take several hours to get the camel on its feet and moving again. What do you think it means to call camels "ships of the desert"?

With all its mean qualities, the camel has many advantages for people of the desert. Nature made this animal just right for desert use. It has a hump, where it stores its food. With this storage area, a camel can travel for days, sometimes even weeks, eating only the dry grass it finds in the desert. Also, the camel can go without water for as long as two weeks. Why is the camel's ability to store food and water important for crossing a desert?

If you ever see a camel in a zoo, look for all the things that make it useful in the desert. But do not get too close. Even in zoos, camels still like to bite and spit.

A Bushman father teaches his son skills that are necessary for survival.

During the few days that it rains in the Kalahari, the Bushmen have no trouble finding food. The desert blooms with all kinds of plants. Hungry animals from surrounding areas move into the desert. Hunting is easy. But the rest of the year the Kalahari is dry. Yet the Bushmen know the desert so well that they can always find food and water. They can follow animal tracks for days. Then they shoot their game with poisoned arrows. If the animal is only wounded, they will run after it for days under the hot sun.

A Bushman can also find water where no one else can. Sometimes he will dig through the sand, looking for the water he knows has seeped in after the rains. Then he will put a hollow reed into the ground. The reed is covered with a blade of grass at one end to keep out the sand. The Bushman will suck the water up through the reed, drawing it out of

▶ Have you ever been in a wilderness area? If there were no signs or paths and you did not have a compass, do you think you could find your way around?

393

◗ An ostrich is a large bird that runs very fast but cannot fly. The shell of its egg is strong and large.

the sand. Whatever water he does not drink, he will store in an ostrich egg shell. He will hide the shell in the sand and remember where he has hidden it. If another Bushman finds the shell, he will not use it—even if he is dying of thirst. He knows that another depends on the water being there.

The women of the tribe also know the desert well. They know where to find the few plants that grow in the desert. They also know how to use all of the things that can be found in the desert. They know which plants have an acid that can take the fur off animal skins. The women can make the skins into clothes and bags.

Nearly everything the Bushmen use comes from the desert. But it takes knowledge and skill to put everything to use. Only with this knowledge and skill can the Bushmen survive in such a harsh homeland.

These women of the Sahara make a home in a rough land. Do they need as many skills as their husbands?

The savannas cannot support large-scale farming. But nomads with their cattle do not take too much from the land. Can you tell from the picture why the nomads and their herds must keep moving on the savannas?

THE SAVANNAS

The areas next to the deserts are called savannas. People in the savannas do not have as difficult a life as the Bushmen. Most do not have to hunt. Instead, many herd animals. There is not enough rainfall in these savanna areas for farming. But there is enough rain for grass to grow. Animal herds can survive here, but only if they keep moving from one area to another.

The savanna may be almost as hot as the desert for part of the year. During this hot time of the year, clouds build up at the desert's edge. Then, a large brown swirl can be seen in the sky. Once this swirl is seen, there is barely time to find shelter. Those who cannot find shelter find themselves caught in a blinding sandstorm. Sand blows fiercely into the eyes, nose, and mouth of a person caught in the storm. Sometimes the sandstorm will blow for several days.

▶ Do you get harsh storms where you live? Do you think they are as bad as these sandstorms? What do you think might happen to a man caught in a sandstorm?

During the dry time of the year, savanna people must keep moving their herds from place to place as the grass is eaten. But, unlike the desert areas, the savanna gets a great deal of water at certain times of the year. The first rains after the dry season are short. They might appear as showers coming every few days. Then heavier rain begins to fall. Finally, real storms drop sheets of rain on the savanna. Within a few days, plants push through the hard sand and the whole region is green again. Now the herd animals can eat as much as they want. In two or three months, though, the rain will stop, and the grass and shrubs will turn brown again.

Herding-people of the savanna Each family of herdsmen usually tends its herds separately. The herds are too large to feed together. One family or a group of families will stay in one area for a few weeks. They will build a camp of small thatch huts. Then each day the men and boys will take the herds out to a different area around the camp. After a few weeks, they will move on and build a new camp somewhere else. Within a year, the herdsmen may travel hundreds of miles.

Each herder knows exactly what land he has a right to use. He may meet other herders only once or twice a year, when they meet in large market towns. Still, he knows which land the other herders use and will probably not use it. To let his herds graze on land that is used by another herder might easily start a war.

Many of the herding people look down on people who have to stay in one place and farm. Some African governments have tried to help the herders. The governments want the herders

▶ To tend means to take care of.

▶ Why do you think herders would be so careful of their rights?

396

Would you enjoy life as a herder? Why might herders look down on a settled way of life?

to make better use of their herds. But the herders are so proud of their way of life that they do not want to change.

THE DODOTH

Among African people who do not want to change are those who own and value cattle. This is certainly true of the Dodoth. They are a proud group who look down on people who do not own cattle. For the Dodoth, cattle are not goods to be bought or sold. They are not animals to be slaughtered.

▶ dō′dōth

For the Dodoth, cattle are the basis of life. Cattle represent wealth. A man pays for his wives with cattle. By giving cattle to his friends, a man gains supporters.

If a drought comes, if the gardens and the grain crops fail, cattle provide the only food. Cows give milk. This is drunk every day and is also made into butter and cheese.

The first food a baby ever eats in his life is a drop of butter. From then on he lives with cattle.

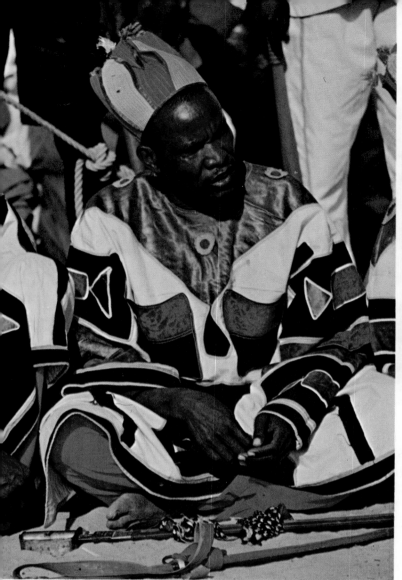

Africans realize that much of their old way of life will change as they move into the modern world. Already machines are replacing the old handicrafts. And governments are taking over the duties of the old tribal chiefs.

Modernization means new cities—
complete with traffic and traffic
jams. It means hard days at work
in factories instead of village fields.
And it means record stores with the
latest popular songs.

Every day and night of his life, his nose will be filled with their smell. His ears will be filled with their sounds. To care for his cattle is his life's work. When he dies, if he dies at home, his body will be wrapped in the hide of his oxen. Then he will be buried in the soft earth of the cattle pen.

If a cow dies, it is eaten. But no one would kill such a valuable animal for its meat. They are grateful for its milk. And they know that each cow can bear a calf every year, and so increase the herd. It is the size of the herd that is the most important thing.

Farming villages of the savanna The Dodoth and other herding cultures live in the dryer part of the savanna. In the wetter woodland sections are the traditional farming villages. In these villages, many Africans practice an ancient form of agriculture called slash-and-burn farming. African farmers clear away the trees and shrubs and leave them to dry out. Then, just before the rainy season, they pre-

Why would permanent farming villages be located in the wetter sections of the savanna?

The members of this African family are eating dinner outside their home.

pare their fields by burning away all the stubble and brush. Trees that are too large to cut down are left standing. Their roots hold down the soil and prevent it from wearing away.

Then the farmers break up the soil for planting. Instead of a plow, most Africans use a broad-blade hoe to break up the earth. The hoe is tiring to use. It takes a great deal of effort just to loosen the thick top layer of soil. But this is desirable soil in Africa. In many parts of the continent, the soil is thin and poor. If it were broken up with a plow, what would probably happen to it when the heavy rains came?

TRADITION AND CHANGE

Farming is a traditional part of African life. But many traditions are gradually losing their force. In the new cities of Africa, few of the old African customs survive. People live in modern houses or apartments with just the closest members of their families.

City life In the cities, the influence of the family fades. People find it easy to form other friendships. They do not need the security offered by their large families. So in the cities, Africans are following new ways. They work in offices and factories that look much like European or American offices and factories.

But only 20 percent of the people in Africa live in cities. The other 80 percent live in villages and in hunting and herding groups. They remain in the savannas, deserts, and rain forests of their huge continent.

Yet their ways of life have changed, too. They have more roads now. They do not have to make everything they need. They can buy many of the things they need in town markets.

Africans have adjusted to the many kinds of land on their giant continent. They have learned to live in the heat and the sand of the desert. They have learned to survive in dangerous and uncomfortable rain forests. And they have built many different ways of life on the broad savannas. They have learned to live in harmony with the many different lands of Africa.

1. Describe the three main climate and vegetation areas of the African continent. Name one group of African people who live in each area.
2. Which climate and vegetation area of Africa would be the easiest to live in? Which area would be the hardest to live in? Explain your answers.
3. In what ways is the traditional way of life in Africa changing?

Case Study: The Ibo of Nigeria

▶ an′ thrə pol′ ə jists

Anthropologists are scientists who study the culture of a people — how they live, how they earn their living, what kinds of groups they belong to, how they educate themselves. One method anthropologists use is living with the people they wish to study.

ONE MAN'S STORY

▶ chēk e′ zē ü chen′ dü
▶ ē′ bō

One anthropologist who studies his own people is named Chikezie Uchendu. Dr. Uchendu is a member of the Ibo tribe in Nigeria.

The most crowded country Find Nigeria on the map on page 379. Nigeria is the most crowded country in Africa. Now look at the southeastern part of Nigeria. Here live Dr. Uchendu's people, the Ibo. There are almost 6 million Ibo in this part of Nigeria.

Scientists consider the Ibo tribe interesting because the Ibo people have tried to change their way of life. For centuries, the Ibo people lived in a traditional way. They farmed the land and lived in villages. In time, Nigeria, their country, began to grow more modern. People began to work in factories and live in big cities. In 1960, a national government took over.

Some people in Nigeria did not want to change their way of life. They did not want to "become modern." The Ibo people, however, wanted to "get up." This means that they wanted to become part of the modern world.

Some of the Ibo people work in cities. And they want post offices, clinics, and other modern things for their home villages.

Scientists are interested in why the Ibo want

to get up—and how they plan to get up. Much of what you will read comes from a book by Dr. Uchendu. As you read, remember that Dr. Uchendu is a member of the culture he writes about. See if you can find things that show the advantages and disadvantages of anthropologists studying their own culture.

Also as you read, ask yourself why the Ibo are so anxious to become part of the modern world? What was their life like in the past?

▶ Do you think that an anthropologist studying his own people can see things that an outsider cannot? Do you think that an outsider might in some ways be a better reporter? Explain your answers.

CHILDHOOD

I grew up in a place made up of five villages. I lived in a big compound. Our **extended family** was a closely knit group. My uncle was in charge of the compound. He was the most successful of his brothers. My uncle loved me like a son. His children were all grown. I was the only boy in the compound old enough to help him. I carried his medicine bag and listened to his stories. He

▶ A compound is a group of family houses surrounded by a fence or a mud wall.

▶ Extended family is a term used by social scientists. It means *all* the members of a family—aunts, uncles, and cousins—as well as parents and children.

Children are very important to the Ibo. Chikezie's mother had feared she would be childless. So when Chikezie was born, his parents gave him a name which means "May God Create Well."

▶ Have you ever heard about the past from an older person? Is this a way of passing on the culture and history of a group? Explain.

▶ Might living with an extended family be an advantage in a farming village with much work to be done? Why or why not?

▶ A palm is a tree that grows very well in hot places. The leaves of the oil palm are used in building and thatching. Palm oil is used to make soap, candles, and margarine.

▶ How did Dr. Uchendu feel about being away from home? Have you ever been away from home? Were you homesick? Do you think an extended family is harder to leave than the one you are growing up in? Why or why not?

▶ Are the Ibo people interested in progress? Do you think progress is always good? Can you name two good things about progress? Can you name two bad things?

knew much about our culture and told it to anybody who would listen. He told me what he could remember about our ancestors and about the coming of the white man.

Growing up was not a hard experience for me. My friends and I played with toys we made. We built traps to catch small animals. We hunted rabbits, too. At night we told stories and sang folk songs. I helped with the farmwork. Since I didn't have any sisters until later, I had to do some of the chores usually done by girls.

SCHOOL DAYS

The time when I finished grade school was a time of poverty for my people. My people could not find markets for palm oil and palm kernels, which were the main sources of income. My father had gone into debt. My family could not afford to give me a high school education.

But this was not too serious. In those days it was rare for boys from my village group to go to high school. Only two boys from my area had been to high school and neither was from my own village.

AWAY FROM HOME

I became a grade school teacher in another village when I was 16. I met many new people through teaching. But for the first time I was alone—without my family and the villagers I had always known.

After I had taught in grade schools for five years, I was admitted to a college. When I graduated from the college, I faced great responsibilities. My family expected me to use my education wisely. My home village saw me as special because of my education. The villagers wanted me to lead them. My village has a great desire to "get up." Our people use this expression to mean progress. Could I help the town get up? This was the question I faced when I finished college.

Long ago Ibo history is unwritten, but we know that people first came to Iboland 500 years ago. When the Europeans began the slave trade, many of the Ibo were sent to the New World to work on plantations. Later, the Ibo had better contact with Europeans — when missionaries came to Africa. The Ibo did not seem to be as united as other tribes in Nigeria. The Ibo were open to new ideas from the missionaries.

New ideas The missionaries showed the Ibo a different way of life. The Ibo judged their culture against that of the Europeans, and many decided they were not satisfied. They wanted to modernize their culture and to have more things. The Ibo wanted to "get themselves up." But how would they do this? What kind of life did they have? How would they change it?

MAKING A LIVING

The land The Ibo live east of the Niger River. The soil there is sandy and not good for farming. But farming is the main way of earning a living for most of the Ibo. The yam is one of the most important Ibo crops.

The people plant their crops in the same plot for a few years. In a while, the soil becomes infertile. Then the farmers move on to an unused area nearby. The old land becomes wild again. It is on this land that the oil palms — an important source of money — grow wild.

A farmer The Ibo have to work very hard to grow enough food. Therefore, they have a strong feeling for their land and crops. This feeling is described by a Nigerian author.

▶ A yam is like a sweet potato. It grows well in warm climates.

407

These cattle are grazing in a small clearing in the rain forest. But in a few years, this area will be overgrown again. When the land becomes wild again, what will happen to the cattle?

♦ ō kon′ kwō

Okonkwo, the hero of the book, is an Ibo farmer. He works hard growing yams.

Okonkwo spent the next few days getting his yams ready. He looked at each yam carefully to see whether it was good for planting. . . . His oldest son and another boy from a neighboring village helped him. They brought the yams from the barn in long baskets. . . .

Okonkwo knew that the boys were still too young to understand how to prepare yams. But he thought that one could not begin to learn too early. The man who could feed his family on yams from one harvest to another was a very lucky man. Okonkwo wanted his son to be successful. . . .

Too many people The density in some parts of Iboland is 1,500 people per square mile. This is one of the highest densities in Africa. Do you think the high population density affects farming? If so, in what way? Many Ibo still think farming is the best way to make a living. But many of them cannot depend only on farming.

▶ Density means the average number of people who live in a certain area.

Trade Today, trading is an important source of income. The Ibo have always traded. Before the Europeans came, the Ibo traded some of their farm products in small village markets. These markets were run mainly by the Ibo women. Later, the Ibo carried on long-distance trade—outside Ibo country. This trade was important since the Ibo needed salt. In exchange, they traded cattle and sometimes even slaves. Men were in charge of these long-distance markets.

▶ What kind of trade was most important after the Europeans arrived?

Women in many parts of Africa frequently carry heavy loads on their heads.

Are new means of transportation important for "getting up"?

▶ Have you ever bargained for something you wanted to buy? If so, describe what happened.

Markets The Ibo markets have changed. Roads have been improved, railroads have been built, and cities have grown. Some markets that were once long-distance markets are now local markets. Why do you think this is so?

The prices in the Ibo markets are set by bargaining. Sellers always ask a higher price than they expect to get. If the buyer thinks the price is too high, he throws the article down. Then the seller might agree to a lower price.

There is a new kind of trader in the Ibo markets now. He buys machine-made things in the cities and sells them to the villagers. He might sell pencils, pens, ink, books, and other things the villagers cannot make for themselves.

Ibo workers Farming, trading, and village handicrafts are still not enough to support all of the Ibo. Many now want other kinds of jobs. People from the most crowded parts of Iboland have always moved to other places looking for jobs. But now more people must do this.

Some workers help farmers in other villages. Some women pick palm kernels on nearby farms. As more roads and industries are built in Nigeria, new kinds of jobs develop. What are some new kinds of jobs a nation becoming modern might have?

The Ibo still try to help each other get used to new ways. In many Nigerian cities, the Ibo organize groups to help newcomers learn about city life. The leaders of these organizations are usually the most educated Ibo workers.

Some workers plan to stay in the cities only a short time before returning home. Sometimes they stay until they make a certain amount of money. But the Ibo who are not successful in the towns do not like to return home penniless. They will often stay and hope their luck will change. They do not want to lose face with their fellow villagers.

GETTING UP

The villagers Most Ibo parents encourage their children to do well in school. They know Iboland is too crowded for everyone to farm. They want their children to find another career. And the children know that their main hope for a good life depends on working outside the village. They hope to find jobs in trade or in government or with big industries.

But even if they leave home, the Ibo never really forget their villages. The Ibo have a strong community spirit. No matter where he moves, an Ibo person wants his or her town to become important and successful—to "get up." The Ibo feel that when a person helps his town, he or she becomes more important, too.

▶ Why do you think more people from the crowded villages look for jobs in other places?

▶ Do you think it is very important among the Ibo people to be successful? How do you know?

AFRICAN WOMEN

When Europeans first came to Africa, they were amazed to find that many African men had more than one wife. Because of this practice, many people thought that African men treated African women like slaves.

But these first impressions turned out to be false. Until about 50 years ago, most African women had more freedom and independence than women in Western nations did. In some sections of Africa, women have owned most businesses and been the chief traders for many years. In Europe, however, there were many places where women were not even allowed to own property.

But what about African marriages? Did the man rule the household—and his three or four wives? Here, too, it seems that first impressions were wrong. When there is more than one wife, each woman depends on her husband less. In a traditional African home, each woman lives in her own hut and runs her own household. Would that kind of living arrangement give the woman more independence?

Privacy and Sharing

Each of the wives in an African marriage owns her own property and raises her own children. But some tasks, like cooking and baby-sitting, are shared with the other wives. Do you think that sharing these chores makes life easier for African women?

Changing Customs

Today, many modern Africans, especially those living in big cities, are changing their ways.

Parents no longer arrange marriages for their children. Most city families are just like ours, with only the husband, his one wife, and their children living at home. The grandparents and other relatives are often left behind in the villages. Why do you think city life has changed the traditional way? Would a city apartment be large enough for the traditional African family?

▶ A symbol is something that represents or stands for something else.

▶ How do you think the importance of cities in your culture is measured today? Name some things that make where you live important.

The Ibo work together to build their villages. Think about the pioneers in America. Do you think cooperation is necessary for a nation to progress?

Symbols of progress The Ibo have always tried to measure the success of their villages. Before the Europeans arrived, the Ibo measured a village's importance by the strength of its warriors, by its nearness to trade centers, and by the size of its markets.

Today, the Ibo use new ways to measure how well a town has gotten up. Dr. Uchendu's village was proud of its symbols of progress: three grade schools, five churches, a marketplace, and many village halls. The Ibo believe that schools, hospitals, and colleges show a village's importance. Buildings show that people have worked to get themselves up.

Working together The Ibo know they can get up only if they work together. They are willing to contribute time, money, and work to make their villages the best. But the Ibo think that education is the key to getting themselves up.

A WORLD OF CHANGE

A description What is the best way to describe the Ibo and the things their culture values? First, the Ibo want to get themselves up. They are very willing to cooperate to reach their goals. But most of all, the Ibo are willing to change and learn new ways.

Some changes Do you think the Ibo have always been willing to adjust to new ways? Think about the coming of the Europeans. The Ibo accepted them. And later the land was overcrowded, and again the people had to find new ways to live.

The Ibo world changes constantly. The people expect change. They believe that if things do not work one way, they must try a different way. The people admire success, and they are willing to experiment until they succeed.

The Ibo have a favorite saying: "One who is too careful is always killed by the fall of a dry leaf." What do you think the Ibo mean? Do you think this saying is a good way to describe the Ibo attitude toward life? Do you think this attitude would be helpful to other groups of people who wish to become modern? Why or why not?

▶ Why do you think a willingness to change is so important for a people?

1. How has the Ibo way of life changed since 1960? Why did this change occur?
2. Explain the Ibo concept of "getting up."
3. In what ways are the Ibo people a model for people who want to become modern?
4. In what ways do the Ibo help one another?

INVESTIGATING THE UNIT

Doing Research

Imagine you are traveling with some-one. You both decide to go on a camera safari to take pictures of lions and elephants. Talk to a travel agent or librarian. What countries in Africa would you be likely to visit? What kind of environment do these animals live in? What kinds of cultures might you find in this environment?

Looking at the Evidence

While skin diving off the eastern coast of Africa, you come across the sunken wreck of a Chinese ship. From coins and pottery found in the wreck, you determine it must have gone down about 700 years ago. The cargo of the ship was gold and ivory. Where do you think the ship might have been coming from? Where do you think it might have been going? Were Europeans trading with the east coast of Africa at that time?

Compare and Contrast

Compare the Bushmen of the Kalahari with the Pygmies of the rain forest. How are their environments different? How are their ways of life difficult? Are their ways of life similar or different? Could we learn anything from the struggle of these people to survive?

Using Maps

You are hitchhiking around the world with a friend. You wind up in Tunis and decide to go as far south as you can, right through the middle of Africa. What countries might you pass through on your journey? What kinds of climates would you go through? What kinds of people could you expect to meet? What kinds of roads do you think you might encounter?

Reading on Your Own

One of the most important and damag-ing events in African history was slavery. Basil Davidson has written two books on this: *Black Mother: The Years of the African Slave Trade* (Boston, Little, Brown); and *The African Past* (Boston, Little, Brown).

LATIN AMERICA

In a nutshell, the Latin-American economic problem is still that of the starving man with a gold mine under his feet. . . . Industry may develop at a fast clip in countries like Brazil and Venezuela, but in the cities, there is great poverty next to luxury. There is not enough for all.

TAD SZULC

Yesterday and Today

THE NEW WORLD

The discovery In 1492, Christopher Columbus set sail from Spain. He was not looking for a new world. He was searching for a new, shorter route to China and the East Indies. Instead, he landed on San Salvador, a small Caribbean island.

Columbus never realized he had passed near two continents unknown to Europeans. But when geographers in Europe retraced his journey, his unknown discovery came to light. Word of the new lands spread fast. The Spanish became interested. They claimed all the land in the Americas for Spain.

Europeans who crossed the Atlantic Ocean after Columbus thought of the new area as the New World. But it was new only to them. Other people had lived there for thousands of years. These were the people called Indians by the Europeans.

▶ Look on the map below. Find San Salvador (san sal′və dôr).

▶ kar ə bē′ ən

▶ How could Spain claim this territory, when it already belonged to the Indians living there?

COMING OF THE INDIANS

No one knows exactly when the first people came to the Americas. They kept no diaries; they had no calendars. Yet they did leave

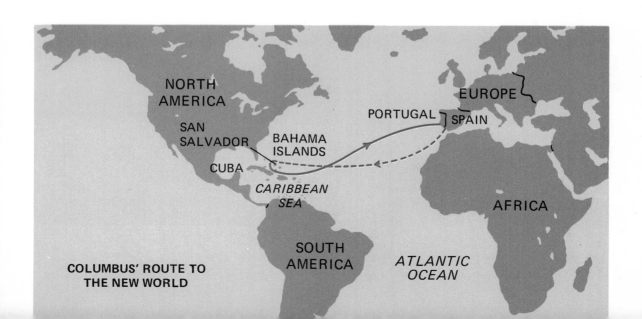

COLUMBUS' ROUTE TO THE NEW WORLD

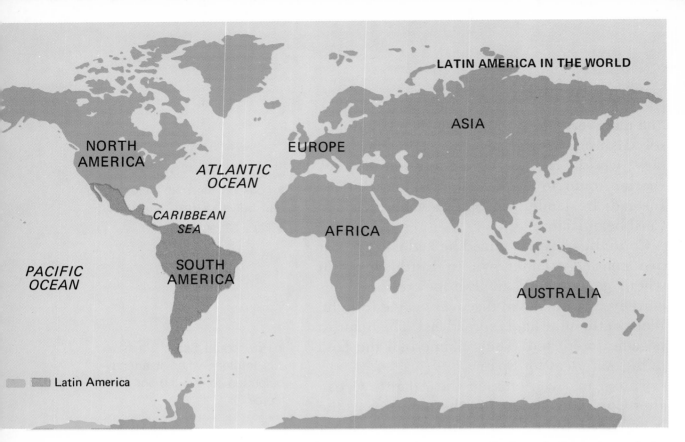

LATIN AMERICA IN THE WORLD

NORTH AMERICA

ATLANTIC OCEAN

CARIBBEAN SEA

PACIFIC OCEAN

SOUTH AMERICA

EUROPE

ASIA

AFRICA

AUSTRALIA

Latin America

● Archaeologists (ar′ kē ol′ ə-jists) are scientists who study ancient cultures by examining such things as tools, housing, and art.

● Anthropologists (an′ thrə pol′-ə jists) are scientists who study people and their ways of life.

▶ Is that land a warm place today? Find out what event in the earth's history caused this change.

records. As they moved, they left tools and the remains of fires behind. Archaeologists and anthropologists have read these records to learn about the earliest Americans.

The land bridge Look closely at the map above. Where are North America and Asia closest? A long time ago, these two areas were connected by a strip of land. This was a warm place where trees and plants grew. Over the years, people wandered across the land bridge. Sometimes they were following animals. Sometimes they were simply wandering with no purpose in mind. They did not know they were crossing into a new continent.

Little by little, these people moved down into the Americas. Some moved east across North America. There they settled into the woods and plains.

Others moved down the west coast to South America. There they settled in mountain lands and rain forests. The last people to come stayed in Alaska. They are the people we call Eskimos.

Isolated peoples For thousands of years, the Indian peoples lived separated from the people of other lands. Different tribes within the Americas did have contact with each other, however. They traded with each other, and they fought with each other. But they lived isolated from the peoples of other lands.

▶ Isolated means separated from others.

Some Indian peoples developed very advanced cultures. One of these cultures was in Mexico. The people were the Aztecs.

INDIAN EMPIRE

Who were the Aztecs? Why were the Aztecs so powerful? Why do we remember them?

At first, they were a wandering tribe. According to Aztec legend, their god had told them that they must wander until they found an eagle with a snake in his beak. The eagle must be sitting on a cactus growing from a rock.

Legend says that the Aztecs found the eagle in Tenochtitlan. Tenochtitlan is now Mexico City.

▶ tā nōch′ ti tlän′

In time, the Aztecs grew stronger. Under their powerful emperor, named Montezuma, the Aztecs spread out. They conquered village

The gold objects on this page are Aztec artifacts found in a tomb in Mexico. Artifacts are
objects that were made by people and used in
their culture. What might the gold perfume bottle
tell about the Aztecs? The Aztec temple, below, is
decorated with the head of the snake god honored
by the Aztecs.

after village and made their conquests part of their empire.

The conquered villages worked to support the Aztecs. Farmers gave part of their crops to support the Aztec lords. Village women wove cloth for their families—and for their conquerors. Many villagers were made slaves. Aztec soldiers kept order among the conquered peoples.

A great market The Aztecs built canals and bridges. They connected their cities with roads. People traveled from all over Mexico to the great market in Tenochtitlan. One traveler described what he saw.

Each day more than sixty thousand people buy and sell things there. Each kind of merchandise is kept by itself on its own street. Each person knows where to go to buy a particular thing.

There is a place for dealers in gold, silver, precious stones, and feathers. There is a slave market where Indian men and women are sold. Next there are traders who sell great pieces of cloth and cotton, and articles of twisted thread. In another part there are skins of tigers and lions, of otters, deer, and mountain cats. There is a place for pottery made in a thousand different forms. And an area for sweet things like honey paste and nut paste.

The empire What kind of an empire did the Aztecs build? Religion and war dominated their culture. The Aztecs built temples and pyramids. Priests took care of the great temples.

Aztec pyramids were decorated with great stone figures of snakelike gods. The Aztecs believed that if the gods were not honored they would get angry and the sun would not

▶ A conquest is a land or a people that has been overcome by force.

▶ Why do you think it was necessary for Aztec soldiers to keep order? How would you react to being made a slave to your conquerors?

▶ Why are good roads important to a strong empire?

▶ How does the market organization show specialization?

The first meeting between Cortez and Montezuma was peaceful. But the Spanish had come to America to add to Spain's wealth and power.

rise. The Aztecs honored the gods by war and sacrifice. Slaves were shot full of arrows and darts and burned alive while drums beat.

ARRIVAL OF THE SPANISH

Cortez   In 1519, the Spanish, led by the explorer Cortez, came to America to search for gold. On his ships, there were 555 men and 16 horses. Their arrival is well documented. One young adventurer in the Cortez expedition kept a journal. In it he described the Spaniards' feelings when they first saw a wondrous city — Tenochtitlan.

> We saw many cities and villages built in the water and other great towns on dry land. Going toward the city we were amazed. It was like the enchantments in legends.
>
> Some of our soldiers even asked if the things we saw were a dream. There is so much to think over that I do not know how to describe it. We saw things that had never been heard of or seen before or even dreamed about. I stood looking and thought that never in the world would there be discovered other lands such as these.

Montezuma   After a few days among the Aztecs, the Spaniards were taken to meet Montezuma, the Aztec emperor.

> Montezuma was about 40 years old. He was of good height, well built, and very neat.
>
> Montezuma had over 200 guards. They had to enter barefoot with their eyes lowered.
>
> Over 30 different dishes were prepared for each of Montezuma's meals. His servants pointed out which foods were best. As he ate, the guards brought him more food, and a chocolate drink in cups of pure gold.

424

The end of the Aztecs The Spaniards were impressed with the Aztec culture. But they were even more impressed with the gold and silver. They decided to conquer the Aztecs.

Cortez claimed all of Mexico for the Spanish empire. The Spanish took millions of dollars worth of gold and silver from the Mexican mines.

SPAIN IN THE AMERICAS

Adventurers and priests The great wealth from the New World helped make Spain the richest, most powerful nation in Europe. By the middle of the 1500s, Spain controlled nearly all of South America and all of Central America.

Spaniards came to the Americas to find gold. They found it. They also came for another reason—religion.

The Spaniards were devout Catholics. They believed that God wished them to carry their religion over all the world. Priests were among the first Spanish settlers in the New World. Their mission was to convert Indians to Christianity. The priests were successful. Today the Catholic religion is the official religion in much of Latin America.

The culture of the Indians changed a great deal after the Europeans arrived. But it did not die. The Indians worked for their conquerors and survived. How do you think working for the Spaniards helped the Indians to keep some of their old ways? Do you think they could have kept these ways if they had fought back?

Agriculture All Spanish rulers encouraged the development of agriculture. Despite the Aztec treasures, there were not great amounts of gold

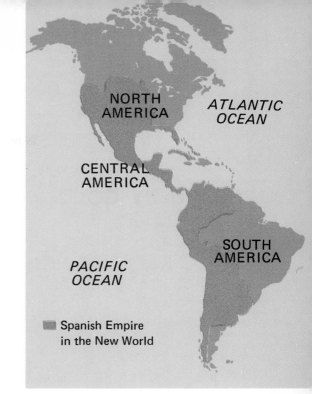

Spanish Empire in the New World

▶ Look at the map on this page. Find where the Spanish settled in North America.

▶ Devout (di vout′) means very religious.

▶ Do you think it is accurate to say the Spanish conquered by the sword and the cross? What does that mean?

▶ Some writers say that the Spanish conquests were a good thing because the Spanish brought Christianity to the Indians. Do you agree with this? Why or why not?

DEATH BY GOLD

Was it possible? Could a Spanish fortune seeker be "fed up" with too much gold? Legend says that one Spanish explorer named Valdivia (val dē′ vē ə) was.

Valdivia came from Spain to lead an expedition to Chile (chil′ ē). Valdivia and his men conquered thousands of Chilean Indians. But even after the conquest, Valdivia was troubled by Indian uprisings.

The Indians finally captured Valdivia. They executed him in a manner they thought appropriate for a Spanish conqueror. They poured hot gold down his throat.

Why would the Indians find that method of execution appropriate?

in the New World. The real wealth for an overcrowded Europe was in the land.

Agriculture was important for several reasons. It provided food and a living for the Spanish settlers. It gave them sugar, tobacco, and cacao for export to European markets. And it helped feed the miners, too.

Encomienda During most of the sixteenth and seventeenth centuries, the Spanish controlled the Indians through a system called *encomienda*. Under this system, the king of Spain allowed settlers to force a certain number of Indians to work for them. In return, the settlers had to provide the Indians with living places and the services of a priest.

The Spanish brought new ideas to Indian farmers. They taught the Indians how to herd cattle, sheep, goats, and hogs. The Spanish brought new tools and new crops—fruits, sugar cane, and cereals. And the Indians, in turn, taught the Spanish to grow corn and squash.

▶ kə ka′o

▶ You have probably eaten or drunk something made from cacao. Look up the word in a dictionary. What is cacao? How have you used it?

▶ en kō mē en′ də

Indian craftsmen made many things, like shoes, that were needed on Spanish plantations.

Indian miners The Spanish also needed people to work in the mines. They forced Indians to work in gold and silver mines.

> Each Monday morning, Indians go up to the mine. They go in and stay until Saturday evening without ever leaving the mines. Their wives bring them food. But they stay underground constantly, digging and carrying out the silver ore.
> They have candles lit day and night. This is the light they work with. And since they are underground, they need the candles all the time.

African slaves The Spanish soon found that Indians made poor slaves. They became ill from changes in the type of work they were doing. And the Indians often ran away from their masters. But the Spanish needed help—especially on large plantations. They found a solution—black slaves from Africa.

What were the advantages of black slaves? They could be bought and transported to the New World cheaply. They were less likely to run away. And they were servants for life. The slave population grew. In time the slaves mixed with the Indians and whites to produce people of mixed ancestry.

Indian slaves were made to do the hardest work on the plantations. Can you see evidence of harsh treatment in this picture?

Social groups The class system in the Spanish colonies was rigid. Birth and race determined social class. And a person could not easily change his class. Indians, black slaves, mulattoes, and *zambos* were in the lowest class. Above them were the *mestizos*. *Mestizos* were craftsmen. They also ran stores and businesses.

Above the *mestizos* were the Creoles. Most Creoles held minor government jobs. Some owned land.

The *peninsulares* were the upper class. They were the real rulers in the Americas. *Peninsulares* were often sent to the New World by the king of Spain to lead the government. They held all top government jobs.

The Catholic church was also powerful in the Spanish colonies. It owned a great deal of land. The priests were an important part of the way of life. They conducted religious ceremonies and ran schools and hospitals.

The Spanish taught few Indians to read or write. And the slaves received even fewer opportunities. The *peninsulares* maintained their control. They kept the class system rigid. The Spanish government did not allow the Indians, the *mestizos*, or the Creoles to govern themselves.

INDEPENDENCE

The rights of man The end of the eighteenth century was a time for ideas. In Europe, and in the English colonies in America, people were talking and writing about the rights of man. People spoke of citizens' right to a voice in their government. Some people spoke out against rule by kings.

◗ Mulattoes (mə lat′ ōz) are people of black and white ancestry.

◗ *Zambos* (zäm′ bōs) are people of black and Indian ancestry.

◗ *Mestizos* (me stē′zōs) are people of white and Indian ancestry.

◗ Creoles (krē′ ōlz) were Spaniards born in the New World.

◗ *Peninsulares* (pə nin′ sü- lä′ res) were Spaniards born in Spain.

▶ Why do you think these two groups would be interested in more privileges and power?

▶ sē mōn′ bə lē′vär
▶ el lē ber tä dôr′

▶ What do you suppose *El Libertador* means?

▶ What effect do you think his European travels had on Bolivar's commitment to the independence struggle?

The old Aztec city of Tenochtitlan once stood on this spot. But the painting here shows only Spanish influence.

Some people in the Spanish colonies — especially the Creoles and *mestizos* — began thinking about revolution and independence, too.

Bolivar In Latin America, the outstanding independence leader was Simon Bolivar. He has been called *El Libertador*.

Bolivar was born in Venezuela. He inherited a fortune from his Spanish parents, who died when he was a child. As a young man, Bolivar traveled in Europe. But he returned home. He devoted his life to the struggle for independence from Spain.

When the Latin American revolutions began in 1810, Bolivar became a troop commander.

Victory For many years, the Latin American movement for independence did not go well. Spanish armies were stronger and better equipped. But finally, Latin American leaders learned to train their armies well and were able to buy arms from European countries. After 1815, they began to win. Ten years later, most of Latin America was free from Spain.

DATES OF INDEPENDENCE IN LATIN AMERICA

Simon Bolivar dreamed of a great union of new Latin American nations. But he was not successful. Bolivar was bitterly disappointed that freedom from Spain had not brought unity. He felt that the revolution had failed. But he said, "All who have served the revolution have plowed the seas."

AFTER INDEPENDENCE

For most Latin Americans, life did not change much after independence. The class system remained. But now it was based more on wealth than on birth.

Indians were no better off. Before, they had worked for Spaniards and received no pay. Now they worked for Creoles and *mestizos* and received very low wages. There were schools,

▶ Had the revolution really failed? Explain your answer.

▶ Think about the plowing of land. What effect does the plow have on the land? Now think about the idea of plowing the seas. What would happen? From Bolivar's statement, do you think he was optimistic?

431

A NEW LIFE

Esteban Pazuj (əs te' bän pä sü') is an Indian plantation worker. But once he was a carpenter in a small village in Guatemala (gwä' tə mä' lə). His way of life has changed. It is better now. But he wonders about the future, too.

Esteban used to make tables and chairs from pine wood. Then he carried a table and six chairs on his back for 12 miles to the market. Esteban bought more wood and a little food from the money he made. But there was still not enough money. Esteban

and his family worked for a few weeks each year on a large coffee plantation to earn more.

A Plantation Job

Then Esteban heard about a new job, on a banana plantation. There he could earn more. And he would have a house free of charge. He would be able to buy food cheaply at the plantation store. If he wished, he could also grow food for himself.

The Pazuj family now has a good house with a kitchen and electric lights. And the children go to school for the first time. He is not completely happy, though. Esteban and his family do not like the hot, wet climate where they now live. They miss the cool, dry highlands of their old home. They miss their friends, too. They do not know their new neighbors. Their neighbors do not speak the Pazuj's Indian language, and the Pazujs learn Spanish slowly. Where they live now does not feel like home to the Pazuj family.

Esteban Pazuj knows that his old life is gone forever. He has become a part of the modern world with its complicated ways. Esteban likes earning more money. His life is a little easier. But Esteban realizes he probably will never earn much more than he does now. He has no education.

Into the Future

Esteban's children are going to school. Perhaps they will learn skills. They might learn to operate a railroad engine or repair a truck. They might learn to do office work. Sometimes Esteban thinks: If life and the future can be so different for Indian children, perhaps other things might change, too.

For centuries, only a few wealthy people have owned land and other property. There have been a few rich families and many poor ones. The rich are the landowners, and the poor work for them. Maybe this will change. To Esteban and other Latin Americans like him, it seems only fair that land be taken from the rich and given to the poor. Then, Esteban thinks, the poor could work for themselves. Then they might not be so poor.

Esteban and many other Latin Americans are changing. They have given up old ways. But they are still puzzled by new ways of doing things. They know they cannot turn back, however. They face the future and hope for a better life.

Why did Esteban and his family move from their highland village?

What problems did Esteban's family find in their new town? Why?

Do you agree with Esteban that giving land to the poor will bring them more money? Why or why not?

Will it be easy to redivide the land by taking some from the rich and giving it to the poor? Explain your answer.

Do you think Esteban Pazuj would have been better off to have stayed in the highland village? Why or why not?

▶ How do you think poor education affects people's ability to govern themselves?

▶ A constitution is a written plan for government.

▶ A dictator is a person with complete power and control.

▶ Why do you think people allowed or supported all these revolutions?

▶ To make an investment means to buy something with the idea that it will be worth more when it is sold.

but very few children attended them. Most people did not learn to read or write.

During colonial times, Latin Americans had been ruled from Spain. The people had no voice in their own government. Now they were not prepared to govern themselves.

New governments After independence, each country wrote out a constitution. The constitutions provided that men would be elected to make laws and that a president would be elected.

But in many countries, dictators ruled. Many of them were important army officers. Sometimes they ignored constitutions. They seized power by force and made laws themselves.

Few Latin Americans could call the government "theirs." Instead, government belonged to those who had power, who had important, rich friends, or who could control the army.

RELATIONS AMONG NATIONS

Dictatorial rule, fighting within countries, and sudden changes of government were the characteristics of much of Latin America in the 1800s.

Outsiders Later, Latin American nations disagreed with the United States and some European countries. Many of these conflicts involved foreign **investments** in Latin America.

Many wealthy Latin Americans wanted to invest their money in land rather than in industries. So the governments welcomed outside investors. These investors put millions of dollars into oil wells and mining. They invested in banana and sugar plantations. And they paid for roads and railroads. All the investors hoped to make profits. Often they did.

Latin Americans take charge Foreign ownership of Latin American wealth has been changing. Some governments have taken over foreign-owned companies. Some governments have made agreements with foreign companies.

▶ Do you think it would be accurate to say that Latin Americans had a tradition of foreign investment and ownership? Why or why not?

WHAT LATIN AMERICA IS TODAY

Every nation is the product of many things: its history, its land, its culture. The nations of Latin America are also the product of these.

Throughout their long history, Latin Americans seldom had control of their own governments. Even today, military governments are common. Governments change rapidly. Constitutions are sometimes ignored.

For hundreds of years, Indians and African slaves performed the hardest tasks for the least pay. Today, all over Latin America, these groups are still not well off.

But change is coming to Latin America. New industries are being developed. New farming methods are being used. All of these will change the history of Latin America.

1. How was the Aztec empire like the Spanish empire? How was it different?
2. Would a system like *encomienda* work in the modern world? Why or why not? Why do you think this system worked in Latin America under Spanish rule?
3. What reasons can you think of to explain why the Indians and slaves were no better off after independence?

The Land and the People

A PLACE TO LIVE

The land of Latin America came first. It was there before the people. The people made their homes, found food, and developed their culture on the land. Then they shaped the land. They used its waters and resources, and they farmed the soil. They built industries, too.

▶ Here the land means the geography—mountains, forests, rivers, plains, climate, and minerals.

How does the land shape people? Geography affects where people live. For instance, the Indians in Latin America often settled by rivers and lakes. The land there was fertile for growing food. The land affects the kinds of houses people build. People who live on a mountainside fit their houses to their environment. People in the desert do the same.

▶ What is another way rivers and lakes might be important to people's food supply?

Looking at Latin America Look at the population map on the next page. Where do most Latin Americans live? Are all parts of the land equally crowded? Density is the number of people who live in a region. Which parts of Latin America have the highest density?

▶ How might natural resources, such as forests, affect housing?

Now look at the landform map. What kinds of landforms have the fewest people? What kinds of landforms have the most people?

Compare the population map with the map showing rainfall. Which areas have the heaviest rainfall? Which areas have very little rainfall? Which areas have the most people? Do you see a connection between these facts?

Now look at the resources map. Where is the most industry found in Latin America? Where is the best grazing land for cattle? Where is the best mining region? Do you think many people like to live in such regions? Do you think there are problems when people prefer to live one place and natural resources are

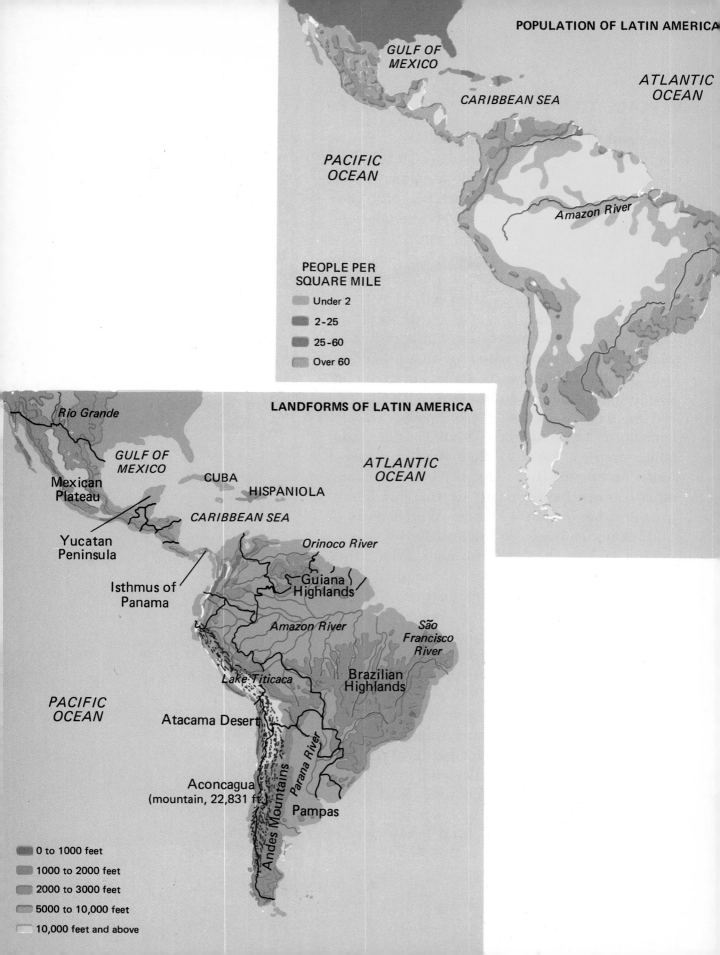

POPULATION OF LATIN AMERICA

GULF OF MEXICO

CARIBBEAN SEA

ATLANTIC OCEAN

PACIFIC OCEAN

Amazon River

PEOPLE PER SQUARE MILE

Under 2

2-25

25-60

Over 60

LANDFORMS OF LATIN AMERICA

Rio Grande

GULF OF MEXICO

CUBA

HISPANIOLA

ATLANTIC OCEAN

Mexican Plateau

CARIBBEAN SEA

Yucatan Peninsula

Orinoco River

Isthmus of Panama

Guiana Highlands

Amazon River

São Francisco River

Lake Titicaca

Brazilian Highlands

PACIFIC OCEAN

Atacama Desert

Aconcagua (mountain, 22,831 ft.)

Paraná River

Pampas

Andes Mountains

0 to 1000 feet

1000 to 2000 feet

2000 to 3000 feet

5000 to 10,000 feet

10,000 feet and above

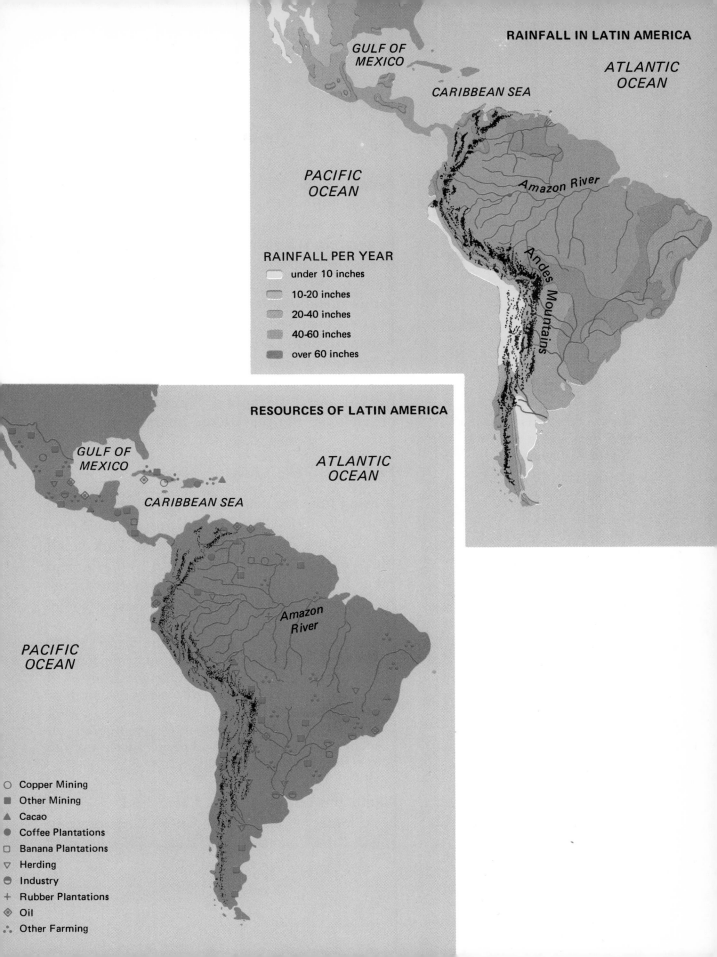

RAINFALL IN LATIN AMERICA

GULF OF MEXICO

ATLANTIC OCEAN

CARIBBEAN SEA

PACIFIC OCEAN

Amazon River

Andes Mountains

RAINFALL PER YEAR

- under 10 inches
- 10-20 inches
- 20-40 inches
- 40-60 inches
- over 60 inches

RESOURCES OF LATIN AMERICA

GULF OF MEXICO

ATLANTIC OCEAN

CARIBBEAN SEA

PACIFIC OCEAN

Amazon River

- ○ Copper Mining
- ■ Other Mining
- ▲ Cacao
- ● Coffee Plantations
- ☐ Banana Plantations
- ▽ Herding
- ⊖ Industry
- + Rubber Plantations
- ◈ Oil
- ∴ Other Farming

located in other areas? If so, what kinds of problems do you think this causes for a country?

People settle The distribution of people has always followed a pattern in Latin America. Areas of dense population are separated by large areas with very few people. Can you tell from the maps on page 438 why this is so? This pattern has affected transportation and communication, too. People have always depended on rivers and inland water routes for transportation. But today some people are trying to overcome the natural barriers such as rain forests. They are trying to build roads right through the jungle. Part of the land is an obstacle, so the people are changing the land.

FARMING THE LAND

A living from the soil In most of Latin America, more people live on farms than in cities. Some farmers live in small villages and work small plots of land. They grow corn, squash, and other foods for their families. Sometimes they have a little food left to sell in a nearby town.

The people crowd together in the market areas. They squat on the ground, waiting for customers. In almost every market, similar goods are sold together. All the people with garden vegetables will be together on one block. Women spin wool on one corner. All the people with pottery to sell occupy another corner. And people with clothing to sell crowd a different block.

Plantations Some farmers live and work on large farms or plantations. These farmers grow sugar, coffee, bananas, and cacao. They are per-

▶ The people of Latin America live and work in different ways because of different climates and resources. And these things gave different interests and problems to the people. Think about this. Could it have affected the unity which Bolivar dreamed of reaching? Discuss your answer.

▶ An obstacle is something that gets in the way of a person or thing.

▶ Do you think the organization of the market into separate areas for different wares is a traditional way of selling? Why do you think so?

440

haps the best off of Latin American farmers. They sell their products mainly in the United States or Europe.

PEOPLE OF THE CITY

Many Latin Americans have left rural areas to seek better lives in cities. Latin American cities are a mixture of old and new. Most of them were first built around a square, or *plaza*. Houses and many other buildings are made of adobe. They have tiled roofs. Each city has a great cathedral and other church buildings.

A job in the city Businesses and factories are in cities. People from the farms hope to find jobs in them. Many Latin Americans who move to cities have a hard time. Many of them have had little or no education. They have no skills. There are few jobs for them. And many of them must live in terrible slums.

▶ The plantation farmers depend for their income on the sale of their products in other countries. If coffee is selling for a high price in the United States, how will that affect the profits of a coffee planter in the Latin American nations?

▶ Adobe (ə dō′bē) is a building material made from mud and straw, then baked in the sun.

Compare the community in the foreground to the one in the background. What are the differences in the two communities?

441

JUNGLE HIGHWAY

Invading the Interior

The interior of Brazil is being invaded. But this time, engineers and construction workers are leading the invasion. They are cutting through the thick growth of the Amazon jungle to build a new road across Brazil.

The new road is called the Trans-Amazon Highway. The map below shows its route. *Trans* is a word part which means across or through. Look at the map. Do you think Trans-Amazon is a good name for the new highway? Why or why not?

The Trans-Amazon Highway will link the cities of Brazil's Atlantic coast with the Peruvian highway which stretches to the Pacific. It will connect cities all over Brazil with new settlements in the country's interior. How will this help new settlements?

The people of Brazil are both anxious and hopeful about the highway project. The land of northeastern Brazil is dry and unproductive. It is difficult for the people to grow enough food or earn much money. Brazilians expect the new highway to provide new farmland and many jobs. They expect new towns and cities to develop along the highway. They believe many people will move from the crowded coastal cities and help develop central Brazil.

The Pioneers

The new highway is a tremendous challenge to Brazilian engineering and skill. Heavy cutting equipment is often used to clear away thick jungle growth. Men with axes cut through the thickest spots.

There are other challenges, too. How do workers deal with heavy rains, thousands of biting insects, disease, and just plain loneliness?

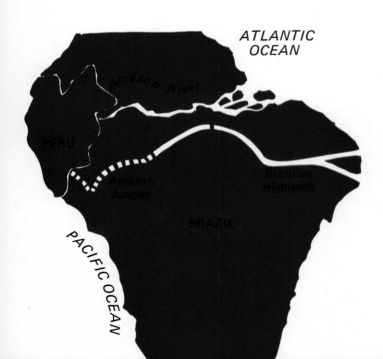

The first arrivals usually reach the site by canoe. They travel along the small rivers leading from the Amazon River. The men must gather and hunt food until they can clear a campsite and receive supplies.

Camp life is especially hard during rainy periods. One engineer said, "The bulldozers and trucks get stuck in the mud. Our clothes are so wet and sticky that they fall apart. Nobody can move. Sometimes it is impossible to work."

And there is always loneliness. Road workers do not bring their families with them. Once the sun sets, there is much time to think about the family and the excitement of the city.

Saving Plants and People

Both ecologists and anthropologists are worried about problems that the new highway may bring.

The rain forest has only a thin layer of rich soil. This layer is now protected by tall trees and fed by decaying leaves and plants. But construction is destroying the Amazonian forest. The trees are being cleared away to make space for the road and new settlements. Ecologists think there will be no good farmland. Some scientists even argue that the jungle may become a desert.

Anthropologists are concerned about the thousands of Indians living in the forests. Many live along the land which is scheduled for construction. Where will they go? What will happen to them?

Why are Brazilians both anxious and hopeful about the Trans-Amazon Highway? Which people do you think would be most worried by the new road? Who do you think would benefit most from it?

See whether you agree or disagree with the following statement: In constructing the highway, man has used his environment to his benefit. But at the same time, the environment is being destroyed.

If you lived in Brazil, how would you feel about the Trans-Amazon Highway?

These pictures show the variety of life in Latin American villages. Have you ever seen a llama in a zoo? The Peruvian man below herds these animals for a living. Poor farmers must plow the hillsides in order to plant their crops. In contrast to the small farmers, the coffee pickers at bottom right work on a large plantation in Brazil. The old woman at right is making lace. Her lace may be sold in a street market like the one on the opposite page.

445

♦ kā rə lē′ nə mä rē′ ə dē hā-süs′

♦ saü pau′ lü

♦ fä ve′ lä

♦ A slum is an area with high density, run-down buildings, and few things like running water and toilets.

♦ Why do you suppose Carolina Maria de Jesus did not leave São Paulo and return to her village?

A story of city life   Carolina Maria de Jesus grew up in a small Brazilian village. She went to school for two years and learned to read and write. When Carolina moved to the city of São Paulo, she had trouble finding work. She and her children had to live in a *favela,* the Brazilian word for slum. Often they did not have enough food.

On old scraps of paper, Carolina kept a diary of what happened to her each day. One day she wrote:

> My children are always hungry. Yesterday I got half a pig's head at the slaughterhouse. We ate the meat and saved the bones. Today I boiled the bones and put some potatoes into the broth. When my children are starving they aren't so fussy about what they eat.

Carolina and her children lived in a small shack she had made from old boards and flattened tin cans. Everyone in the slum had to get water from a single faucet. They stood in long lines each day to fill their buckets. People washed their clothes in a nearby river that smelled terrible because it was polluted.

BUILDING INDUSTRY — AUTOS IN CHILE

Some changes have come to Latin America in the twentieth century. But many people think more change must come. They think governments should help produce more food, build factories to provide jobs and goods, and improve people's lives.

Assembling cars   Chile is one of the narrowest countries in the world. Most of Chile's people live in a huge valley in the center of the country. Santiago, the capital, and other cities are located here.

sän′ tē ä′gō

For a long time, Chile imported many manufactured goods. In recent years, however, Chile has worked to build up its own industries. The Chilean government decided to strengthen the country's automobile industry.

The government ordered that fully assembled cars could no longer be brought in from foreign countries to be sold in Chile. Instead, Chilean companies would buy parts from other countries but assemble the automobiles themselves. Chilean companies would also make some of the parts. And each year the auto assembly companies would have to use more parts made in Chile.

To assemble means to put together.

• Major cities in Chile

These were the government's reasons for its rules:

1. Less money would leave Chile for importing foreign auto parts.
2. The assembly plants would help build up Chile's industry and would also provide jobs for workers.
3. Chile would depend less on other countries.

Helping a city There was one other government requirement. Companies could not build assembly plants just anywhere. They had to build them in Arica.

Arica is a city of 20,000 people. It is in the far northern part of Chile. Find Arica on the map on page 447. What kind of land is Arica near? Arica is on the Pacific Ocean and almost on the border of Peru. It is about 1,000 miles from Santiago, Chile's capital. Find Santiago on the map. Arica is also a long way from other cities where cars assembled in Arica would be sold.

Why did the government choose Arica for its auto plants? The city and the surrounding area once belonged to Peru. But even after Chile had won the area, the people of Arica felt more like Peruvians than Chileans. They thought the government at Santiago paid little attention to them. It did not help them find jobs. From time to time, the people of Arica threatened to make their area once more a part of Peru. How do you think they would do that?

The Chilean government wanted to make sure Aricans would be loyal to Chile. The government thought: If there were auto assembly plants in Arica, the people would have jobs. And they would thank the government.

▶ ə rē′ kə

448

Made in Chile Assembling cars in Chile turned out to be a seasonal business. It was like growing crops—some times of the year were busier and more productive than others. Many companies produced no cars during the first part of the year. Production began about June. When no cars were being assembled, the companies let many of their workers go. Do you think the seasonal nature of auto assembly would make people want to work in the factories? Why or why not? Some workers came back to the plants when production began again. Others did not. Each year many new workers had to be trained.

Besides having workers come and go each year, the Arica factories had other problems. Some of the parts needed to assemble cars were imported. But many of the parts—bumpers, front doors, tires, seats—were produced in or near Santiago. One factory manager bought his front doors from Santiago. But he ordered his back doors from Europe. Why would this present problems? Look again at the map on page 447.

Sometimes, parts made in Santiago did not arrive on time. Assembly plants then had to close until the needed parts got there. How do you think this affected the workers?

Another problem was that the parts made in Chile often did not fit. They had to be changed or remade at the assembly plants. And the parts made in Chile were often more expensive than imported parts. Sometimes they cost eight times more!

Asking why Why have Chilean companies had so much trouble manufacturing automobile parts? One reason is a lack of skilled workers.

The assembly line above never stops. Each worker works on the same part of every car that passes.

▶ What problems of manufacturing parts and assembling cars might be overcome if all parts were made in Chile?

▶ Do you think it is likely that the problem of poorly fitting parts will be overcome? Why or why not?

▶ Do you think Chile's automobile program could be called successful? Explain.

Another is too little money for factories and machines.

There was still another problem. Chileans had to pay more for cars assembled in Chile than they did for imported cars. Why do you think the cost of the cars was so high?

PROBLEMS AHEAD

Poverty remains a serious problem in many Latin American countries. Governments realize more people must have schooling and jobs. Carolina Maria de Jesus was different from many poor Latin Americans mainly because she could read and write. In her country, Brazil, more than half the people are not literate. That means they cannot read and write. The situation is worse in some countries and better in others. The idea that everyone should go to school is new in Latin America.

Latin America has more than 200 million people now. And the population is still growing. More food is needed. More land must be put into farming. More schools and factories must be built. And all these things are needed in a hurry.

1. How does the geography of Latin America affect where the people live and how they make their livings?
2. How is farming different in Latin America and the United States? How would that affect the way people live?
3. Why does Carolina Maria de Jesus live the way she does? What opportunities does she have?
4. Why is it important for Latin American nations to develop their own industries? What do you think might happen if they do not? What help will industry bring?

Case Study: Chile and Marxism

SALVADOR ALLENDE

säl′və dur ä yen′dā

A government career Salvador Allende was born into a well-to-do family in Santiago, the capital of Chile. He studied medicine, but he never practiced it. He was more interested in politics. Allende wanted to be president of Chile.

Three times Allende ran for president. Three times he lost. A man once asked him what he did when he was not running for the presidency. Allende replied: "I sit and dream about being president." In 1970, Allende's dream finally came true.

märk′ siz əm

Marxism for Chile Why is Allende's election important? Because he is a Marxist. And he is the first Marxist anywhere in the world to be selected as head of government in a free and open election.

The word **Marxism** comes from the name of Karl Marx, a German who lived in the 1800s. A Marxist believes that *workers,* with the help of their government, should own and operate a nation's factories, farms, transportation, and communication. Is this different from the United States? If so, how? Is it similar to the United States in any way? If so, how?

Salvador Allende, a Marxist, won more votes than any of the other candidates. More than a third of the voters cast ballots for him. To find out why the voters selected Allende, let us look at Chile as a social scientist would.

Like all scientists, we begin by asking questions. What problems do Chileans face today? What programs did Allende have to meet these problems? Who stood to gain by Allende's election? Let's look at the issues.

WHO ARE THE LANDOWNERS?

A handful of owners Chile has long had a land problem. A few wealthy people have owned much of the land. Most farmers have had no land of their own. They are too poor to buy any. Instead, they have been working for large land-owners who pay low wages.

Even the farmers who have owned land barely raise enough food to eat. They have hardly ever had enough to sell. Landowners have not managed their farms well. And farmers have used old-fashioned growing methods.

This picture shows Salvador Allende, in a hard hat, campaigning among some miners.

▶ Do you think agriculture is a profitable business in Chile? Why?

POLITICAL SCIENCE

Why do people vote the way they do? How do different governments work? How are government decisions made? These are some of the questions people ask about politics and government.

And these are some of the questions that **political scientists** try to answer. Political scientists analyze and compare governments. They try to find out how policies are made and how they change. Who could use these studies?

Voter Studies

Political scientists spend a long time researching. To analyze an election, for example, these scientists compare many sets of figures. They relate voting results to figures showing education, age, family income, and past voting of the voters.

Political scientists might find that poor people vote differently from rich people. They might find that young people vote for different candidates than their parents. Why might these groups vote differently? From their research, political scientists might even be able to predict how certain people would vote in the future. Would this be useful information? To whom?

Land reform Even before Allende's election, the Chilean government had begun to take land from wealthy landowners and divide it more equally. The government paid what they considered a fair price for the land they took. Then they divided it into small farms and gave land to many landless farmers. But still many people remained without land.

Farmers march A group of landless farm workers marched 60 miles to the Department of Agriculture in Santiago. They were protesting the slowness of land reform.

A worker from the department called to the demonstrators, "I support your actions. It's the only way we'll get things done."

Candidate Allende pledged to speed up land reform. Do you think poor farmers would support Allende? Why? How do you think landowners would feel about Allende? Why?

Most of Chile's land is not good for farming. It is necessary to use modern methods to cultivate what good land there is.

▶ Is land reform fair? Will it help solve Chile's problem? How?

455

WHO OWNS THE FACTORIES?

▶ Do you think there is a pattern of ownership of land and money in Chile? If so, give your evidence.

There had only been a few factory owners in Chile, and they controlled most of the money. But there were many factory workers.

Many Chileans felt that it was unfair for one owner to control a company. They believed that the owner often became too rich from the company profits. The worker, however, always received a set salary—one that often seemed too low to support a family.

▶ Do you think the workers would be willing to work harder if they were part owners? Why or why not?

Workers as owners Marxist supporters believed that if the government and the workers took over and ran the factories, things would be better for everyone. No one group would have too much. The workers, the government, and all of Chile would share the factory profits. When Allende's government took over, it made some changes in factory ownership. It took over some large businesses. It gained control of railroads, truck routes, and telephone systems. The government hoped to run businesses better than before.

▶ Do you think the factory owners agreed that things would be better for everyone? Explain.

HOUSING CRISIS

The countryside A fifth of all Chileans do not have decent housing. In the country, where most people are farmers, people live in one-room houses made of woven branches and whitewashed mud. The roof may be thatched or made of red tile to keep out the rain. Many of these houses are on the edges of large estates.

▶ An estate is a large area of land which often has a big house on it.

The cities In the cities, many poor people have no permanent place to live. Some live

456

in alley doorways. Others live in run-down wooden and tar paper shacks. These run-down developments pop up so quickly that Chileans call them "toadstool towns."

The outskirts of Santiago are crowded with poorly built huts standing along muddy paths. Some architects want to help. They have a plan to design large communities for the poor people, rather than single houses for the rich.

Many Chileans thought their living conditions would improve under the new government. They hoped Allende would build more and better homes for them. Certainly, they thought, their lives could be no worse. As a political scientist, are you beginning to find reasons for Allende's election?

WHO OWNS THE MINES?

The Chilean soil is rich in metals. Chile is a major exporter of copper. In fact, copper is the backbone of Chile's economy.

But for many years, American companies owned Chile's copper mines. These companies

▶ What are toadstools? Are they planted by people? Do you think that is a good nickname for these city living places? Explain.

▶ An architect (är′ kə tekt) is a person who plans buildings.

▶ What does the "backbone" of the economy mean?

The American-owned mines in Chile use the most modern equipment. When the Chilean government took over the mines, it sometimes could not find skilled people to service this equipment.

457

had both money and technical experience. Chile had neither of these things — only copper. The Chilean government had hoped that new jobs would be created after foreign companies set up mines in Chile. The government had hoped that Chileans would learn to operate and manage their own mines. However, things did not develop this way.

Chileans worked the mines, but the profits, the power to make decisions, and the important jobs belonged to the foreign owners. Often the profits left Chile. The money from Chile's copper was spent in other countries.

Chile for Chileans   Before Allende's election, the Chilean government persuaded the mine owners to share their profits more equally. But many Chileans were unhappy. They believed that Chileans, not North Americans, should work, control, and manage the copper industry.

The companies had already invested money and built the factories, however. They felt they should continue to manage the companies and share in the profits. After Allende's election, though, the government took over all the copper mines. The foreign companies were forced out. The government did not decide immediately how much to pay the companies for their property. However, workers' wages were immediately increased.

PEOPLE TAKE SIDES

Fears grow   People inside and outside Chile soon realized that Allende was talking about making important changes in the country. Many foreign companies moved to pull out their investments, even before the election.

▶ Why would the profits leave the country? How would this hurt Chile?

▶ Do you think the Chilean copper workers supported Allende? Why or why not?

458

One American company was accused of interfering to help Allende's opponents.

A brighter future Many college professors and students voted for Allende. They did not hope to gain higher wages or ownership, but they believed the future might be better for everyone if Allende were elected.

AFTER THE ELECTION:
A CHILEAN FAMILY

You have read about the problems Chileans had before Allende's election. You know some of the groups who were for and against Allende. Now let us meet the members of a real family in Santiago and see how they feel about Allende since his election.

The family have lived in their house for 30 years. The house is comfortable, but not fancy. There is a small garden for corn and tomatoes. A maid and a cook live with the family. They are paid $10 a month.

▶ What do you think Alberto meant by his remark? Do you think he had reason to worry? Explain.

▶ What would you have done in Alberto's place? Would you have waited to see what changes came?

▶ An opposition is a group which is against the people in power.

▶ Where would the government get the money to build houses and pay higher wages? Is this always easy to do?

Alberto The head of the family is Alberto. He came to Chile when he was only 16. Alberto worked hard. He saved, invested, and gradually built a large business. Today his businesses include a farm, a small factory, several apartments, and some stores.

Alberto seems to be a wealthy man. But since Allende was elected president, Alberto has lived with a constant fear. He is afraid of losing everything he has worked for. He is afraid he will end up "an old man working for the state." Alberto and his wife did not vote for Allende.

Some people closed their businesses or stores and left Chile after Allende's election. They were worried about the future. Why didn't Alberto leave? He says, "My family and friends all live here. My business is here, and I'm not happy if I'm not working."

Miguel Alberto's older son, Miguel, is a professor. He and his wife are strong Allende supporters. Though they understand what is troubling Alberto and his wife, they do not think the old people should worry. "Don't forget," they say, "the important thing here is that there is an opposition. You can speak out and protest." Alberto does not answer, but he is thinking, "There may be a chance to speak out now, but for how long?"

Carlos Alberto's younger son, Carlos, voted for Allende, too. But now he has doubts about Allende's policies. Carlos says, "Allende gives the poor people a feeling that they can do what they want—even take over farms and factories. And the poor people want everything—nice houses, cars, good jobs. But the government can't give it to them right away. So now the people are becoming impatient. The time may come when the government won't be able to control them."

LIVING WITH THE NEW GOVERNMENT

After two years of Allende's government, no one knew what would happen next. The road to public ownership proved to be hard.

Food for the people   Chile has never been able to grow enough food for its people. It has always imported much of its food. The new government hoped that food production would increase when farmers got their own land.

But the government was wrong. Food production was not able to meet food demand. Beef became scarce in stores. Wheat and bread supplies were very low. Butter disappeared from stores. Prices had doubled by 1972.

Housewives grew more and more unhappy with the Allende government. They protested against shortages and high prices. Once, the housewives marched through the streets of Santiago, beating wooden spoons against metal pans.

Workers react   Some farm workers added to Allende's problems. Many of them did not wait for the government to take over farmland. They took it over themselves and forced the owners to leave. The landowners received no money for their land. This made them even more unhappy with the Allende government.

The housing situation also did not immediately improve. Many poor people still had to live in shacks in slums.

▶ Can you explain why prices doubled when there were food shortages?

461

▶ A technician (tek nish′ ən) is someone who knows the details of how to do a job. Is a technician a specialist? Why do you think so?

▶ Why were workers on strike against themselves?

Copper industry Things did not go well in the copper industry. When the government took it over, Chilean technicians replaced many of the American technicians. But some of the Chilean technicians did not know their jobs well. They had not yet had enough training.

Copper production fell. The price of copper fell. The government was getting less income from the copper industry than it expected. At one mine, miners went on strike for higher wages. They did not seem to care that they were really on strike against themselves.

462

AN UNCERTAIN FUTURE

Chile has been one of the more peaceful Latin American countries. In Chile, governments have come and gone through elections, not revolutions. Chileans have been able to solve their problems peacefully.

But the people of Chile have become anxious. By 1972, after Allende had been president for two years, many Chileans were concerned about the future. The wealthy feared they would lose everything. Farmers and factory workers feared that Allende was not moving fast enough. A few people even feared that Allende would make himself the dictator of Chile. And everyone, even some of his supporters, blamed Allende for their fears. Do you think it is fair to blame all of Chile's problems on Allende's government? Why or why not?

▶ Do you think people often blame their leaders for all of their country's problems? Explain.

Allende loses an election In 1973, the people of Chile showed their anxiety by voting against Allende's party in the legislative elections. The opposition parties had combined to work against Allende and his policies. The opposition parties got a majority of the seats in Chile's Senate. But they did not get enough votes to veto Allende's program. Can you think of reasons why the people of Chile voted as they did?

1. What kinds of feelings and attitudes do you think Salvador Allende appealed to in his campaign?

2. What advantages do you think foreign-owned companies brought to Chile? Where do their profits go?

463

INVESTIGATING THE UNIT

Doing Research

Pick a town in Latin America that is about the size of your community. Find out as much as you can about the town and the people who live there. What are the main industries? How does the town affect the rest of the region or the country? How do the people of the town live? What are the differences between their lives and your life?

Looking at the Evidence

Imagine you are an officer in an American foundation that is trying to help Latin America. You have a million dollars to give away to the town you studied. But you want to spend it in the best possible way. From your research, what do you think are the most urgent needs of the town? What evidence is there that a million dollars would really help solve one of its problems? What evidence would you look for to see if your grant was working?

Using Maps

Cape Horn and the Strait of Magellan are two of the most dangerous sea passages known. Find them on a good map of South America. What is the difference between them? How can ships sailing from the Atlantic to the Pacific coasts of North America avoid these dangerous passages?

Comparing and Contrasting

Compare Carolina Maria de Jesus' attitudes with the opinions of Carlos and Miguel. How are the backgrounds of the two families different? Do you think that some of Carlos' comments would apply to Carolina and her family?

Reading on Your Own

Why not try finding out some more about Latin America's interesting past? Here are some books to start with: *Simon Bolivar: The George Washington of South America,* by Bob and Jan Young (New York, Hawthorn Books); *Gold and Gods of Peru,* by Hans Bauman (New York, Pantheon Books).

SOCIAL STUDIES DICTIONARY

KEY TO PRONUNCIATION

The pronunciation of a word is shown in this way: **abbreviate** (ə brē′vē āt). The letters and signs used are pronounced as in the words below. The mark ′ is placed after a syllable with primary or heavy accent, as in the example above. The mark ′ after a syllable shows a secondary or lighter accent, as in **abbreviation** (ə brē′vē ā′shən).

a	hat, cap	j	jam, enjoy	u	cup, butter
ā	age, face	k	kind, seek	u̇	full, put
ã	care, air	l	land, coal	ü	rule, move
ä	father, far	m	me, am	ū	use, music
		n	no, in		
b	bad, rob	ng	long, bring		
ch	child, much			v	very, save
d	did, red	o	hot, rock	w	will, woman
		ō	open, go	y	young, yet
e	let, best	ô	order, all	z	zero, breeze
ē	equal, be	oi	oil, voice	zh	measure, seizure
ėr	term, learn	ou	house, out		
f	fat, if	p	paper, cup	ə represents:
g	go, bag	r	run, try	a in about
h	he, how	s	say, yes	e in taken
		sh	she, rush	i in April
i	it, pin	t	tell, it	o in lemon
ī	ice, five	th	thin, both	u in circus
		ҭн	then, smooth	

From THORNDIKE-BARNHART JUNIOR DICTIONARY by E. L. Thorndike and Clarence L. Barnhart. Copyright © 1968 by Scott, Foresman and Company. Reprinted by permission of the publisher.

agricultural revolution—The time when people first learned to domesticate plants and animals to produce more food.

apprentice (ə prent′ tis)—A person who worked for low wages in order to learn a trade. He usually worked under a master.

anthropologist (an' thrə pol' ə jist)—A social scientist who studies people and their ways of life.

archaeologist (är' kē ol' ə jist)—A social scientist who studies ancient cultures by examining the material remains of those cultures.

artifact (är' tə fakt)—Any material object that people use as a part of their culture.

barter (bär' tər)—Trading one thing for another without using money.

capitalism—A system which features the private ownership of land, property, and, often, the means of production—like factories.

caste (kast)—A Hindu social group into which a person is born and which determines his position and status in Indian society.

chattel slavery (chat' l)—A form of slavery in which people were bought and sold just like goods.

city-state—A city which is really like an independent state. City-states, such as Athens and Sparta, governed themselves in their own way.

civilization—The name given to the complex ways of living of a group of people. Civilization involves cities and higher levels of trade, art, and government than are possible in small villages.

collective farm—A type of farm in the Soviet Union in which most of the land is owned jointly by the farmers who work it.

communism—A system in which property is owned by the people as a group, not as individuals. The government controls most land and business.

culture—The complete way of life a group of people practice and pass on to their children.

cuneiform (kū nē' ə fôrm)—A system of writing with wedge-shaped marks in clay used by the ancient Sumerians and Babylonians.

domestic slavery—A milder form of slavery practiced long ago in Africa. Slaves could usually manage to purchase their freedom after a few years.

domestication (də mes' tə kā' shən)—Human control over plants or animals for the raising of food.

economic system—The way that cultures produce goods and services.

economist—A social scientist who studies how goods and services are exchanged, owned, and managed.

ethnocentrism (eth nō sen' triz əm)—The way that some people judge the rest of the world according to their own values.

466

extended family—A more complicated social group in which parents, young children, grown children, grandparents, and other relatives live together in the same household.

feudal system—The medieval way of government in which men gave a lord help in war, or some other kind of help. In return, the lord gave them protection and the use of land.

food-gathering—Finding things to eat rather than growing them.

GNP (Gross National Product)—The total value of all the goods and services produced in a country in a year.

hieroglyphics (hī′ ər ə glif′ iks)—The Egyptian system of writing using pictures to represent things and ideas.

historian—A social scientist who studies written records to learn how people lived in the past.

hypothesis (hī poth′ ə sis)—An explanation, or educated guess, which can be proved or disproved.

imperialism (im pir′ ē əl iz əm)—The system of conquering other nations to build an empire.

Industrial Revolution—The time in history when people learned how to use machines and new sources of power to produce the things they needed.

Marxism—A set of ideas which says that workers, with the help of their government, should own and operate a nation's factories, farms, transportation, and communication.

material culture—The tools, clothes, houses, art, and other things that a people make and use.

migrant workers—People who leave their native homes to find jobs in another place or country.

monotheism (mon′ ə thē iz′ əm)—A religious belief that there is only one God.

monsoons (mon sünz′)—Winds that blow at certain times of the year in areas near the equator and bring heavy rains.

nationalism—A strong feeling of pride in one's country.

New Stone Age—The ancient time when people still used stone tools, but had learned how to domesticate plants and animals.

nuclear family (nü′ klē ər)—A simple type of social group made up of parents and their children or of just a husband and wife.

Old Stone Age—The ancient time when stone was used to make tools and when people were mostly food-gatherers or hunters.

peasants (pez′ nts)—Owners of small farms or people who work for other farmers.

political scientist—A social scientist who studies government and its powers.

polytheism—A belief in more than one god.

population density—The term used to describe the average number of people who live in a certain area.

Renaissance (ren′ ə säns)—A period in Europe about 600 years ago, when art and learning underwent a "rebirth."

roles—The parts that a person plays in a group or social situation.

serfs—Unfree medieval peasants who lived on the land of a lord. The lord gave them protection in exchange for their labor.

social institutions (in′ stə tü′ shənz)—Complicated social groups such as educational systems or governments.

socialization (sō′ shə lə zā′ shən)—The process by which people learn to be part of their culture.

society—The group of people in a culture.

sociologist (sō′ sē äl′ ə jist)—A social scientist who studies how different people in societies live with each other.

specialist (spesh′ əl ist)—A person who does just one particular job.

status (sta′ təs)—The degree of importance that a person or a social group has in a society.

surplus (sėr′ pləs)—More than a person or group *needs;* something extra.

symbol (sim′ bl)—Something that stands for or is a sign for something else.

technology (tek nol′ ə je)—All the skills and ways of doing things that a people develop. Tools + knowledge = technology.

time-binding—How cultures pass on knowledge from one generation to the next so that each generation can build on all previous knowledge.

urban revolution—The change in human history that took place when people first began to live in cities.

vassals (vas′ lz)—Medieval people who held land from a lord or superior. In return, vassals gave help in war, or some other kind of help. A great noble could be a vassal of the king and have many other men as his vassals.

ACKNOWLEDGMENTS

Design by Mulvey/Crump Associates, Inc.

Illustrations by Marbury Brown and Ed Sibbett

Maps by Eric Hieber

PHOTOGRAPHS

Authentic—Authentic Pictures; Bettmann—the Bettmann Archive; Culver—Culver Pictures DPI—Design Photographers International, Incorporated; FPG—Free Lance Photographers Guild; Granger—The Granger Collection; N.Y.P.L.—New York Public Library Shostal—Shostal Association
Front Cover: Adele Brodkin
Back Cover: E. J. Ross

Unit 1
1: Woodfin Camp (Kal Muller). 2: *l* De Wys (Victor Englebert), *r* Magnum (Leonard Freed). 5: De Wys (B. Morgenroth). 6: *l* Black Star (T. S. Satyan), *r* Shostal (Barkha). 7: *t* Woodfin Camp (Kal Muller), *bl* Woodfin Camp (Jehangir Gazdar), *br* Woodfin Camp (Jehangir Gazdar). 8: Photo Researchers (George Holton). 9: *t* Photo Researchers (Maslowski), *b* Magnum (Eric Hartmann). 10: Rapho Guillumette (Sam Bettle). 11: *t* Rapho Guillumette (Pat Hartley), *b* Photo Researchers (Victor Englebert. 13: Photo Researchers (Gianni Tortoli), *b* Photo Researchers (E. Bubat). 15: Photo Researchers (Joe Rychatnik). 16: *l* Nancy Palmer (Barry Schlachter), *r* Photo Researchers (Guy Gilette). 18: *t* China Photo Service from Eastfoto, *bl* Paula Henderson, *br* Photo Trends (Horst Schafer). 20: *l* DPI (Dunn), *r* Woodfin Camp (Marc and Evelyn Bernheim). 26: *l* Magnum (Ian Berry), *r* Black Star (Flip Schulke). 27: *tr* Museum of the American Indian, *tl* Joseph Martin/SCALA, *b* Joseph Martin/ SCALA. 29: *t* Woodfin Camp (Jehangir Gazdar), *b* William G. Froelich, Jr. 32: *l* Granger, *r* Magnum (Marc Ribaud). 33: *l* Photo Researchers (George Holton), *r* Museum of the University of Pennsylvania, Joseph Martin/SCALA. 35: Woodfin Camp (Peter Keen). 40: Authentic. 41: *l* Granger, *tr* SCALA New York/Florence, *br* Metropolitan Museum of Art, Rogers Fund 1934. 42: William G. Froelich, Jr. 43: Granger. 44: Shostal (K. Scholz). 46: *l* Culver, *r* Woodfin Camp (John Marmaras).

Unit 2
Rapho Guillumette (Georg Gerster). 50: Photo Researchers (John G. Ross). 54: Federico Borromeo/SCALA. 55: Photo Researchers (Tomas D. W. Friedmann). Rapho Guillumette (Georg Gerster). 58: Metropolitan Museum of Art, Harris Brisbane Dick Fund, 1959. 61: Bettmann. 63: Metropolitan Museum of Art, Museum of Excavations 1928–29, Rogers Fund 1930. 64: *l* Rapho Guillumette (C. A. Peterson), *r* SCALA New York/Florence. 65: *t* SCALA New York/Florence, *b* Federico Borromeo/SCALA. 69: Woodfin Camp (Peter Keen). 72: SCALA New York/Florence. 73: Metropolitan Museum of Art, Rogers Fund 1955. 74: Photo Researchers (George Holton). 79: Photo Researchers (Dr. Richard Dranizke). 85: *t* Photo Researchers (J. J. Scherschel), *bl* Photo Researchers

(Frank Screider), *br* Photo Researchers (Len Jossel). 87: Rapho Guillumette (Paolo Koch). 89: DPI (Marvin Newman). 91: Rapho Guillumette (Gene Badger). 92: *tl* Rapho Guillumette (Georg Gerster), *tr* Photo Researchers (Frank Maroon), Photo Researchers (Katrina Thomas). 95: Rapho Guillumette (R. G. Everts). 96: Rapho Guillumette (Paolo Koch). 97: Photo Researchers (Carl Frank). 99: DPI (Paul Stephanus). 101: Photo Researchers (William Carter). 104: DPI (Paul Stephanus).

Unit 3
113: Rapho Guillumette (Paolo Koch). 114: Photo Researchers (G. Tomsich). 115: Photo Researchers (George Holton). 118: N.Y.P.L. 119: DPI (J. Alex Langley). 122: N.Y.P.L. 123: N.Y.P.L. 125: Courtesy of the J. Pierpont Morgan Library. 126: N.Y.P.L. 128: *l* and *r* Courtesy of the J. Pierpont Morgan Library. 129: *l* and *r* Courtesy of the J. Pierpont Morgan Library. 131: Bettmann. 132: N.Y.P.L. 134: N.Y.P.L. 135: N.Y.P.L. 136: *l* Metropolitan Museum of Art, Gift of J. Pierpont Morgan, 1916, *b* Metropolitan Museum of Art, Rogers Fund 1924. 139: Editorial Photo Color Archives. 143: N.Y.P.L. 145: N.Y.P.L. 148: Monkmeyer (Terry Buchanan). 150: Woodfin Camp (Adam Woolfit). 154: *l* Rapho Guillumette (Paolo Koch), *bl* Monkmeyer (Michal Heron), *br* Rapho Guillumette (A. L. Goldman). 155: DPI (Sandy Nixon). 158: Photo Researchers (John Reichel). 161: *tl* Rapho Guillumette (Paolo Koch), *tr* Rapho Guillumette (E. Heiniger), *b* Rapho Guillumette (Bullaty Lomeo). 163: Woodfin Camp (Tony Howarth). 164: Rapho Guillumette (Paolo Koch). 166: Monkmeyer (Holzgraf). 168: AFP from Pictorial. 172: Michal Heron. 173: *t, m,* and *b* Michal Heron.

Unit 4
177: DPI (J. Alex Langley). 178: N.Y.P.L. 182: N.Y.P.L. 184: N.Y.P.L. 185: N.Y.P.L. 188: Culver. 189: Culver. 191: Culver. 193: Rapho Guillumette (Bernard G. Silberstein). 195: *t* Charles Phelps Cushing, *b* Culver. 198: DPI (J. Alex Langley). 199: Sovfoto. 200: Charles Phelps Cushing. 204: Monkmeyer (Warren Slater). 210: *tl* Rapho Guillumette (Roland and Sabrina Michaud), *tr* Monkmeyer (Warren Slater), *b* Rapho Guillumette (Roland and Sabrina Michaud). 212: UPI. 213: *t* Woodfin Camp (Adam Woolfit), *bl* Rapho Guillumette (C. A. Peterson), *br* DPI (J. Alex Langley), 214: Charles Phelps Cushing (Stockwell). 215: Photo Trends (Lou Wilson). 216: DPI (J. Alex Langley). 222: DPI (J. Alex Langley).

Unit 5
225: Photo Researchers (Vau Bucher). 226: Photo Researchers (George Holton). 229: *t* SCALA New York/Florence, *b* Information Service of India. 234: Black Star (T. S. Satyan). 235: *t* and *b* Harrison Forman. 236: Authentic (Chris Hansen). 242: *l*

SCALA New York/Florence, *r* Harrison Forman. 243: DPI (Paul Stephanus). 244: Woodfin Camp (Raghibur Singh). 245: Harrison Forman. 249: Bettmann. 250: Photo Researchers (Vau Bucher). 255: Wide World. 259: Photo Researchers (Hermann Schlenker). 261: Authentic (Chris Hansen). 265: Rapho Guillumette (Brian Brake). 266: *t, bl,* and *br* Authentic (Chris Hansen). 267: *t* and *b* Authentic (Chris Hansen). 270: *t* Rapho Guillumette (Paolo Koch), *m* Harrison Forman, *b* Photo Researchers (Vau Bucher). Rapho Guillumette (Brian Brake). 277: *t* Photo Researchers (Hermann Schlenker), *b* Woodfin Camp (Marc and Evelyn Bernheim). 282: Authentic (Chris Hansen). 284: *t* Authentic (Chris Hansen), *bl* Dell, *br* Photo Researchers (Vau Bucher). 286: Authentic (Chris Hansen).

Unit 6

289: Photo Trends. 290: Peabody Museum, Salem. 297: *t* and *b* N.Y.P.L. 299: Woodfin Camp (Vittoriano Rastelli). 301: Wide World. 302: N.Y.P.L. 304: N.Y.P.L. 305: Photo Trends. 309: Authentic (Chris Hansen). 311. N.Y.P.L. 313: *tl* Magnum (Marc Ribaud), *tr, b* Peabody Museum, Salem. 318: *tl* Woodfin Camp (Vittoriano Rastelli), *tr* and *b* Photo Trends. 320: N.Y.P.L. 322: Lee Ambrose. 327: *t* and *b* Magnum (Rene Burri). 330: *tl, tr,* and *b* Lee Ambrose. 331: *l* and *r* Lee Ambrose. 332: *t* and *b* Lee Ambrose. 333: *t* and *b* Lee Ambrose. 335: *t* and *b* Lee Ambrose. 336: Lee Ambrose. 337: *t, bl,* and *br* Lee Ambrose. 340: *tl, tr,* and *b* Authentic (Chris Hansen). 342: Authentic (Chris Hansen). 345: *tl* DPI (Watanabe), *tr* and *b* Authentic (Chris Hansen). 347: Woodfin Camp (D. Turner Givens).

Unit 7

353: Black Star (M. Philip Kahl, Jr.). 354: DPI (Sidney Glatter). 357: Woodfin Camp (Marc and Evelyn Bernheim). 360: Photo Trends. 361: Monkmeyer (Herbert Lanks). 363: N.Y.P.L. Map

EXCERPTS AND QUOTATIONS

Unit 1

Page 1: Adapted from *People and Places* by Margaret Mead. World Publishing Company. Copyright © 1959. Pages 3–4: Adapted from *Savage Africa* by William Winwood Reade. Harper and Brothers, 1864. Page 10: Adapted from *Never in Anger: Portrait of an Eskimo Family* by Jean L. Briggs. Harvard University Press. Copyright © 1970. Pages 20–21: Adapted from *The Forest People* by Colin Turnbull. Clarion Books. Copyright © 1961. Page 34: "Ha! The butterfly!" from *Japanese Lyrics* by Lafcadio Hern. Reprinted by permission of Houghton Mifflin Company. Copyright © 1963: "A giant firefly" from *An Introduction to Haiku* by Harold Henderson. Doubleday & Company, Inc. Copyright © 1965. Page 46: Adapted from *The Study of Man* by Ralph Linton. Appleton-Century-Crofts. Copyright 1936.

Unit 2

Page 58: Adapted from *History Begins at Sumer* by Samuel Noah Cramer. Doubleday & Company, Inc. Copyright © 1959. Page 61: Adapted from *Our World Civilizations*. The Board of Education of New York City, Copyright © 1967. Page 70: Adapted from *History Begins at Sumer* by Samual Noah Cramer. Doubleday & Company, Inc. Copyright © 1959. Pages 76–77: Adapted from *The Middle East Yesterday and Today* by David Miller and Clark Moore. Charles Scribner's Sons. Copyright © 1970. Pages 89–90: Adapted from "The Sword and

Collection. 365: Monkmeyer (Sarah Errington). 367: N.Y.P.L. 369: N.Y.P.L. 371: *t, m,* and *b* N.Y.P.L. 373: N.Y.P.L. 374: Culver. 377: Monkmeyer (Hilda Bijur). 380: Monkmeyer (Toge Fujihira). 381: *l* Woodfin Camp (Marc and Evelyn Bernheim), *r* Monkmeyer (Warren Slater). 383: Monkmeyer (W. Holzgraf). 385: Bruce Coleman (M.P.L. Fogden). 388: Monkmeyer (Warren Slater). 389: Monkmeyer (Toge Fujihira). 391: Black Star (Victor Englebert). 393: Central Color (Cyril Toker). 394: Rapho Guillumette (Sabine Weiss). 395: DPI (Michael Lee). 397: Monkmeyer (Halperin). 398: *tl* Woodfin Camp (Marc and Evelyn Bernheim), *tr* Monkmeyer (Lanks), *b* Black Star (M. Philip Kahl, Jr.). 399: *tl* Monkmeyer (William Mares), *tr* Monkmeyer, *b* Monkmeyer (Lanks). 400: Woodfin Camp (Marc and Evelyn Bernheim). 401: Woodfin Camp (Marc and Evelyn Bernheim). 403: James Foote. 405: James Foote. 408: James Foote. 409: James Foote. 410: James Foote. 414: James Foote.

Unit 8

417: Photo Researchers (Carl Frank). 418: Photo Researchers (Jane Latta). 422: *tr* Shostal, *b* Jack Haynes-Shostal, *tl* Joseph Martin/SCALA. 424: Culver. 427: Joseph Martin/SCALA. 428: Bettmann. 430: Joseph Martin/SCALA. 432: Photo Researchers (Stephanie Denkins). 433: Rapho Guillumette (Nicholas Sapieha). 436: Photo Researchers (Stephanie Denkins). 441: Photo Researchers (Carl Frank). 442: Woodfin Camp (Toby Molenar). 443: Woodfin Camp (Toby Molenar). 444: *t* Photo Researchers (Carl Frank), *b* Rapho Guillumette (Allyn Baum). 445: *tl* Rapho Guillumette (Davis Pratt), *tr* Photo Researchers (George Holton), *b* Photo Researchers (H. Sternberg). 449: Photo Researchers (David Magurian). 451: Photo Researchers (Russ Kinne). 453: Pool Fotografico Empresa Educatinal Nacional (Quimantu). 455: Monkmeyer (Herbert Lanks). 457: FPG.

the Sermon'' by Thomas Abercrombie in *The National Geographic,* July 1972. Pages 91–93: Adapted from "Nasser's 'True Face of Egypt' Is a Poor, Hard-Working Village" from The *New York Times,* June 4, 1960. Reprinted by permission. Page 93: Adapted from *The Arab World* by Desmond Stewart. Time-Life Books. Copyright © 1962. Page 94: Adapted from *Tunisia* by John Anthony. Charles Scribner's Sons. Copyright © 1961. Pages 105, 106, 108: Tables from *The Statistical Abstract of Israel.* Copyright © 1972. Page 107: Adapted from *Israel Inside* Out by Herbert Geduld. Abelard-Schuman Limited. Copyright © 1970. Page 110: Adapted from *Time,* February 14, 1972.

Unit 3

Page 130: Adapted from *Medieval People* by Eileen Power. Methuen & Co., Ltd., Copyright 1924. Page 144: Both excerpts adapted from *An Economic and Social History of Britain* by M. W. Flinn. The Macmillan Company. Copyright © 1961. Pages 157–158: Adapted from *The Land People of England* by Alicia Street, J. B. Lippincott Company. Copyright © 1969. Page 159: Adapted from The *New York Times,* January 15, 1971. Pages 167, 169: Tables adapted from *Migrants in Europe* by Arnold Rose. University of Minnesota Press. Copyright © 1969.

Unit 4

Page 211: Adapted from *The Kremlin's Human Dilemma* by

470

Maurice Hindus. Doubleday & Company, Inc. Copyright © 1967. Pages 214–215: Adapted from *The Russians* by Leonid Vladmirov. Copyright © 1968. Reprinted by permission of Praeger Publishers, Inc., New York. Pages 218–220: Reprinted by permission of The *New York Times.* Copyright © 1962.

Unit 5

Page 232: From *The Golden Womb of the Sun* by P. Lal. Calcutta Writers Workshop Publications. Copyright © 1965. Page 244: Adapted from *Sources of the Indian Tradition* edited by William de Bary et al., Columbia University Press. Copyright © 1958. Page 253: Adapted from *Nonviolent Resistance* by M. K. Ghandi. Schocken Books, Inc. Copyright 1951 by the Navajivan Trust. Page 265: Adapted from *Nectar in a Sieve* by Kamala Markandaya. The John Day Company, Inc. Copyright 1954. Pages 268–269: Adapted from *India: A World in Transition* by Beatrice Pitney Lamb. Copyright © 1963. Reprinted by permission of Praeger Publishers, Inc. New York. Page 271: Adapted from *The Roots of Change* by The Ford Foundation. Copyright © 1961. Page 278: Adapted from *Village on the March* by S. N. Bhattacharyya. Metropolitan Books. Copyright © 1959. Page 279: Adapted from *Mother India's Children* by Edward Rice. Pantheon Books, Inc. Copyright © 1971. Pages 280–281: Adapted from "India's Traditional Arranged Marriage Takes a Modern Turn" by Judith Weinraub. Reprinted by permission of The *New York Times,* June 3, 1973. Pages 286–287: Adapted from *India Changes* by Taya Zinkin. Oxford University Press, Inc. Copyright © 1958. Page 287: Adapted from *India and South Asia* by Seymour Fersh. The Macmillan Company. Copyright © 1965.

Unit 6

Page 293: Adapted from *Birth of China* by Herrlee G. Creel. Frederick Ungar Publishing Co., Inc. Copyright 1937. Page 303: Adapted from *Sources of Chinese Tradition* edited by William de Bary. Columbia University Press. Copyright 1960. Page 317: Adapted from *Quotations From Chairman Mao Tse-Tung* by Mao Tse-Tung. Page 323: From *The Ways of Man: An Introduction to Many Cultures* by Bertha Davis. Copyright © 1971 by The Macmillan Company. Pages 328–329: Adapted from *The Good Earth* by Pearl S. Buck. Copyright 1931, 1949, 1958 by Pearl S. Buck. By permission of The John Day Company, Inc., publisher. Pages 343–344: Greatly adapted from *A History of Modern Japan* by Richard Storry. Cassell. Copyright © 1962. Pages 350–351: "A Japanese Youth Lectures Sato on Pollution" The *New York Times,* September 22, 1971. Reprinted by permission.

Unit 7

Pages 370, 372: Adapted from *The Interesting Narrative of Oulaudah Equiano.* London, 1789. Pages 376–378: This adaptation of "To a Farm in the White Highlands" by Solomon Kagwe from *Origin East Africa,* edited by David Cook, 1965, is reprinted by permission of the publishers, Heinemann Educational Books, London. Pages 397, 400: Adapted from *Warrior Herdsmen* by Elizabeth Marshall Thomas. Alfred A. Knopf, Inc., Copyright © 1965. Pages 405–406: Adapted from *The Igbo of South-Eastern Nigeria* by Victor C. Uchendu. Copyright © 1965 by Holt, Rinehart, and Winston, Inc. Reprinted by permission. Page 408: Adapted from *Things Fall Apart* by Chinva Achebe. Copyright © 1959 by Fawcett Books.

Unit 8

Pages 423–424: Adapted from *Readings in Latin American Civilization* edited by Benjamin Keen. Copyright © 1955 by Houghton Mifflin Company. Page 428: Adapted from *Readings in Latin American Civilization* edited by Benjamin Keen. Copyright © 1955 by Houghton Mifflin Company. Pages 432–433: Adapted from "The Uprooted: A Guatemala Sketch" by Richard R. Behrendt. *The New Mexico Quarterly Review,* Vol. XIX, No. 1. Copyright 1949 by Richard R. Behrendt. Page 440: Adapted from *Peru, Bolivia, Ecuador: The Indian Andes* by Charles Paul May. Copyright © 1969 by Thomas Nelson. Page 446: Adapted from *Child of the Dark: The Diary of Carolina Maria de Jesus* translated by David St. Clair. Copyright © 1962 by E. P. Dutton and Company. Pages 459–460: Adapted from "A Chilean Family Chronicle—Living Through the Allende Revolution" by Sara Davidson in The *New York Times Magazine.* October 17, 1971. Reprinted by permission.

INDEX

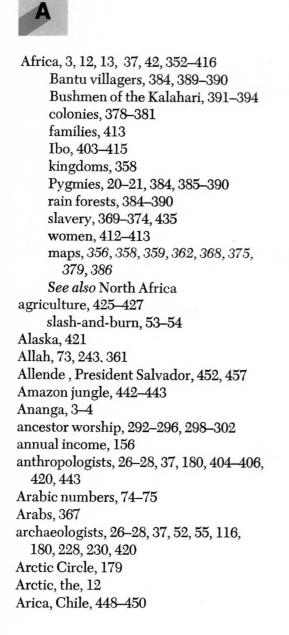

Africa, 3, 12, 13, 37, 42, 352–416
    Bantu villagers, 384, 389–390
    Bushmen of the Kalahari, 391–394
    colonies, 378–381
    families, 413
    Ibo, 403–415
    kingdoms, 358
    Pygmies, 20–21, 384, 385–390
    rain forests, 384–390
    slavery, 369–374, 435
    women, 412–413
    maps, *356, 358, 359, 362, 368, 375,*
       379, 386
    See also North Africa
agriculture, 425–427
    slash-and-burn, 53–54
Alaska, 421
Allah, 73, 243, 361
Allende, President Salvador, 452, 457
Amazon jungle, 442–443
Ananga, 3–4
ancestor worship, 292–296, 298–302
annual income, 156
anthropologists, 26–28, 37, 180, 404–406,
    420, 443
Arabic numbers, 74–75
Arabs, 367
archaeologists, 26–28, 37, 52, 55, 116,
    180, 228, 230, 420
Arctic Circle, 179
Arctic, the, 12
Arica, Chile, 448–450

artifacts, 25, 26–28, 55, 355
Aryans, 230, 231–234
Asia, 420
Atlantic Ocean, 153
Australian aborigines, 28
automobile plant, 164
automobiles, 446–450
Aztecs, 421–425
    empire, 423
    pyramids, 423
    religion, 423
    slaves, 423–424
    war, 423
    women, 423

Baltic Sea, 179
Bangladesh (East Pakistan), 256–258
    population density, 258
Bantu villagers, 384, 389–390
barbarians, 124
barter, silent, 360–361
beauty, 33–34
Belgium, 381
Ben-Gurion, David, 107
Benin, 359
Bible, the, 67
Bolivar, Simon (*El Libertador*), 430–431
Bolshevists, 200
Brahmans, 286–287
Brazil, 442, 450
British East India Company, 248
bronze, 41, 67, 292

Buck, Pearl S., *The Good Earth,* 328–329
Buddhism, 237–240, 244, 308–311
    four noble truths, 309
    many Buddhas, 309–311
    Nirvana, 308, 311
    rules for living, 237
buildings
    apartment, 95
    factory, 44
    houses, 15, 93
    mosques, 94
    office, 95
    pyramids, 64
Bushmen. *See* Africa
business, 460

C

camels, 392
caravans, 359
caste system, 24, 231–287
    Brahman, 231, 237
    Kshatriya, 231
    outcastes (untouchables), 234
    Sudra, 231
    Vaisya, 231
capitalism, 194–196
Caribbean Sea, 153
cataracts, 357
Catherine II (the Great), 192–194
Catholic Church, the, 127, 129, 429
cattle, 397–400
chattel slavery, 369
Chile, 451–463
    and Marxism, 451–463
    technicians, 462
    map, *447*
China, 42, 46, 186, 291–319, 326–336, 338
    Buddhism, 308–311
    Chiang Kai-shek, 315
    Chou dynasty, 299–304
    civilization, 291
    commune, 333–336
    Communism, 315, 317–319
    Confucianism, 302–304

farming, 323, 331–336
Formosa, 315
geography, 326–331
government, 333
Great Wall, 312
Han dynasty, 304–308
loess, 326–329
Mao Tse-tung, 315
Middle Kingdom and the Outer
    World, 311–315
natural resources, 323
population, 326
rice, 331
Shang dynasty, 291–299
ways of life, 332
World War II, 315
Yangtze River, 326, 330
Yellow River, 292, 299, 326–331
maps, *294, 295, 324, 325, 334*
Chinese legends, 291
Chou dynasty, 299–304
Confucianism, 302–304
Christ, 71–72
Christianity, 374
cities, 411, 441, 456–457
    and factories, 212–215
    life in, 401–402, 446
citizens, 174
city jobs. *See* work
civilization
    Arab, 74
    and cities, 52–55
    cradle of, 52
    Western, 51–78
class system, 429, 431
climate (weather), 151
    in China, 331–336, 338
    dry seasons, 151
    and farming, 153
    floods, 151
    and geography, 12–15
    Gulf Stream, the, 153
    in Japan, 336–339
    landforms, 205–208
    rainy seasons, 151
    regions, 205, 384
    maps, *14*

colonies, 374–382
Columbus, Christopher, 419
Common Market, 160–162
communism, 194–196, 199, 201–202,
    in China, 315, 317–319
Communist Party (U.S.S.R.), 216–223
Confucianism, 302–304
constitutions, 434
cooperation, 21
copper, 457–462
Cortez, Hernando, 424–425
counting, 107
countryside, 456
credit, 30
Creoles, 429, 430, 431
Crusades, 131–133
culture, 4, 11, 12, 355
    African, 356
    contact, 11, 12, 356
    defined, 4
    patterns of, 17
    revolutions, 38–46, 140–145
cultures
    African, 357–358, 360
    Arab, 73–76
    Aryans, 231–235
    Babylonians, 59–62
    Bantu, 384, 389–390
    Bushmen, 391–394
    Chukchi, 15
    Dodoth, 397–400
    Egyptians, 62–69
    Eskimos, 10, 13, 15
    Hebrews, 67–72
    Ibo, 403–415
    Iranians, 92, 181
    Phoenicians, 68
    Pygmies, 20–21, 384, 385–390
    Rembos, 3–4
    Rus, 180–182
    Sumerians, 55–59
    Tasadays, 39
    Tivs, 12
    Turks, 73–74
    Yemenites, 102
customs, 3, 4
    Bedouin hospitality, 89

Declaration of the Rights
    of Man and Citizen, 140
deserts, 51, 390
dictators, 434, 463
domestic slavery, 369
domestication, 40, 231
drought, 387

East Africa, 26–28
East Asia: China and Japan, 289–352
    See also China; Japan
Eastern Europe: the Soviet Union,
    174–224
    See also Russia; Soviet Union
eating, ways of, 8–9
ecologists, 443
economics, 28–30, 45
economists, 23, 167–169
encomienda, 427
Ecuador, 11
education, 406, 414, 432, 442
    in U.S.S.R., 217
Egypt (United Arab Republic), 181, 357
elections, 219–223, 434, 457, 463
    in Chile, 434, 457, 463
    in the United States, 219–221
    in U.S.S.R., 219–223
Elizabeth I, Queen, 248
England (Great Britain), 158, 159–160,
    181, 200, 378
    and Ireland, 181
    and Scotland, 181
Eskimos, 421
equality, 111
Europeans, 367, 374–382
extended family, 405–406

factories, 144–145, 160, 456

families, 19, 45, 402
farmers, 56, 81, 115–116, 131, 461
farming, 180, 390, 407–408, 410, 440–441,
    450, 455
        slash-and-burn, 400–401
favelas, 446
feudal system, 125–130, 134
        castles, 126
        guilds, 134
        knights, 125
        lords, 125, 128–129
        serfs, 126–128, 129–130, 187–189
floods, 230
food, 461
forests, 180–182
France, 130, 200
        Revolution, 139–140

G

Gandhi, Mohandas, 252–256
        assassination, 254, 256
        march to the sea, 254
        nonviolence, 253
gathering, 38
        and hunting, 53
geographic features, 150, 151, 357
geography, 12–15, 149–155, 427
        and climate, 12–15, 151
        and industry, 153–155
        minerals, 151
        soil, 116, 151
        maps, *14*
geologists, 37
"getting up," 406, 411
gold, 363, 364, 365, 366, 368
government, 61–62, 86, 110–111, 120, 127,
    138, 139, 140, 429, 434, 435, 447–448,
    454, 455, 461, 462
        in Europe, 124
        U.S. Constitution, 219
        in U.S.S.R., 212, 218–223
Great Way. *See* Confucianism
Greece, 24, 116–120
        democracy, 116, 118
        reason, 120

groups, 17–19, 88–89

H

Hammurabi's Code, 61–62
Han dynasty, 304–308
herding, 88, 90, 395–400
Heyerdahl, Thor, 66
historians, 22–23, 180, 243, 244
Hitler, Adolf, 201
hunters, 115–116
hunting, 20–21, 38, 385–388
        and gathering, 53

I

Ibn Battuta, 362–367
Ibo, 403–415
        and Europeans, 407
        "getting up," 406, 411
        women, 409
ideas, 122, 149
        borrowing, 149
immigrants, 99–111
imperialism, in India, 246–254
income, 105
independence, 77, 378, 380–382, 429, 430
        problems, 381
India, 7, 24, 40, 46, 225–288
        agriculture and industry, 282–283
        Brahmans, 286–287
        and British government, 248–254
        caste, 278, 280–281, 285–287
        city life, 269–271
        climate, 261–265
        economic and social change,
            272–287
        education, 285
        Gandhi, Mohandas, 252–256
        geography, 260–265
        Hindu-Moslem war, 254–258
        independence, 252–258
        industrial revolution, 279–282
        marriage, 280–281
        monsoons, 264–265
        and Pakistan, 255–258

India–(*Continued*)
    population growth, 275–276
    maps, *230, 248, 262, 263*
    time line, *241*
Indians, Latin American, 419, 421,
    427–429, 432, 435, 443
industry, 86–98, 378, 382, 437
    and agriculture, 170–171
    in Africa, 375
Indus Valley civilization, 228–230
Industrial Revolution, 140–145
    steam engine, 143
    technology, 141
inventions, 58–59
Iran (Persia), 46, 181
irrigation, 81
Islam, 73–74, 97–98, 243–245
    in Africa and Asia, 245, 361, 362
    and Hindus, 245
    Mohammed, 73–74, 243–245
Israel, 78, 99–111
    immigrants, 99–111
    Law of Return, 100
Italy, 121, 158–159

J

Japan, 320–321, 336–351
    agriculture, 347–348
    Chinese influence on, 320
    clans, 320
    Communist party, 344
    crowding and pollution, 349–351
    economy, 346–351
    exports and imports, 341, 349
    family, 343–344
    gross national product, 346
    industry, 339–341, 350–351
    population, 348
    standard of living, 326
Jerusalem, Palestine, 71
jobs. *See* work

K

Kalahari Desert, 391–394

Kiev, U.S.S.R., 182–183, 212
Koran, the, 73

L

land, 437, 450
    barren, 103
    features of, 80–81
    fertile, 60
    infertile, 59
    reform, 86
    Russia, 204–208
    and salt, 59
    use, 208
land bridge, 420–421
landforms, 437
languages, 4, 31, 155, 175, 180
    Arabic, 355
    complete, 32
    differences, 160
    English, 233
    Hebrew, 107
    Latin, 233
    Persian, 181
    Sanskrit, 230–233, 239
    sounds, 31
    symbols, 31
    uses, 31
    Yiddish, 107
Latin America, 417–464
    Aztecs, 421–425
    Brazil, 442, 450
    Chile, 451–463
    cities, 441
    Peru, 448
    revolutions in, 430, 463
    and the Spanish, 424–431, 432
    maps, *419, 420, 425, 431, 438, 439,*
        442, 447
latitude and longitude, 261
Leakey, Dr. Louis, 26–28
Leakey, Maeve (Mrs. Richard), 37
Leakey, Mary (Mrs. Louis), 26–28
Leakey, Dr. Richard, 37
learning, 5–6
Lenin, Nikolai (Vladimir Ilich Ulyanov),

199–201
Leningrad, U.S.S.R., 212

M

machines, 44–45, 140–145
Mali, 358, 362–367
Mao Tse-tung (Chairman Mao), 315, 317–319
Marx, Karl, 194–196, 201, 452
material culture, 25
Mead, Margaret, 1
Mecca, Saudi Arabia, 73
Mediterranean Sea, 49–112
mestizos, 429, 430, 431
metals, 41–42, 458
Mexico, 423
Middle Ages, 124
middle class, 140, 190
Middle East, 42, 49–111
    maps, *52, 56, 60, 67, 75,*
      77, 82, 83
    time line, *53*
    See also names of individual
      countries
migrant workrs in Europe, 163–175
Milan, Italy, 159
Mohammed, 73–74, 243
Mongols (warriors on horseback), 185–186, 310
monotheism (God), 70–74
    Christianity, 72, 127, 129
    Islam, (Moslems, Muslims), 73–74, 97–98, 133, 243–245, 362
    Judaism (Jews), 8, 70–72, 100–111
Montezuma, 421, 424
Moscow (Muscovy), U.S.S.R., 186, 212, 222-223
Moslem. *See* Islam
mountains, 51, 116, 117
mulattoes, 429
Muscovy, Russia, 185–186

N

natural resources, 86

Near East, 46
New Stone Age, 40
New World. *See* Latin America
Nicholas II, Tsar, 196–198, 201
Niger River, 407
Nigeria, 404
Nile River, 62–69, 357
nomads, 12
    Aryans, 230, 231–234
    Bedouins, 88–90
North Africa and the Middle East, 49–112
North Tropic Line, 261

O

oases, 51, 88, 360
oil, 87
oil palms, 407
Old Stone Age, 36–39
    today, 38
Olduvai Gorge, 26–28
Ottoman Empire, 76

P

Pacific Ocean, 179, 442, 448
Palestine, 69, 71
palm oil, 382, 406
paper, 306
papyrus, 66
peasants
    fellahin, 84, 93
    serfs, 126–128, 129–130
Peking man, 316
peninsulares, 429
Persia (Iran), 46, 181
Peru, 442, 448
Peter the Great, 191–192
Philippine Islands, 39
plantations, 432, 440
poetry, 33–34
political scientists, 23, 454–463
pollution, 47
Polo, Marco, 310
polytheism, 69–70
    Aztec gods, 423

polytheism–*(Continued)*
    Buddhism, 237–240
    gods, 58, 62, 70
    Hinduism, 236–237
population, 437
    density, 81–84, 155–157, 409, 440
    chart, *84*
    map, *440*
Portugal, 368
power, 44
    electricity, 15
    people and animals (muscles), 44, 141
    running water, 141
    steam, 44, 141, 143
    wind, 141
profit, factory, 456
pull forces, 168–171
push forces, 168–171
Pygmy hunters, 384, 385–390
pyramids, 64, 423

R

railroads, 382, 425
rain clouds, 81
rain forests, 421, 440
rainfall, 80, 384, 395, 437, 442
Reade, William Winwood, 3–4
records, 45, 57–58, 63, 420
religions
    ancestor worship, 292–296, 298, 302
    Aztecs, 423
    beliefs, 30
    Buddhism, 237–240, 244, 308–311
    Catholicism, 127, 129, 425
    Christianity, 72, 74, 133, 183, 425
    Confucianism, 302–304
    Hinduism, 236–237, 240, 245
    Islam (Moslems, Muslims), 73–74, 97–98, 133, 243–245, 361, 362
    Judaism (Jews), 8, 70–72, 100–111
    monotheism, 70–74
    pagans of Kiev, 183
    polytheism, 69–70
    Russian Church, 183

Yoga, 238–239
Rembo people, 3–4
Renaissance, the, 135–139
resources, 437
role, 24, 133
    men, 89, 97
    women, 89, 97–98, 118
Romanov, Michael (Russia), 187
Romanovs, the (Russia), 187–198
Romans, 71, 120–124
rules, 19, 20–21, 24–25, 122
Russia (Soviet Union, U.S.S.R.), 177–224
    elections in, 219–223
    farm life in, 208–211
    Kiev, 182–183
    Mongols, 185
    Muscovy, 185–186
    Revolution in, 196–201
    Romanovs, 187–198
    Rus, 180–192
    World War I, 197–198
    World War II, 201–202
    maps, *179, 183, 186, 190, 197, 206, 207, 209*

S

Sahara Desert, 12, 355, 360, 362, 390–391
salt, 360–361, 364, 365
San Salvador, 419
Sanskrit, 232–233, 239
Santiago, Chile, 447, 448, 449, 452, 457
São Paulo, Brazil, 446
Sato, Eisaku, Premier (Japan), 350–351
savannas, 395–401
    life in, 396
schooling, 431, 450
serfdom, 187–189
Shang dynasty, 291–299
Shansi province, China, 333–334
Siberia, 15
skills, 157, 175, 449
slash-and-burn farming, 400–401
slavery, 188–189, 369–374
social institutions, 17
    families, 19, 45

government, 19–20
social scientists, 22, 452
    anthropologists, 180, 404–406, 420
    archaeologists, 22, 26–28, 37, 180, 420
    economists, 23, 167–169
    historians, 22–23, 180, 243–244
    political scientists, 23, 454–463
    sociologists, 23, 101, 110–111, 167–169, 171
socialization, 10
society, 10
sociologists, 23, 101, 110–111, 167–169, 171
Solzhenitsyn, Alexander, 203
Songhai, 358
South Asia: India, 225–288
    and European trade route control, 246–247
    landform map, *262*
    mountain ranges map, *263*
    population density map, *273*
Spain, 419, 423, 430
Spanish, the (Spaniards), 424–431, 432
    colonies, 429
specialists, 43, 54–55, 96–97, 211
Stalin, Joseph, 201–202
standard of living, 146
status, 24, 103–111, 175, 187–190
    caste system, 24, 231–287
suburbs, 95–96
surplus, 42–43

taming. *See* domestication
Tasadays, 39
taxes, 185
technology, 28, 39, 44–47, 141, 228
telling time, 58–59
Tenochtitlan (Mexico City, Mexico), 421, 423, 424
Tigris and Euphrates rivers, 60, 62
tools, 25, 26–28, 38, 39, 40–41, 116, 141, 420
trade, 56, 57, 131, 133, 182, 357, 360, 409, 410, 423
    barter, 28
    exchange, 88
    patterns of, 359
    silent barter, 360–361
    map, *359*
Trans-Amazon highway, 442
transportation, 15, 45, 142, 208, 382, 440
tribe, 404
tsar, 187, 217

Uchendu, Dr. Chikezie, 404
Ukraine, 211
United States, 3, 24, 200
untouchables (outcastes) *(Harijans)*, 286

Vedic (Aryan) literature, 232–233
Venezuela, 430
Victoria, Queen (England), Empress of India, 249
villages, 115, 388–390, 400, 411, 440–442

wages, 165, 167
warfare, 41, 357
wars, 78, 120, 146–147
water, 80–81, 90, 446
ways of life, 87–98, 145–146
weapons, 41–42, 116
West Africa, 3, 359
West African kingdoms, 360
Western Europe, 113–176
    maps, *117, 121, 137, 147, 149, 152*
    See also names of individual countries
White Highlands, Kenya, 376
work
    jobs and half-jobs, 96, 441
    jobs in Russian cities, 212–215
    jobs of untouchables, 234

work–(*Continued*)
    labor, 158
    specialization, 43, 54–55, 96–97
World War I, 146, 197–198
World War II, 146–147, 201–202
writing
    Chinese, 292–296
    cuneiform, 57–58
    hieroglyphics, 63–66
    Phoenician alphabet, 68
    signs, 66
written records, 241

Yemenites, 102
Yin and Yang, 296
Yoga, 238–239

Zaire, Republic of, 381
zambos, 429